61-12912

7-3-62

TEXAS UNDER THE CARPETBAGGERS

Edmund J. Davis, Governor of Texas throughout the Carpetbag Period, 1870–1874. Ellison Photo Company.

TEXAS UNDER THE CARPETBAGGERS

by W. C. NUNN

UNIVERSITY OF TEXAS PRESS • AUSTIN

PUBLISHED WITH THE ASSISTANCE OF A GRANT FROM THE FORD
FOUNDATION UNDER ITS PROGRAM FOR THE SUPPORT OF
PUBLICATIONS IN THE HUMANITIES AND SOCIAL SCIENCES

TO MY PARENTS,

WILLIAM H., NOW DECEASED, AND MATTIE E. NUNN,

ALSO TO WALTER PRESCOTT WEBB,

AND TO THE MEMORY OF

CHARLES W. RAMSDELL

THIS BOOK IS DEDICATED.

ACKNOWLEDGMENTS

Professor Charles W. Ramsdell and Professor Walter Prescott Webb made the completion of this study possible by their considerate aid. A generous grant from Texas Christian University provided for the preparation of the material for publication. Kind librarians, forbearing readers, and a patient family also rendered valuable assistance.

W. C. Nunn

Fort Worth, Texas

TABLE OF CONTENTS

ILLUSTRATIONS

TEXAS UNDER THE CARPETBAGGERS

BACKGROUND

TEXAS SUFFERED LITTLE during the Civil War in comparison with other Southern states. Still, there was no government worthy of the name as summer began in 1865. The Confederate governor, Pendleton Murrah, had fled to Mexico along with many of his associates. Maximilian, the puppet emperor south of the Rio Grande, beckoned, and the prospect of extensive lands there to be had almost for the asking was too much to resist, especially when possible arrest and imprisonment awaited the former Confederate leader at home.

As a part of President Andrew Johnson's ill-fated policy of restoring the South to the Union, General A. J. Hamilton was appointed provisional governor on June 17, 1865. Hamilton had been a prominent figure in the state before the war, and, at the beginning of the conflict, he had entered the United States Army.[1] At the time of his appointment, Hamilton was in New Orleans. He set out for Texas and landed at Galveston on July 21, 1865.[2]

The new provisional governor at once began organizing the government under the Johnson plan of reconstruction, which granted amnesty, with certain exceptions, to those who had served in the Southern forces during the war, provided that they executed an oath of allegiance.[3] Hamilton filled the various appointive offices of the state with Unionists whenever he could, but when this was impossible he named former secessionists known to be capable and trustworthy. He became aware that the jurisdictions of the provisional civil courts were being

[1] Charles W. Ramsdell, "Texas in the New Nation," *The South in the Building of the Nation*, III, 417.

[2] Statement of Mrs. L. H. Maloney, daughter of Governor Hamilton; Ramsdell, "Texas in the New Nation," p. 417.

[3] H. H. Bancroft, *History of the North Mexican States and Texas*, XVI, 479.

gradually usurped by military authority. He did not strenuously object to this, however, for he felt that civil court juries were not inclined to give justice to former slaves or to those who had served the Union cause. In fact, Hamilton was quite willing to see these juries replaced by officials whose views were more in keeping with the desires of the government.[4]

Four distinct social classes then existed in Texas. First, there were the former Confederate soldiers, many of whom had returned home bitterly convinced that their hardships in the army had not been shared in any way by those who had remained behind. These men also felt that the resources of the country had been wasted by the incompetent and unscrupulous men in control. Some veterans held that the personal property of the defunct Confederacy belonged to them, and a great deal of it was thus confiscated. Soldiers of Fayette County, meeting late in May, 1865, at La Grange, named a committee to collect government property in the county and distribute it to indigent soldiers or their families. Later at the same town and also at San Antonio government stores were pillaged. Private property, however, was generally left undisturbed.[5]

The second distinct class, composed of Unionists, who were looked upon as traitors by the former Confederates,[6] fell into two divisions: (1) conservatives who did not favor drastic reconstruction policies for the state and who were, in fact, willing to subordinate everything to the restoration of normal relations with the Union;[7] and (2) radicals, who themselves fell into two groups: renegade secessionists called scalawags and extreme Unionists. Both groups, usually working together, desired to build up a political machine by disfranchising "Rebels" and enfranchising all Negroes whose votes they could control.[8] Radicals who came to Texas from the North with a view to controlling political and economic affairs were called carpetbaggers. Their arrival did not become evident until several years after the end of the war.[9]

[4] Ramsdell, "Texas in the New Nation," p. 417.
[5] Charles W. Ramsdell, *Reconstruction in Texas*, pp. 34–35.
[6] Bancroft, *History*, XVI, 480.
[7] Louis J. Wortham, *A History of Texas from Wilderness to Commonwealth*, V, 140.
[8] Clarence R. Wharton, *Texas under Many Flags*, II, 131.
[9] *Ibid.*, p. 167.

The third group, the military, appeared in Texas soon after May 29, 1865, when General Philip Sheridan was assigned to the command of the Military Division of the Southwest. On June 10, from his headquarters at New Orleans, Sheridan ordered General Gordon Granger to proceed with 1800 men to Galveston. As quickly as possible these troops were posted at the most important points in the state to effect the surrender provisions and to preserve order until establishment of civil government. Other troops, numbering 52,000 men, under Sheridan himself, were ordered to the Rio Grande by General U. S. Grant as a demonstration against the French in Mexico. Granger's troops, which were sent to the interior, were thoroughly inadequate for the policing of the state, as the posts were widely separated.

Comprising the fourth group were the freedmen; General Granger proclaimed their emancipation as soon as he assumed military control of Texas.[10] The former slaves, unconstrained and eager to test the extent of their new liberty, assembled in crowds or wandered aimlessly from place to place. They flocked to towns where offices of the Freedmen's Bureau were located, and many who had been brought to Texas during the war returned to their old homes.

The Freedmen's Bureau was organized in 1865 by the War Department to serve as a prop for the Southern Negro in his new life. Purposes of the Bureau were to feed and educate the Negro and to help him adjust. At first the Bureau rendered commendable service, but, as will be shown, it later became a tool of the ultrapartisan Republicans of the North.[11] The Bureau thus victimized its charges, who also faced other perils. One was posed by the "poor whites," who were especially bitter about the present and fearful of the future and who were so vindictive toward the recently-freed Negroes that they murdered numbers of them. The luster of liberty thus became tarnished for a good many freedmen, and by 1866 they had begun to settle down into another routine—as free laborers.[12]

On November 15, 1865, Governor Hamilton issued a proclamation calling for an election, to be held January 8, to choose delegates to a convention for reframing the state constitution.[13] This action stemmed from President Johnson's reconstruction plan: the provisional gover-

[10] Ramsdell, *Reconstruction in Texas,* p. 40.
[11] Thomas A. Bailey, *The American Pageant,* p. 464.
[12] Bancroft, *History,* XVI, 480–484.
[13] Ramsdell, "Texas in the New Nation," p. 418.

5

nor, after re-establishing normal operation of the courts, was to arrange for a convention which would change the state constitution to take into consideration social conditions evolving out of the war. Delegates were to be elected from among the "loyal" citizens—those who took an oath of allegiance prescribed by the President. Specifically, the convention was required to do three things: to nullify the act of secession; to declare slavery abolished and fix the civil status of the freedmen; and to repudiate state debts contracted in support of the Confederacy. The President's reconstruction plan further stipulated that all of this must be ratified by a vote of the people. Once this was accomplished, Texans were to elect a governor, a legislature, and other state officials. When the elected legislature met it was to ratify the Thirteenth Amendment to the federal Constitution, prohibiting slavery. After that the state was to be accepted as fully restored to the Union.[14]

Election of delegates was held as scheduled on January 8, 1866.[15] A month later the delegates gathered in Austin.[16] Three parties were represented: Secessionists, Radical Unionists, and Conservatives of both Union and Secessionist groups who desired to subordinate all issues to Union restoration for Texas.[17] After much argument, the convention declared the secession ordinance void, disclaimed forever the right to secede, repudiated the Confederate debt, and prohibited slavery forever. The convention also assured freedmen certain civil rights. Near the end of the session Conservatives and Secessionists agreed on the nomination of J. W. Throckmorton for governor and George W. Jones for lieutenant governor. Throckmorton had been a member of the Secession Convention of 1861, when, as a Conservative, he had cast one of seven votes against secession. But after the war began he organized a company of men for Confederate service. Radical Unionists, dissatisfied with this choice, nominated ex-Governor E. M. Pease for the highest office and L. Lindsay for lieutenant governor.[18]

All of President Johnson's prerequisites for readmission having

[14] Wortham, *History of Texas*, V, 2; Louis M. Hacker and Benjamin B. Kendrick, *The United States since 1865*, p. 16.

[15] Bancroft, *History*, XVI, 482.

[16] Ramsdell, "Texas in the New Nation," p. 418.

[17] Wortham, *History of Texas*, V, 5.

[18] Ramsdell, "Texas in the New Nation," p. 418.

been agreed upon, the convention submitted them in the form of an amended constitution to be voted on by the people.[19] On June 25 the election was held; the amended constitution was adopted, and Throckmorton and Jones were elected by a large majority over the Radical candidates. President Johnson's plan for reconstruction had thus been accepted by Texans,[20] and only legislative ratification of the Thirteenth Amendment remained to be accomplished.

With the inauguration of Throckmorton the new civil government went into operation. Former Secessionists controlled the Legislature, however, and they exhibited tactlessness in sending O. M. Roberts, former president of the Secession Convention, and David G. Burnet, ex-president of the Republic of Texas and a Secessionist, to the United States Senate. Former Confederates were also elected to seats in the House of Representatives. Northerners looked upon this as an affront, and neither the senators nor the representatives were allowed to take their seats in Congress.[21] A strong faction in Washington was dissatisfied with Johnson's reconstruction plan, and this group gained control of Congress. It contended that the new governments of Texas and other Southern states were unconstitutional, since they had been created without congressional sanction, and that the restored states were in the hands of still-rebellious leaders who did not guarantee protection of life and property.[22]

Texas had committed other acts suspicious in the eyes of Congress. When the Thirteenth and Fourteenth Amendments had been submitted to the Texas Legislature they were not ratified. In submitting the Thirteenth Amendment Governor Throckmorton had declared that its acceptance was unnecessary, for it was already a part of the federal Constitution, having been ratified by three fourths of the states. He presented the Fourteenth Amendment at the same time but expressed his unqualified disapproval and recommended rejection. The Thirteenth Amendment was returned to the Secretary of State without action, and the Fourteenth was rejected by a vote of sixty-seven to five.[23]

Congressional distrust of Texas was to increase as a result of laws—

[19] Dudley G. Wooten, *A Comprehensive History of Texas,* II, 324.
[20] *Ibid.,* p. 156.
[21] Ramsdell, "Texas in the New Nation," p. 420.
[22] Bancroft, *History,* XVI, 487.
[23] *Ibid.,* p. 485.

"black codes"—passed by the Legislature concerning the freedmen labor problems. (Other Southern states passed similar legislation.) In Texas the first of these was the general apprenticeship law,[24] providing that any unmarried minor, with the consent of parents or guardian, could be bound out by the county judge until he had reached the age of twenty-one. The apprentice was to be taught a trade and to be protected against harsh treatment; anyone who enticed away an apprentice working under contract or who harbored a runaway was to be punished.[25] But the most stringent "black code" was the contract labor law, providing that common laborers who desired to contract their services for periods longer than one month must record the contract before magistrates and witnesses. The laborers were free to choose employers, but once they had taken employment they could abandon it only by forfeiting their wages. Freedmen's Bureau officials refused to recognize such contracts and ordered that the law be disregarded.[26] A third measure, similar to those in the North, was enacted on November 8, 1866[27] in an attempt to control the vagrancy problem. Under this law the convicted vagrant was required either to pay a fine of ten dollars or to work at a dollar a day until that assessment was paid.

Governor Throckmorton faced a critical domestic problem created by the presence of United States soldiers quartered in Texas. Before the federal government would remove them he had to prove that lawlessness could be controlled. He worked diligently toward this end, but he faced great difficulties, for Texas had all of the disorder characteristic of the frontier, plus a lawless element produced by the war. Conditions improved slowly.

This progress was nullified by the Congressional Reconstruction Act of March 2, 1867. Texas lost its statehood by this law and became only a "conquered province" governed by military rule. Throckmorton ceased to be the regularly elected executive, although for some months he remained provisional governor. He attempted, with great difficulty, to administer state government according to the wishes of the military commanders and at the same time according to his sense of duty. General Sheridan removed him on July 30, 1867 to satisfy the constantly

[24] Ramsdell, "Texas in the New Nation," p. 420.
[25] H. P. N. Gammel, *Laws of Texas,* VI, 979–981.
[26] *Ibid.,* pp. 994–997.
[27] *Ibid.,* pp. 1020–1022.

clamoring Radicals and Major General Charles Griffin, head of the United States Army in Texas, who disliked Throckmorton intensely.[28] Appointed military governor in his place was E. M. Pease.

Texans were afforded some consolation in that military rule was intended to be temporary. In the Reconstruction Acts, Congress provided machinery for setting up the kind of government that its radical members wished. There was to be a general registration of all voters, black and white, who would swear that they had never voluntarily aided the Confederacy. These people were then to vote on a proposal to hold a constitutional convention, which would frame a form of government acceptable to the Radicals. During the election a number of registered voters stayed away from the polls, hoping to defeat the proposed convention by preventing a majority turnout. But the plan failed, and the convention met in Austin on June 1, 1868. Most of the delegates were Radicals, and a number of them were Negroes.

At the convention the Radicals soon began to quarrel among themselves. The extreme radical element was led by E. J. Davis and Morgan C. Hamilton, the more moderate wing by ex-Governor A. J. Hamilton and Governor E. M. Pease. Extremists contended that all state acts passed during the recent Throckmorton administration and during the Confederacy were void, and they also advocated disfranchising all who had taken part in the recent "rebellion." The moderate Union men disagreed heartily, and the argument between the two factions became heated. After two tempestuous sessions, the Conservatives were successful in getting the convention to accept a constitution in full accord with the recent acts of Congress but free of certain objectionable features favored by the Davis wing. Each faction named a ticket, but the details of the campaign of 1869 will be discussed in the following chapter.[29]

[28] Ramsdell, "Texas in the New Nation," p. 422.
[29] *Ibid.*

SECTION I THE POLITICAL HISTORY OF THE REGIME OF E. J. DAVIS

THE RESUMPTION OF CIVIL GOVERNMENT AND THE WORK OF THE TWELFTH LEGISLATURE

ELECTION OF 1869

CONSERVATIVE REPUBLICANS desired a state election in 1869 to ascertain whether the constitution drawn up by the recent convention would be acceptable to the people, and to choose district and county officers under the new constitution. The Radicals, of course, since they had fought against the constitution as it was accepted at the convention, were strongly opposed to the calling of a ratification election.

Each Republican faction sent a delegation to Washington. The Radicals, led by Davis and Morgan C. Hamilton, declared that Texas was not yet ready to vote on the constitution. Opposed to this view were the Conservatives, led by A. J. Hamilton, who presented a synopsis of Texas political history since the war and won support of the national administration concerning the needs of the state. Congress provided for the election, and the field of political battle was again transferred from Washington to Texas.

Although most of the Democrats favored the constitution, they chose not to fuse with Conservative Republicans. Instead, they put up their own candidates for the legislature and for state and county offices.[1]

A. J. Hamilton announced for governor from Washington, after it became evident that Congress would not object to the new constitution. He and other members of his Conservative faction met in the national capital and drafted the remainder of the Conservative ticket. A few

[1] Charles W. Ramsdell, *Reconstruction in Texas*, p. 268.

13

Conservatives wanted E. M. Pease to run for governor, but he declined. They also discussed at length the advisability of fusing with the Democrats, and debated the propriety of calling a state convention. Both propositions were eventually rejected.

No strong newspapers favored the Radical Republicans and they seemed to have no great strength over the state. Their scheme for dividing the state and disfranchising all ex-Confederates had failed. They were at first undecided about a platform that would best promote their cause, but one thing was certain: if they continued to fight against the constitution they would almost surely be defeated. Reconciliation with Conservative Republicans was out of the question, because the Conservatives would not tolerate them. They finally decided on a middle path and constructed a platform similar to that advocated by the Conservatives at the convention of 1868.[2] For governor they nominated E. J. Davis; for lieutenant governor, J. W. Flanagan; for commissioner of the land office, Jacob Kuechler; and for state treasurer, George W. Honey.[3]

A strong friend of the Radical Party was General J. J. Reynolds, military commander of Texas. Largely because of Reynolds' influence President Grant gave his support to the Davis faction. But Reynolds had not always been an ally of the Radicals; for a time he had supported the Conservatives. At the reconstruction convention Reynolds had advocated only white men for voting registrars, and he had condemned disfranchisement, division of Texas into smaller states, and other Radical Republican suggestions. Reynolds had censured the Radicals for bolting from the Republican state convention in August of the previous year.

Then Reynolds had been present at a Hamilton-Davis clash in Congress, when Davis denounced the new constitution and urged the President and Congress to prevent its submission to a vote. A. J. Hamilton had defended it and pleaded for reconstruction, and on that occasion Reynolds had endorsed Hamilton and recommended Hamilton men for office. Reynolds also urged that A. P. McCormick be put on the same ticket with Hamilton for lieutenant governor. When Reynolds returned to Texas the angry Davis men—Radicals—met in convention and voted on a resolution denouncing the General and

2 *Ibid.,* pp. 269–272.
3 Houston *Tri-Weekly Union,* June 16, 1869, I, 70.

14

asking for his removal. This resolution was defeated by only one vote.[4]

But Reynolds' warm conservatism was soon to cool because of a political slight. It became known to A. J. Hamilton that Reynolds liked the Texas climate and might enjoy becoming United States senator from the state. Hamilton did not approve, feeling that the party could make a stronger nomination. This infuriated Reynolds, who deserted the Conservative faction of Hamilton and gave his support to the Radicals.[5]

The Texas election was set by President Grant to extend from November 30 through December 3. Paving the way, in the summer and fall of 1869, federal patronage was taken away from the Hamilton supporters and given to the Davis group. On September 4 General Reynolds wrote the President that if Hamilton won the election it would mean a reinstatement of Confederate government in Texas and that the only bona fide Republican Party in the state was the E. J. Davis faction. On hearing this, Pease resigned his military governorship, leaving the chair vacant, and threw all of his support to the Hamilton campaign, declaring that eight-tenths of the educated Republicans favored A. J. Hamilton. Conservatives called the Radicals a "carpet-bagger and Negro supremacy" party; and Davis' followers retaliated by saying that the Conservatives had "sold out to the rebels."[6]

The Radicals were able to line up the Negro vote by doing three things: (1) gaining the support of G. T. Ruby, state president of the Union League;[7] (2) convincing the Negro that the Conservative Re-

[4] Ramsdell, *Reconstruction in Texas,* p. 274.

[5] Austin *Daily Republican,* January 3, 1870, II, 178.

[6] Ramsdell, *Reconstruction in Texas,* p. 281; *Daily State Journal,* February 17, 1870, I, 17.

[7] The Union League of Texas, the state branch of the Union League of America located at New York City, was a secret organization designed primarily to educate the Negro to vote the radical Republican ticket, to guard him against intimidation, and to obtain his donations to the campaign fund. It was usually spoken of as the "Loyal League."

The society in Texas was controlled by a state council led by a president who was assisted by an executive committee of which he was a member. Below the state council and under its supervision were subordinate councils located in the various counties that possessed Negro populations.

The office of the state council after June, 1870, was evidently located at Austin, for at that time James P. Newcomb, the secretary of state, superseded G. T. Ruby as president.

15

publicans intended to disfranchise him; (3) persuading him that the federal administration would guarantee the freedman's political rights.

To counter Davis' Negro vote it was necessary for Hamilton to gain the support of the Democrats. The Davis faction, however, realized this and was instrumental in getting the Democrats to run an independent ticket. Several Democratic editors met in Brenham in September and nominated one of their own number, Hamilton Stuart, editor of the Galveston *Civilian*, as their candidate for governor.

On October 1, in preparation for the election, General Reynolds issued an order: voter registration was to begin November 16 and continue for a period of ten days. Only Davis men were appointed registrars in most of the counties.[8]

Much dissatisfaction with the rulings of the registration boards developed in Travis, Bastrop, and adjoining counties; in Travis the board ruled that all applicants who had been rejected at the previous registration were to be summarily rejected again. Most rejected applicants were certain that this was not according to the reconstruction acts or to the orders of the commanding general, for the law made it an obligation of the new board to revise the lists. Such revision was not made. Moreover, the previous board had turned down many men who were actually entitled to register; they had been Unionists throughout the war, but had not been allowed to register because they had held an office in Texas before the war.

In Bastrop County the board rejected every man who had volunteered for the Confederate service, even though he had held no office. At the same time all names of those who had been previously registered, but who had proved obnoxious to the Radicals, were struck off. Appeals were made to General Reynolds, but without success. He was reported to have given a verbal opinion against this action of the board, but he refused to go further, leaving the board free to do as it wished. This was not the only instance of injustice, for the registration orders

---

Ritual, Constitution, and By Laws of the National Council, Union League of America. Together with All the Necessary Information for the Complete Working of Subordinate Councils. Miscellaneous Pamphlets in The Pearson Newcomb Collection; G. T. Ruby to James P. Newcomb, August 11, 1869, Pearson Newcomb Collection, MS.; Thomas Baker to James P. Newcomb, June 20, 1870, Pearson Newcomb Collection, MS.

[8] Ramsdell, *Reconstruction in Texas,* p. 281; *Daily State Journal,* February 17, 1870, I, 17.

issued by General Reynolds were drawn up in a manner that permitted serious abuses. Those who supervised registration suited the orders to their own partisan interests and numbers of qualified voters were disfranchised.[9]

Voting began with troops stationed at all polling places, and any disturbance was considered a just cause for closing the polls. In every county the election officers were the same men who had composed the board of registration. Of the registered whites in the state only about one-half cast ballots. The registered Negroes took a more active part.

The election resulted in a victory for Radical Republicans. In its report military headquarters gave Davis a majority of about 800. Reynolds stated in a general order issued on January 11, 1870, that the new constitution had been ratified, and declared that the following officials had been duly elected: governor, Edmund J. Davis; lieutenant governor, J. W. Flanagan; comptroller, A. Bledsoe; treasurer, G. W. Honey; land office commissioner, Jacob Kuechler. He also announced the names of the new members of Congress and of the Twelfth Texas Legislature. Winning Congressional candidates were G. W. Whitmore, First District; J. W. Conner, Second District; W. T. Clark, Third District; E. Degener, Fourth District.

Many accusations of fraud were made following the election. Its legality was protested to President Grant by E. M. Pease and other prominent Texas citizens. They charged that thousands of fraudulent votes had been cast and that in numerous instances neither the laws

[9] Frank Brown, "Annals of Travis County and the City of Austin," Ch. XXVII, pp. 19–22, MS. Concerning the provisions of General Reynolds' order Brown declared:

It provided that an applicant might be registered in a given county and make a statement that he was about to remove to another county. As the registration continued ten days, there was no means of preventing a person, whose identity was unknown at the county seat, from procuring registration papers and voting in at least two counties. There was probably no intention to provide means for repeating, but the order was liable to abuse in that respect.

The order also provided for four challengers. This was liable to abuse, because there were likely to be partisans. And there was no appeal to the district commander, or to any other authority, against the improper registration of an applicant. The decisions of the registrars was final.

Boards of registration were invested with power to suppress disturbances and have a detachment of soldiers at the county seat.

There is no doubt that in numerous cases throughout the State applicants were rejected who were entitled to register from the standpoint of the Democrats and moderate Republicans. And there can be no doubt that many were rejected who were clearly entitled to register and vote in the opinion of General Reynolds himself.

17

of Congress nor the orders of the Commanding General had been complied with.[10] They requested an official investigation.

General Reynolds finally reported the election to Washington. The Conservatives hoped that the President would submit this report and other documents relating to the Texas election to Congress, although they suspected that Grant would be governed to a great extent by what Reynolds might say.[11] This must have been true, for there was never any federal investigation of the election.

Several counties submitted no final report of the votes cast, and Navarro held no election at all, for the chairman of the board of registrars absconded with a list of the registered voters.[12] The Radicals claimed he had been forced to flee as a result of intimidation: he had been without aid or military protection, and the sheriff had purposely resigned a day or so before the election. Had the voters in Navarro been counted, it was generally agreed, the majority of them would have been for Hamilton.

Nor did Milam County fare any better. There a dispute between the chief of the board of registrars and a citizen prevented the counting of the votes. The Waco *Examiner,* a Democratic paper, declared, according to Charles W. Ramsdell in his *Reconstruction in Texas,* that on the second day of the election a Cameron citizen informed Lieutenant Benham, the registrar, that he had brought to the polls a number of Negroes who were to vote as he, the citizen directed. A fight ensued, and both men were wounded. The majority vote of this county probably would have gone to Hamilton.[13]

Many Conservative Republicans, including Governor Pease, thought that Hamilton would have been elected had the votes of Milam and Navarro counties been counted.[14] Elsewhere there were other questionable acts. Hill County reported a majority of 149 for Davis, but it later

[10] Houston *Tri-Weekly Union,* January 18, 1870, II, 46; Dudley G. Wooten, *A Comprehensive History of Texas,* p. 185. The returns of the votes announced by General Reynolds were as follows: For the constitution, 54,447; against it, 4,655; for governor, E. J. Davis, 39,901; A. J. Hamilton, 39,092; Hamilton Stuart, 380; for lieutenant-governor, J. W. Flanagan, 35,401; Wells Thompson, 19,583; Boulds Baker, 10,327; A. H. Latimer, 6,801; registered voters in the state, 78,648 whites; 56,905 colored.

[11] *Flake's Bulletin,* January 4, 1870, V, 165.

[12] Ramsdell, *Reconstruction in Texas,* p. 284.

[13] *Ibid.*

[14] Houston *Tri-Weekly Union,* December 25, 1869, II, 39.

developed that the ballots had been removed to an adjoining county and counted there by one member of the board.[15] Fraud was charged in Cameron County and in El Paso County, where over twice as many votes were cast for Hamilton as were actually counted for him. In El Paso the local district commander found, upon examining the ballots, evidence of tampering, and he advised General Reynolds that an investigation was needed. In a number of counties it was charged and admitted that election officers had not sworn as to the correctness of the election returns. Voters whose ballots had apparently not been counted swore before magistrates that they had voted the Conservative ticket,[16] but no official investigation was ever conducted.[17] The Conservatives clamored in vain for Reynolds to study the fraud charges and to order a special election in Milam and Navarro counties.

The election left the Radicals jubilant. One party organ proclaimed. "Reconstruction has come to an end at last. There is no Andy Johnson 'policy,' no Throckmorton 'Confederate record,' no Jack Hamilton 'rebel coalition' in the present programme. Let the people of Texas rejoice. 'Come thou with us, and we will do thee good.' "[18]

General Reynolds appointed all of the newly elected candidates as provisional officers on January 8, 1870, the day he announced the result of the election.[19] The Davis administration thus began. Conservatives greeted it with a spirit of resignation, but at least military government was at an end.

Edmund J. Davis was a Southern man, born in Florida on October 2, 1827. Although biographical information is incomplete, he apparently came to Texas in 1848 with his widowed mother and her three other children. The family settled in Galveston, but Davis soon moved to South Texas, living for a time at Laredo, Corpus Christi, and Brownsville. He studied law, but at what time or place is not known.[20]

In 1850, at Laredo, he became deputy customs collector of the Rio Grande and held this position until 1852. In 1853 he was elected dis-

[15] Ramsdell, *Reconstruction in Texas,* p. 284.
[16] Austin *Daily Republican,* January 24, 1870, II, 196; also see Cruse Carson to Governor E. J. Davis, January 12, 1870, Executive Letters of Governor E. J. Davis, MS.
[17] Ramsdell, *Reconstruction in Texas,* p. 285.
[18] Houston *Tri-Weekly Union,* January 18, 1870, II, 46.
[19] Austin *Daily Republican,* January 10, 1870, II, 184.
[20] Seth S. McKay, "Texas under the Regime of E. J. Davis," p. 95, MS.

trict attorney; the next year he was named state district court judge at Brownsville, and retained this position until 1861. In 1858, at Corpus Christi, he was married to Miss Anna Britton, daughter of Major Forbes Britton, a former United States Army officer who had seen service in the Mexican War.

At the outbreak of the Civil War Davis was still judge of the state district court at Brownsville.[21] Opposed to secession, he campaigned for the post of delegate to the Secession Convention but was defeated because of his Unionist stand.[22] Soon after the war began he was forced to flee to Mexico to escape a group of secessionists determined to kill him.[23] In 1862 he raised a cavalry regiment for the federal army, recruiting Texans of Unionist convictions who had fled to Mexico. Davis was commissioned a colonel.

[21] *Ibid.*, pp. 95–96; Wooten, *Comprehensive History of Texas,* p. 185.

[22] An account by James P. Newcomb of an interview between E. J. Davis and Robert E. Lee in November, 1860, indicated the way both men looked at the secession question, and since it threw light upon the character of Davis, it is incorporated below:

After General Twigg's surrender, among other United States officers, Colonel Robert E. Lee stopped at San Antonio on his way North. Judge E. J. Davis was personally acquainted with Lee and regarded him as the most able man in the Federal Service. They met by appointment in the parlor of the hotel then kept by Mrs. Philips situated on Main Plaza, James P. Newcomb having been invited to be present. The meeting was purely a friendly and social one, but Davis took advantage of this opportunity to make a strong appeal to Colonel Lee to stand by the Union and resist secession. He called his attention to his having been educated at West Point, and being a native of Virginia, the home of Washington. He reviewed the question of secession from a legal point of view. Davis, in his appeal, stated his own Southern history,—that his family had been of South Carolina, and had taken part with Washington—that he, Davis had never been North and bore no enmity towards the people of the Northern States. He regarded the preservation of the Union as paramount to all other considerations. Lee made little reply to the argument advanced by Davis. Rising from his seat, he paced the room, showing visible feeling, and remarked that the argument offered by Davis was correct and unanswerable, that while secession was suicidal and disaster certain to the people of the South, he felt that he must go with his State.

The interview deeply affected young Newcomb, who was an ardent Unionist. The two men presented to him a remarkable contrast. Lee was a superb man, a perfect soldier, compact in frame, handsome in countenance, bronzed by the suns of service on the frontier. Davis was a cavalier in appearance—taller in height than Lee by five or six inches, but graceful in manner—a splendid face, intellectual and strong. He wore his hair long, as was the custom in the South. It was a memorable meeting. Unpublished account by James P. Newcomb, Pearson Newcomb Collection, MS.

[23] McKay, "Texas under the Regime of E. J. Davis," pp. 95–96, MS; Wooten, *Comprehensive History of Texas,* p. 185.

He and five of his men were captured in Mexico in March, 1863, by Confederate Army forces, and were carried across the Rio Grande into Texas. At the time he was seized he was below Matamoros, enlisting men for his regiment. Other Union officers in Mexico urged the governor of Tamaulipas to intercede in his behalf, and the governor protested to Brigadier General H. P. Bee in command of Confederate force at Brownsville, who released the prisoners. Davis' regiment then went by sea from Mexico to Union-held New Orleans and from there to the federal army in Louisiana.

Later, in March, 1864, Davis led an unsuccessful attempt to capture Laredo. During that same year he was made brigadier general and early in 1865 was assigned to the Department of the Gulf. He was mustered out of the service in August, 1865, at San Antonio.[24]

In the constitutional convention of 1866 Davis began to assert his leadership over the Radical Republican faction. He urged that all acts of the Legislature be made void from the date of secession, and he advocated unrestricted Negro suffrage and disfranchisement of former Confederates. His faction was in the minority in this convention, however, and did not reach its full strength until 1868.

Davis was the acknowledged leader of the extreme radical faction in the reconstruction convention of 1868, and he was elected chairman of the convention. Opposing him was the moderate wing of the Republican party, led by A. J. Hamilton. Davis' Radicals wanted to divide Texas into three states and to disfranchise all ex-Confederates, but these two schemes were defeated by the Moderates. As a result, ex-Confederates were not disfranchised except when they were affected by provisions of the Fourteenth Amendment.

Davis then tried to adjourn the convention without waiting for the state constitution to be finished. He hoped thus to be able to retain military government in Texas for an indefinite period, or at least until his faction could gain control. Some delegates did go home, but a majority remained, and these supervised the printing of the constitution and its submission to the people.[25]

Now, however, the Radicals had gained full control of the state and Davis, winner of the 1869 election, was about to take office as

[24] Homer S. Thrall, *A Pictorial History of Texas,* p. 530; Austin *Daily Statesman,* February 8, 1883, XII, 164.

[25] Ramsdell, *Reconstruction in Texas,* pp. 255–260.

governor. On January 11, 1870, General Reynolds issued a proclamation convening the Legislature on the eighth day of February.[26] On January 17 Davis qualified as provisional governor and immediately commenced discharging official duties.[27] One of his first acts was to appoint James P. Newcomb of San Antonio as secretary of state. Commenting on this selection, the Radical Republican *Tri-Weekly Union* of Houston said: "The appointment is an eminent proper one. Mr. Newcomb is a cultivated gentleman, a man of ability and enterprise, and a fast and long friend of Davis. We cordially approve the appointment and heartily congratulate Mr. Newcomb."[28]

A day or two before the Legislature convened, General Reynolds appointed Major B. Rush Plumley temporary speaker of the House of Representatives. This elicited an observation from at least one newspaper that the appointment of the speaker by a military officer appeared to be a rather strange proceeding,[29] but that it was necessary before the civil government could be put into operation. A number of the newly elected legislators had their seats contested, and such cases were referred to military headquarters for a decision by General Reynolds. One Conservative Republican newspaper commented:

From present appearances not less than twenty seats in the Legislature will be contested. This is extraordinary and may well cause reflection. It was not infrequently the case in the past that a member's seat was contested, but it was only when the vote was exceedingly close or where there was palpable fraud. Now we see men contesting seats where their opponent was elected by a thousand or more majority. Candidates who were so badly beaten that everybody had forgotten they were in the field, respond promptly to General Reynold's order, and are here ready to claim their seats.[30]

On February 10 Ira H. Evans of Corpus Christi, a personal friend of Governor Davis, was elected permanent speaker of the House. J. W. Flanagan, the newly-elected lieutenant governor, was expected to serve as president of the Senate,[31] but the Legislature was soon to

---

[26] Houston *Tri-Weekly Union*, January 18, 1870, II, 46; *Tri-Weekly State Gazette*, January 14, 1870, III, 18.

[27] Austin *Daily Republican*, January 19, 1870, II, 192.

[28] Houston *Tri-Weekly Union*, January 18, 1870, II, 46.

[29] Austin *Daily Republican*, February 7, 1870, II, 208.

[30] *Ibid.*, February 7, 1870, II, 46.

[31] Brown, "Annals of Travis County," Ch. XXVII, p. 5, MS.; Ramsdell,

elect him to the United States Senate, and he then relinquished the position of lieutenant governor to Don Campbell.[32]

In the Senate of this provisional Legislature were seventeen Republicans, seven Conservative Republicans, and six Democrats. Two Republican senators were Negroes. In the House were fifty Republicans, nineteen Conservative Republicans, and twenty-one Democrats.[33] Eleven Negroes were elected to the House.[34]

Soon after the provisional Legislature was organized General Reynolds referred to it, for settlement, certain cases arising over contested seats, but he presented only those cases which did not arise under reconstruction laws. Eight of these contests were for seats in the House; only one was for a Senate position. In each house Radical Republicans outnumbered the combined strength of Conservative Republicans and Democrats, and by controlling the committees on elections they were able to seat Radicals in nearly every instance. Some ten other contests, involving reconstruction laws, were reserved for a military board decision.[35]

General Reynolds had convened the provisional Legislature for the

---

Reconstruction in Texas, p. 289; McKay, "Texas under the Regime of E. J. Davis," p. 107, MS.

[32] Ramsdell, *Reconstruction in Texas,* p. 296; McKay, "Texas under the Regime of E. J. Davis," p. 107, MS.

[33] Brown, "Annals of Travis County," Ch. XXVII, pp. 5–6, MS.; Thrall, *Pictorial History of Texas,* p. 429.

[34] Unpublished manuscript writings of James P. Newcomb, Pearson Newcomb Collection, MS.; *The House Journal, 12th Legislature,* 1870, pp. 3, 4, 83. The colored members of the Senate were G. T. Ruby and Matthew Gaines, and those in the House were: Shep Mullins, Ben Williams, Richard Allen, Goldstein Dupree, Silas Cotton, M. Kendall, D. W. Burley, Henry Moore, Williams of Walker, David Medlock, J. J. Hamilton, and J. Mitchell.
Senator Ruby, a mulatto, was the most prominent Negro of the group and a man of some ability. Born in New York in 1841, he was educated in the free schools of Maine. In March, 1861, he went to Haiti as correspondent of the *Pine and Palm,* a Boston paper. Ruby remained there until 1864, when he left the island for New Orleans. Soon he was appointed principal of a grade school in the city, but was promoted to the position of school agent for Louisiana. In September, 1866, Ruby came to Texas. He was elected a member of the constitution convention in 1868, and the following year was chosen to represent the Galveston district in the state senate. It has been mentioned that at one time he was president of the state council of the Union League.

[35] McKay, "Texas under the Regime of E. J. Davis," p. 105, MS.; Ramsdell,. *Reconstruction in Texas,* p. 289.

dual purpose of having that body adopt the reconstruction amendments to the federal Constitution and having it elect members to the United States Senate. The Fourteenth and Fifteenth amendments were adopted easily on February 18,[36] and two Radical Republicans were elected to the United States Senate less than a week later.[37]

Reynolds himself had been urged by some of his Radical friends to become a candidate for the United States Senate, but he refused, at least for the present. His election would have been certain, however, because he exercised a great deal of power in keeping the Radical faction in control of the Legislature. Reynolds explained his refusal in an open letter to the *Daily State Journal:*

I am not a candidate for any civil position whatever, and have never authorized the use of my name in such connection. The proper discharge of my duties has required of me the performance of many acts of a political character, but my convictions of right and sense of propriety would preclude the acceptance on my part of any political office at the present time and under existing circumstances, at the hands of the Legislature of Texas. I have, to be sure, resided in the State with a trifling interval, for more than three years, but this residence has been as an officer of the army, charged in addition to the ordinary duties of my profession, with the execution of the reconstruction laws of Congress.

Nothing but the existence of an unprecedented emergency would warrant the Government in placing in the hands of a single individual the vast powers entrusted by these laws to a District Commander. I doubt whether a residence under such conditions constitutes me "an inhabitant of that State" in the sense in which this phrase is used in the Constitution of the United States.[38]

Chosen for a full term in the United States Senate beginning March 4, 1871, was Morgan C. Hamilton. He was also selected to serve out the unexpired part of the term that would end March 3, 1871. He was a Radical who had no sympathy whatever for the views of A. J. Hamilton, his Conservative brother.

Lieutenant Governor J. W. Flanagan was elected for the term ending March 3, 1875.[39] Flanagan, too, was a leading member of the

---

[36] *Daily State Journal,* February 19, 1870, I, 19.

[37] Austin *Daily Republican,* February 25, 1870, II, 224.

[38] *Daily State Journal,* February 16, 1870, I, 16.

[39] Austin *Daily Republican,* February 25, 1870, II, 224; C. Appleton (ed.), *American Annual Cyclopaedia,* 1871, XI, 15.

Radical Republican Party of Texas, but Morgan Hamilton was more prominent.[40]

Its work now complete, the reconstruction session of the Twelfth Legislature adjourned on February 24, to meet again on the call of the Governor as soon as the state was readmitted to the Union.[41]

WORK OF THE TWELFTH LEGISLATURE

PARTY LEGISLATION

The act readmitting Texas into the Union was approved by President Grant on March 30, 1870. Governor Davis at once issued a call for the Legislature to convene on April 26.[42] General Reynolds, in an order dated April 16, relinquished the state government to civil authorities.

Reynolds' order further provided that newly elected state officers would take the oath of office prescribed in the act of Congress that restored Texas: each officer would swear that he had never taken an oath for a federal or state office wherein he had sworn to support the United States Constitution and had later rebelled against it. The officer would also take the oath required by the state Constitution.

General Reynolds ordered all civil officials to continue in their present duties until relieved by qualified successors, to whom they were to turn over all records and public property pertaining to their respective offices. To facilitate the establishment of new county organizations, General Reynolds laid down certain instructions in his order which were in accordance with existing laws and the state constitution. He ordered the supreme and district courts of the state to continue to discharge their respective duties until the new courts should be inaugurated. Since no provisions had been made in the new constitution with reference to county surveyors and county treasurers, General Reynolds

[40] Thrall, *Pictorial History of Texas*, p. 549. Hamilton was a native of Alabama and had come to Texas in 1830. For six years he had acted as a clerk in the war department of the Republic, and at a later date had served as both Secretary of War and Secretary of the Treasury. In 1867, he was appointed comptroller of the state treasury by E. M. Pease. He played an important role in the convention of 1868 where he took a decided stand in favor of the disfranchisement of all ex-Confederates; this position had added much to his prominence in the Radical Republican faction. *Ibid.*, pp. 549, 427; Louis J. Wortham, *A History of Texas from Wilderness to Commonwealth*, V, 56.

[41] Austin *Daily Republican*, February 25, 1870, II, 224.

[42] *Flake's Daily Bulletin*, April 3, 1870, V, 242.

decreed that the present incumbents of these offices would retain their positions under the existing laws, pending the action of the legislature.

The specific instructions facilitating the establishing of the new county organizations were as follows: 1. Each justice of the peace elect was to give bond to the sum of five hundred dollars, payable to the presiding justice of the police court of the county, to be approved by the county court. 2. The new clerk of the district court for each county was to give bond in the sum of seven thousand dollars, payable to the governor of the state, which was to be approved by the county. 3. The sheriff elect of each county was to give bond in any sum not less than five nor more than thirty thousand dollars, payable to the governor, and to be approved either by the then present county court, or by the new police court when organized; the amount of the bond was to be determined by either of the said courts to which it might be presented.

The instructions the post commanders were to follow in disposing of the civilian prisoners were: 1. Those persons held for offences under the laws of Texas against whom indictments had been found, or for whom warrants or other process of arrest had been issued were to be surrendered at once to the civil officers producing the proper legal process and receipts taken for them. In all cases where the post commander was able to do so, he was to cause complaints to be made to some examining and committing magistrate, and cause the necessary process to be issued to enable prisoners to be turned over to the civil authorities. All information in reference to their cases would be turned over with the prisoners, and care was to be exercised to protect the interest of witnesses and informants. 2. Persons who were held under the authority of the United States would be detained in custody to await the United States marshal, or his deputy, on proper demand, based on competent legal process.

Under the new constitution the office of assessor and collector was abolished, and taxes were to be assessed by the justices of the peace and collected by the sheriffs. To prevent, however, the great confusion and delay that would arise if the assessment rolls were then turned over to the justices of the peace, the present assessors would complete the assessment of taxes in their respective counties and return their rolls to the comptroller of public accounts on or before the first day of June, 1870. The offices of county judge, county commissioners, and coroners, were also dispensed with. The five justices of the peace in each county constituted the police court. The civil and criminal jurisdiction of the county judge was vested in the district court, district clerk, and the justice of the peace.[43]

Governor Davis was inaugurated on April 28 and delivered his message to the Legislature the following day.[44] He declared that a matter of vital importance was the establishment of a state militia, and recommended the creation of a state police system which would incorporate the local police and sheriffs, sheriff's deputies, and constables. He wanted the criminal code modified, a state school system established, and further frontier defense provided. He stated that if Texas wanted to subsidize railroads it should confine itself to building a road from the Red River to the Rio Grande. Then he concluded by saying that he trusted the work of the Legislature would result in the establishment of security and harmony throughout the state.[45]

A few days later, on May 9, in a most unusual caucus of the Radical legislators, it was decided that there could be no state election until November, 1872. The Radical lawmakers were thus extending their term of office twelve months longer than the period allowed by the state Constitution. The extremists, who were in the majority, argued that the people of the state were in no condition for a political contest, since they had not undergone sufficient reconstruction to face the discordance that an election would create. This decision was at once denounced by Morgan C. Hamilton, who had been, until that time, a staunch Radical Republican. He began to write caustic newspaper articles calling this proposed extension of tenure unconstitutional. But the Legislature was determined to give its plan the force of law; the act, was passed and, on August 15, 1870, was signed by Governor Davis. The Twelfth Legislature adjourned its first session on August 15, reconvened on January 10, 1871, and remained in session until May 31. Then it adjourned to meet on September 12, and this final session lasted from that date until December 2.[46]

Certain measures were passed in the early weeks of the first session dealing with the organization of civil state government machinery. One was a joint resolution authorizing the newly elected officers—sheriffs, county clerks, justices of the peace, and constables—to con-

[43] Houston *Daily Union,* April 22, I, 70; II, 38.
[44] Wortham, *History of Texas,* p. 63.
[45] *Daily State Journal,* April 30, 1870, I, 79.
[46] Brown, "Annals of Travis County," Ch. XXVII, pp. 6–7, MS.; McKay, "Texas under the Regime of E. J. Davis, p. 107, MS.

tinue to serve under the existing laws until further legislation should be enacted.[47] But this resolution failed to make adequate provision for the assessing and collecting of taxes pending the time that the newly elected officers took office. The fault was temporarily remedied by the order of General Reynolds which provided for the inauguration of civil government.[48]

Another law divided the state into thirty-five judicial districts.[49] Each of these districts was to have an elected judge, who was required to hold three terms of his court annually in each county of his district.[50]

At this time, also, two bills startling in character were considered. Each would increase the power of the governor to a greater degree than he ordinarily exercised, and, if strictly enforced, would involve arbitrary and despotic government. The first, known as the militia bill, provided for the enrollment of the militia and the organization and discipline of the state guards. The other bill called for the creation of a state police.

Specifically, the militia bill provided that all able-bodied male citizens between the ages of eighteen and forty-five were to be subject to military duty. The governor was to be commander in chief of the state military forces, which would consist of two classes: the State Guard and the Reserve Militia. The State Guard was to be composed of those who voluntarily enrolled and equipped themselves for service, and the Reserve Militia was to be composed of all others liable to military duty who had not enrolled in the State Guard. Provision was made for reserve-militia enrollment in every county once every two years. But the bill added that anyone liable for service in the Reserve Militia could avoid duty by paying fifteen dollars. The governor was to appoint an adjutant general, to hold the rank of colonel, who was also to act as quartermaster and commissary general.

The bill placed great discretionary power in the hands of the governor. It permitted him to declare martial law in any county whenever he believed it necessary to do so and to suspend the laws until the Legislature convened. Then that body might take any action it deemed proper. In the event of a martial law declaration the governor could call on the State Guard, Reserve Militia, or State Police to sup-

[47] H. P. N. Gammel, *Laws of Texas,* VII, 415.
[48] Houston *Daily Union,* April 22, 1870, II, 38.
[49] Gammel, *Laws of Texas,* VI, 195–197.
[50] Appleton, *American Annual Cyclopaedia,* 1870, X, 716.

press the disorder. During this period the expense of maintaining forces could, at the discretion of the governor, be assessed upon the people of the county where civil laws were suspended. The governor could also provide for the trial and punishment of offenders while martial law existed.[51]

The militia bill passed the House with ease, but when it reached the Senate it encountered difficulty, for there a fight occurred between fifteen Radicals who favored it and eleven Democrats and three Conservatives who opposed its passage.

Webster Flanagan had introduced a substitute to the original bill, more conservative than the original proposal in providing that local authorities instead of the governor should decide on the necessity of calling the militia. Moreover, Flanagan's proposal said nothing about martial law or assessing counties for maintenance costs. But Flanagan's substitute was defeated by one vote on June 21.[52] Then, in violation of an earlier agreement, the original bill was moved to be voted on. Thirteen of the minority immediately withdrew, evidently for a consultation, and broke the quorum. These persons were arrested at once, and with the exception of four who were necessary to make a quorum they were excluded from their seats. The Senate passed the original bill a few minutes later.[53] Senator E. L. Alford, one of the members released to make a quorum, was expelled a few days later by the "rump" Senate on the pretext that he had resisted arrest.[54]

[51] Gammel, *Laws of Texas*, VI, 185–190.

[52] Ramsdell, *Reconstruction in Texas*, pp. 296–297; *Senate Journal, 12th Legislature*, 1870, pp. 248–249.

[53] *Senate Journal, 12th Legislature*, 1870, pp. 248–249. The senators who absented themselves and were placed under arrest were: Alford, Bowers, Broughton, Clark, Cole, Dohoney, Douglas, Evans, Flanagan, Latimer, Pickett, Pyle, and Shannon. But Evans, Shannon, Dohoney, and Alford were released from arrest to make a quorum.

[54] Austin *Daily Republican*, January 10, 1871, III, 186. Alford was expelled while the other eight members were still under arrest, and as soon as they returned, they forced the Senate to repeal the resolution expelling him. But regardless of his re-instatement, Davis declared Alford's seat empty and called for a new election from his district. The newly elected Radical candidate, Hillebrand, was accepted by the Senate, and Alford was permanently unseated.

Virtually the same experience was forced upon Senator Dillard in April, 1871. Dillard, a conservative Republican, had been elected to fill the vacancy in the Senate left by Priest whom Davis appointed to a district judgeship. Dillard had been elected in his district by a majority of 441 votes. Evidence showed

For more than three weeks the Senate kept its Conservative members under arrest, and during that time it disposed of a number of party measures, with the aid of a Radical lower house.[55]

One of these acts provided for the establishment of a state police force of about 250 men, led by a chief of police but controlled by the governor. This law was approved by the Governor on July 1, 1870.[56]

Another measure passed by the "rump" Senate that received much criticism from the Conservative Republicans and Democrats alike was the "enabling act," which was approved by the Governor on June 28, 1870. It increased the governor's appointive power to an extraordinary degree by authorizing him to name a district attorney for each judicial district, a treasurer and a surveyor for each county, a sufficient number of cattle and hide inspectors, public cotton weighers, a mayor and a board of aldermen for each incorporated city and town, and a city recorder for Houston and Galveston. When a vacancy occurred in the position of sheriff or district clerk he could fill it by appointment. Much patronage was thus given to the governor, and for that reason the measure was severely criticized.[57]

---

that this election was both peaceable and fair. Yet he was ejected from the Senate when there was no just reason for the act. During his trial, Senator E. B. Pickett made a motion that Dillard be allowed to appear by counsel, a privilege which the Constitution of the State guaranteed, and which each member had sworn to observe. This privilege had never been denied in either of the houses of Congress, but in this instance it was refused, and under the call of the previous question, Dillard was unseated. *Flake's Daily Bulletin,* April 15, 1871, VI, 208. Also see the Austin *Daily Republican,* January 10, 1871, III, 186, and *Tri-Weekly State Gazette,* April 12, 1871, IV, 31.

[55] Ramsdell, *Reconstruction in Texas,* p. 297.

[56] Details of the provisions and outcome of the measure are given in Chapter II.

[57] McKay, "Texas under the Regime of E. J. Davis," p. 126, MS.; San Antonio *Herald,* October 20, 1871, XIV, 250. A letter of the Dallas citizens to Carl Schurz written at a later date gives an example of the type of criticism it received. An excerpt from the letter follows:

Davis now appoints directly:	Salary
3 Supreme Judges	$ 13,500.00
35 District Judges	132,500.00
1 Attorney General	3,000.00
35 District Attorneys	42,000.00
1 Adjutant-general	3,000.00
200 General Staff Officers	?
33 District School Supervisors	42,000.00

The minority report of the House committee on judiciary, to which the measure was referred, was strong in its denunciation of the bill, recommending its rejection for the following reasons:

FIRST: Because the act is unconstitutional in that it is in strict contravention to section twelve, article five of the State Constitution, which provided that district attorneys shall be elected by the qualified voters of each judicial district.

SECOND: Because it robs the people of the elective franchise, and attempts to clothe the Chief Executive with power not conferred upon him by the Constitution.

THIRD: Because it contravenes section one, article six of the Constitution, which confers upon every male citizen of the United States of the age of twenty-one years and upwards, without distinction of race, color, or former condition, who shall be a resident of the State at the time of the adoption of this Constitution, the right to vote for all offices that are now elected by the people.

258	Regular State Police	68,080.00
2,620	Special Police for each Election	188,640.00
1	State Geologist	10,000.00
6	Officers of Asylums	12,000.00
2	Officers of Penitentiaries	6,000.00
133	County Registrars paid in 25 cents fees	?
293	County Election Managers	about 23,500.00
1	Secretary of State	3,000.00
3	Clerks	3,000.00
393	County Surveyors, 60 Ocean and Bay Pilot Pilot Fees	?
300	County Officers to fill vacancies (fees)	?
500	Officers of Towns and Cities	?
35	Official Newspapers, enjoying a forced monopoly of all legal state, judicial and county advertising in judicial districts, in return for defense of Davis and slander of people	?

Indirectly he appoints:

393	County School Examiners	70,740.00
About 3,275	local school directors	1,200,000.00
	TOTAL	$1,842,685.00

Here are 8,538 persons directly and indirectly appointed by Davis to places of trust, honor or profit, or all combined. It will be seen that $1,842,685.00 are paid out in salaries, besides the amount in fees paid to 1,386 other people.

Not all of this appointive power came to the governor through the "enabling" act. A great part of it came through the public school act, the State Police act, the election law, and the public printing act, all of which were passed by the Twelfth Legislature. All of these acts have been or will be discussed in this study.

FOURTH: Because the Legislature have no authority to confer upon the governor any appointing power reserved by the people to themselves, and that any attempt to do so is subversive of republican institutions, and in violation of the Constitution of the State, which declares "that the privilege of free suffrage should be supported by law."

Wm. E. Hughes
J. E. Hawkins
J. W. Posey[58]

Another act passed by the Twelfth Legislature that was subjected to much criticism from Conservative Republicans and Democrats was a measure regulating the public printing. This law, approved by the Governor on August 13, 1870, provided for the election of a public printer, to be chosen by a joint vote of both houses, who would supervise the publishing of all material required by the various state offices. He was also to publish a newspaper in which were to be printed the journals of both the House and Senate, the laws of the state, and other official matters. This newspaper was to be designated as the official state journal. The governor was further authorized to designate certain newspapers to perform county and judiciary printing and judicial-district advertising.[59]

Conservative Republicans and Democrats complained about the cost of public printing under the new act, and both declared that it was likely to be more than the entire expenses of the state government before the war.[60]

In January, months before the act was passed, J. G. Tracy, a Radical with an eye for business, went to Austin to establish a party organ there. He bought the *State Gazette,* changed its name to the *Daily State Journal,* and obtained the consent of James Newcomb, secretary of state, to become its editor.[61] It was designated as the official state organ.

Soon thereafter the San Antonio *Herald* quoted the Houston *Telegraph* as saying that the firm of Tracy, Quick, and Company should not be allowed to hold the office of state printer since it already possessed from one to three state and federal offices. But the *Herald* disagreed, declaring, "We have no idea that a little thing like a constitu-

[58] *House Journal, 12th Legislature,* 1870, p. 116.
[59] Gammel, *Laws of Texas,* VI, 249.
[60] *Daily State Journal,* June 15, 1870, I, 118.
[61] Ramsdell, *Reconstruction in Texas,* pp. 286–287.

tional prohibition will prevent their handling the $200,000.00."[62] Statewide criticism caused the Twelfth Legislature the following year to repeal that part of the measure providing for official organs in each judicial district. The *State Journal,* however, was retained as the official newspaper.[63]

During the summer of 1870 came the first organized movement against the Davis administration. It was led by A. J. Hamilton, E. M. Pease, and J. W. Throckmorton, who sponsored a conference held at Austin in July. There they vehemently condemned the Davis policies and drew up a "Petition of the People of Texas to Congress to Guarantee to the People a Republican Form of Government."[64] As the title suggests, it asked Congress to give Texans the representative form of government guaranteed by the Constitution and to restore lost civil liberties.

The sponsors hoped that two-thirds of the voting population would sign the petition in time for presentation to Congress immediately after its convening in December. They planned to distribute copies of the petition over the state in pamphlet form and to circulate half a dozen in each county for signature.[65]

[62] McKay, "Texas under the Regime of E. J. Davis," p. 129, MS.; San Antonio *Herald,* February 12, 1871, XIV, 37.

[63] Gammel, *Laws of Texas,* VII, 33.

[64] Wortham, *History of Texas,* p. 73.

[65] Austin *Daily Republican,* July 27, 1870, III, 148. In the petition, relief was asked from five laws, as follows:

1. The state militia act, which they claimed created a standing army and provided for its support.

2. The state police act, and of this the petitioners said:

It will be observed that this police force is endowed with extraordinary powers; that these policemen may be employed as detectives; that they are invested with the authority belonging to all peace officers, thus making them judicial as well as executive officers, that their jurisdiction is co-extensive with the state; that they can act independently of the local peace officers, and that they are absolutely at the beck and nod of the Executive. There is also another insidious power conferred upon the Executive in this act in making all executive officers of the counties and municipalities of the state a part of this force and directly responsible to the Executive, and their tenure of office dependent on his will.

3. The "enabling act" which was a measure whose provisions allowed the governor to appoint the district attorneys and all county and municipal officers of the state who were declared elective by the state constitution.

4. An act, providing for the registration of voters, whose purpose seemed to the petitioning citizens to be to keep the white men of Texas from registering.

The petition was indeed widely circulated and then submitted to Congress, but nothing more was heard of it.[66]

RAILROAD LEGISLATION

Railroad construction was stimulated by state legislation. Fifty-two bills were introduced into the Twelfth Legislature for incorporation or relief of as many railroads.[67] To hasten action on some of these bills bribes were reportedly offered and accepted.

The first of these measures was an act, which became law on August 5, 1870, incorporating The International Railroad Company. By provisions of this act the International was to form a junction with the Cairo and Fulton Railroad at or near Fulton, Arkansas, and to build through Texas in a southwesterly direction, passing through or near Jefferson and crossing the state by way of Austin, San Antonio, and Laredo. To help this project Texas was to donate to the company, state bonds in the amount of $10,000 a mile for road actually constructed. These bonds were in denominations of $1,000 each, payable to the company within thirty years and with annual 8-per-cent interest, payable semiannually. Before presentation of the bonds to the railroad they were to be signed by the governor and state treasurer and countersigned and registered by the comptroller.[68]

In the passage of this and other railroad acts Twelfth Legislature members were charged with corruption. *Flake's Daily Bulletin,* a Conservative Republican newspaper published at Galveston, declared that they sold their votes, that proof was evident, and that the Radical press never denied it. Sudden wealth, new residences and farms, gold watches, fine horses and buggies, and fat bank accounts all indicated dishonesty, the publication declared. Another observer also commented on the alleged bribery.

It is within the knowledge of this writer that a prominent lawyer then at Austin about the time of the passage of the I. and G. N. railroad charter of the famous Twelfth, was given a check for $2,500.00—the consideration being that he would do nothing and keep his mouth closed.

---

5. An act regulating elections, which was believed to be an act to perpetuate and insure frauds at all future elections.

[66] Wortham, *History of Texas,* p. 73; Ramsdell, *Reconstruction in Texas,* p. 304.

[67] Ramsdell, *Reconstruction in Texas,* p. 300.

[68] Gammel, *Laws of Texas,* VI, 606–612.

DEMOCRATIC MEMBERS
OF THE
House of Representatives, 12th Legislature, April 18, 1871.

PLATE 1. Democratic members of the House of Representatives, Twelfth Legislature, April 18, 1871. Ellison Photo Company.

PLATE 2. James P. Newcomb, Secretary of State in the Davis Administration. From the University of Texas Archives.

It is well known at Austin that a prominent member of the Senate, since deceased, had been given a check for $2,500.00 for his vote and influence in favor of the same measure. When the time nearly arrived for a decisive vote, he was absent. A corruptionist was dispatched to the Raymond House where the Senator had a room and was boarding, with a request that he attend the sitting of the Senate at once. The member played sick. The lobbyist soon saw what the trouble was. A check for $2,500 was promptly handed the Senator, when he at once recovered, proceeded to the capitol, and cast his vote for the charter carrying an enormous money bonus . . .[69]

Conservative Republican and Democratic newspapers vigorously denounced the measure.[70] This criticism perhaps had some effect on the Governor, for he began using his veto to curb the zeal of legislators in granting other charters and donations. Had Davis not used his veto during the special session a debt of as much as $30,000,000 would have accrued.[71]

Following passage of the International Railroad Incorporation Act a large number of bonds were signed by the Governor and the State Treasurer, but Comptroller A. Bledsoe refused to add his signature, declaring that the law was unconstitutional. Court proceedings were entered against him to compel him to sign, and the case went from the Travis County District Court to the State Supreme Court. Much delay was caused by appeals and the infrequency of court sessions, and when the E. J. Davis regime ended a decision was still pending. Later the question was brought before the State Supreme Court during Richard Coke's administration, and Bledsoe was sustained.[72] During Coke's term, also, the Democratic Legislature was to compromise with the International Railroad Company by providing a gift of twenty sections

[69] Brown, "Annuals of Travis County," Ch. XXX, pp. 17–19, MS. It is also from Brown that the quotation from *Flake's Bulletin* is taken.

[70] The *Tri-Weekly State Gazette,* July 6, 1870, III, 69, declared:

It is needless to speak of the lobby influences brought to bear in getting this monstrous scheme through the Legislature. By an overwhelming vote, the Bill passed the House, and the money of the People goes into the pockets of the corporators, if the Senate or Governor does not put a quietus that will weaken its vertebrae. The plan of giving away money without any other return than the general beneficial results that flow from all internal improvements and especially when the corporators will make fortunes out of their naked enterprise, is an outrage on the People as a mass, and an injustice to other roads. The plan is like one of those hideous monsters that ought to be strangled at birth.

[71] *Daily State Journal,* August 16, 1870, I, 169.

[72] *Bledsoe v. The International Railroad Company,* 40 Texas 537, 1874.

of land for every mile of road built—instead of the $10,000 in bonds promised by Radical lawmakers in 1870.[73]

The Twelfth Legislature, at a later session, granted the Southern Pacific and the Southern Trans-Continental Railway companies money subsidies: thirty-year 8-per-cent state bonds amounting to 6 million dollars, with the stipulation that the two railroads unite at a point near the eastern boundary of Shackleford County. But the bonds were not to be delivered until the junction of the lines had been effected. The Legislature was further allowed to exchange these bonds any time before January 1, 1874, for public lands at the rate of twenty-four sections for every mile.[74] Under the old law the railroads were entitled to only sixteen sections a mile; now they had an opportunity to obtain a total of more than 22 million acres of land.

Earlier, House Speaker Ira H. Evans had argued against the bill, after first calling W. H. Sinclair, representative from Galveston, to the chair. Despite this opposition, however, the measure passed the House, 61 to 15. The Senate having concurred, the bill was sent to Governor Davis. But he vetoed it, declaring that if the measure became law it would burden Texans with an annual tax greater than that needed for the maintenance of state government. The bill was passed, however, over his veto.[75]

During the Thirteenth Legislature, on May 2, 1873, the Texas and Pacific bill was also enacted. This measure defined the rights of the newly organized Texas and Pacific Railroad Company, formed by a merger of the old Southern Pacific and Southern Trans-Continental lines, and enabled the state to sidestep the money subsidy provision of the earlier act. A grant of twenty sections of land for every mile of road constructed was substituted instead of the money stipulated.[76]

The Constitution of 1869 had declared railroad land grants illegal, and not until 1873 did an amendment remove this obstacle. The change, proposed in 1871 by the Twelfth Legislature, was voted on by the people in November, 1872, and ratified by the Legislature in March, 1873. Speaker Evans declared that the action was taken in answer to the "general sentiment of the people of Texas" and to avoid

[73] Gammel, *Laws of Texas,* VIII, 659–663.
[74] Gammel, *Laws of Texas,* VI, 1623–1628.
[75] Ramsdell, *Reconstruction in Texas,* pp. 307–308.
[76] Gammel, *Laws of Texas,* VII, 1018–1027.

"the bankruptcy of the state through granting bonds in aid of internal improvements." During the time that land grants had been prohibited thirty-one companies were chartered, and nine of these began actual construction. Of the nine, one obtained land through prior legislation and seven were given land by subsequent laws.[77]

On April 12, 1871, the Twelfth Legislature enacted a bill authorizing any county, city, or town to donate or subscribe bonds to aid in railway construction.[78] Under the provisions of this act a number of the cities and counties voted bonds. Incomplete figures show that cities issued a total of $347,000 and counties a total of more than one million.

Democrats did not approve of this type of aid, and when they came into control in 1874 they repealed the law. Furthermore, when they drafted their new constitution in 1875 they inserted a clause prohibiting the Legislature from authorizing such aid.[79]

During the Davis administration an old law providing for loans to railroads from the permanent school fund threw certain companies into financial difficulties. This law, which dated from 1856, stipulated that when a railroad company could show at least twenty-five miles of finished track it was to be allowed to borrow from the public school fund $6,000 for every mile completed. In return, the company was to execute its bond to the state for the amount received and to pay thereon 8 per cent per annum, 6 per cent as interest and 2 per cent to form a sinking fund for the retirement of the bonds at maturity. During the war years and the troubled times immediately following the war a number of the companies who had borrowed from the public school fund were unable to make these yearly payments, and in 1868 the reconstruction convention demanded the sale of some of these companies in order to discharge debts to the permanent school fund. Only one of them, however, was actually sold—the Houston Tap and Brazoria, the transaction being completed in Austin in February 15, 1871. Other companies were saved by the Twelfth Legislature, which passed a relief act on August 13, 1870, providing that railroads might avoid sale by paying six months' interest on the amount due, as it stood on May 1, 1870; depositing an additional 1 per cent for the

[77] Charles Shirley Potts, *Railroad Transportation in Texas, pp.* 99–100.
[78] Gammel, *Laws of Texas,* VI, 931–934.
[79] Potts, *Railroad Transportation in Texas,* p. 88.

sinking fund; and continuing semiannual payments, at these rates—on May 1 and November 1 of each year.[80]

OTHER LEGISLATIVE ENACTMENTS

The Twelfth Legislature, justly condemned for its arbitrary measures and its extravagant railroad legislation, nevertheless enacted some laws of merit. Among them were those providing for frontier protection.

The first act, passed in 1870, called for the raising of twenty companies of Rangers[81] to guard the northern and western frontiers.[82] Another law authorized bonds to be sold to provide for the Rangers' maintenance.[83] This protection soon proved to be expensive, however, and in 1871 a third act was passed substituting the use of Minute Men for Rangers. Pay for the Minute Men was to come out of the balance of money left from the act of 1870.[84]

Two other commendable measures were the homestead acts. The first of these, passed on August 12, 1870, allowed 160 acres of public domain land to every head of a family not already in possession of a homestead, provided that he occupied it for three years and paid office fees on it. Under the same provision, single men twenty-one and older were allowed eighty acres; and any person—single or married—who settled on not more than 160 acres of the public domain was entitled to buy the land at a dollar an acre. Such a purchase might also be made by one who already possessed a homestead.[85]

The second measure defined property exempted from forced sale. It declared that a family homestead of not more than two hundred acres of land in the county or of not more than five thousand dollars valuation in city lots, (both valuations at the time of designation as a homestead) would not be subject to forced sale for general debts. But it could be ordered sold if the debt was for the purchase of the prop-

[80] Gammel, *Laws of Texas,* VI, 260; Potts, *Railroad Transportation in Texas,* pp. 89–90.

[81] Not to be confused with the *Texas Rangers* of historical fame. Although Davis' force carried the same name, the resemblance was otherwise slight, for Davis' law officers almost invariably proved obnoxious to citizens. The real Texas Rangers were held in abeyance from the Civil War to 1874, when Coke became governor.

[82] Gammel, *Laws of Texas,* VI, 179–182.

[83] *Ibid.,* VI, 219–220.

[84] *Ibid.,* VII, 36–38.

[85] *Ibid.,* VI, 242–244.

erty itself, and it could be sold for labors and materials expended upon it and for taxes. This act became law on August 15, 1870.[86]

Another Twelfth Legislature act, which was then a forward step in state-wide education but which was afterward discredited, established a free school system. This act was passed in August, 1870,[87] in compliance with a stipulation in the 1869 constitution that public schools be created. The authors of the measure were unpopular, however, and the law was not well enforced; few schools came into being as a result of it. The Radicals, displeased by the lack of consideration the law received, resolved to enact a more stringent measure. So, in April of 1871, the Twelfth Legislature passed another free school law, the first workable one.[88] This statute is described in detail elsewhere in this study.

SENATOR HAMILTON VERSUS SENATOR REYNOLDS

The provisional session of the Twelfth Legislature, as has been mentioned, in February of 1870 elected Morgan C. Hamilton to the United States Senate to fill both the unexpired term ending March 4, 1871, and the full term expiring six years later.[89] At that time Hamilton was recognized as one of the stanchest leaders of the Radical faction,[90] but, as mentioned, he broke with the Radical legislators when they unconstitutionally lengthened their term of office. Nor could Hamilton approve of the militia law, the state police law, and certain other measures passed by the called session in 1870. He declared that these acts were violations of his party's pledges, believing that the Radical faction was obligated by its platform and by all its other promises to support the same liberal principles as those advocated by his brother,

[86] This measure further reserved to every family free from forced sale for debts, all household and kitchen furniture, all implements of husbandry, all tools and apparatus belonging to any trade or profession, all books belonging to private or public libraries, two yoke of work oxen, two horses and a wagon, a carriage or buggy, a gun, twenty hogs, twenty head of sheep, all provisions and forage on hand for some consumption, all saddles, bridles, and harness necessary for the use of the family; and to every citizen not a head of a family, a horse, bridle, and saddle, all wearing apparel, and all tools, apparatus, and books belonging to his private library. Gammel, *Laws of Texas,* VI, 301.

[87] *Ibid.,* VI, 287–292.

[88] Frederick Eby, *The Development of Education in Texas,* p. 157.

[89] Austin *Daily Republican,* February 25, 1870, II, 224.

[90] *Daily State Journal,* February 23, 1870, I, 22.

ex-Governor A. J. Hamilton.[91] In retaliation, the extremists plotted Senator Hamilton's political demise.

On January 10, 1871, the Twelfth Legislature reassembled and immediately began considering the legality of electing a new United States senator to replace Hamilton[92] for his full six-year term.[93] The legislators argued that because of the reconstruction laws, while Texas was out of the Union it was not a state, and the senators merely represented the people of a territory, who were given the authority by a congressional act to take the first steps toward representation in Congress. The Radicals now argued that former state laws did not become effective until the state was readmitted to the Union in 1870. Since Hamilton had been elected under such a law in February, 1870, one month before the state was readmitted, this contention, if upheld, would invalidate his election. The final decision in the matter rested with the United States Senate.

On January 19 the Texas House of Representatives passed, by a large majority, a resolution to elect a new United States senator; every Republican voted for it. Then, less than a week later—on the twenty-fourth—the House chose General J. J. Reynolds for the office. Governor Davis wired Reynolds his congratulations, and the General, stationed at San Antonio, replied by asking the Governor to convey his appreciation for the honor.

Reynolds was also elected by the state Senate, but not without opposition. A Democrat, Captain H. H. Bowers, read an excerpt from one of Reynolds' letters in which the General stated that he was not a citizen of Texas. Republican Senator A. J. Fountain countered with the argument that this information was of a private nature, but most Democrats nevertheless voted for Senator E. B. Pickett.

Many Texans believed that the United States Senate would not seat General Reynolds. Even before the vote had been cast by the Legislature Senator Morgan Hamilton had written to friends in Austin advising them not to take part in the election. He asserted that no matter how the vote went in the Legislature, the question would be

[91] Austin *Daily Republican,* October 14, 1870, III, 115.

[92] McKay, "Texas under the Regime of E. J. Davis," p. 107, MS.

[93] Brown, "Annals of Travis County," Ch. XXX, p. 15, MS.; Appleton, *American Annual Cyclopaedia,* 1870, X, 716; Gammel, *Laws of Texas,* V, 864.

settled by the judiciary committee of the United States Senate.[94] But the *Daily State Journal* reported that every Republican in the Legislature voted against Hamilton, that the twelve votes cast for him were all by Democrats.

A Conservative Republican paper commented adversely on the election:

Yesterday General Reynolds received a majority in both houses on the first ballot for United States Senator. This action will astonish the country at large and will be especially mortifying to the people of Texas.

We had hoped, and we believe the Republican party of the Nation hoped that with the completion of reconstruction, the rights, interests, and wishes of the people would be everywhere respected. There were so many wicked and foolish things connected with reconstruction of the Southern States, that the Republican party is already seriously injured thereby. The action of the Legislature yesterday will prove a bad day's work for the party.

We have no idea he will be permitted to take the seat. The position is already filled by a distinguished citizen of the state who was elected by this Legislature, and at the time fixed by law. He has never been expelled, neither has he died or resigned. . . . Were he [General Reynolds] a citizen of our State, and a vacancy really existed, we should oppose this election and so would the masses. He is in no manner identified with the interests of this state. He is totally without experience as a civil officer. He has performed no feats that indicated that he is in any sense of the term, a statesman. He has done nothing for the people of Texas that entitles him to be so highly honored by them. On the contrary as their appointed ruler he has done much to humiliate and injure them. In the U. S. Senate he could no more command the respect of his brother Senators than he could that of the people of Texas.[95]

Senator Charles Sumner of Massachusetts corroborated this, stating in a telegram to Austin that Hamilton would not be removed. Nevertheless, General Reynolds went to Washington in February, and soon after his arrival he conferred at length with President Grant, who was expected to use his influence to have Reynolds seated on the ground that the General had been legally elected. But some question still remained as to whether General Reynolds would contest Hamilton's seat, for although it was known that he had proceeded to the

[94] Brown, "Annals of Travis County," Ch. XXX, pp. 12–15, MS.
[95] Austin *Daily Republican,* January 25, 1871, III, 199.

41

capital by the order of the President, some of Reynolds' friends asserted he would not insist upon a seat. They believed that Reynolds considered the Legislature's action in electing him nothing more than a compliment. Moreover, they quoted the President as saying that he had no information on Reynolds' views in regard to a Senate seat, and that Grant did not believe the General would give up his military position to accept it.[96]

Finally, in March, 1871, the United States Senate decided against General Reynolds and authorized Hamilton to serve his full term. At the time the decision was made Texas was without representation in the Senate, for Senator Flanagan had left the city and Hamilton had absented himself while the question was being settled.[97] Thus, the attempt to displace Hamilton as Senator from Texas was thwarted solely by non-Texans.[98]

[96] Brown, "Annals of Travis County," Chs. XXX and XXXI, pp. 13–15, MS.

[97] *Ibid.*, p. 15; Appleton, *American Annual Cyclopaedia,* 1870, X, 715–716.

[98] Reynolds was a native of Kentucky from which state he received an appointment to the United States Military Academy at West Point. He graduated from this institution in 1843, and entered military service in July of that year with the rank of brevet second lieutenant of the Fourth Artillery. He was commissioned on May 11, 1846, to be second lieutenant of the Third Artillery, which position he held nearly a year, when he was promoted to be first lieutenant. On February 28, 1857, he resigned and entered the grocery business in Terre Haute. He joined the volunteer service during the war as colonel of an Indian regiment and was soon promoted to rank of brigadier general. After the battle of Stone River, he was placed in command of a division in General Thomas' Fourteenth Army Corps. With distinction, he led his division through the battle of Chickamauga. When the army was reorganized before the Atlanta campaign, he was assigned a command in the Southwest, and after the war he was made commander first of the District of Texas, and then of the Fifth Military District. At the time of his election to the United States Senate, he was colonel of the cavalry in the regular army. *Daily State Journal,* February 17, 1871, II, 19.

THE STATE POLICE

INTRODUCTION

THE STATE POLICE played an important role in the administration of Governor E. J. Davis. The organization was in existence almost three years, and during that time it acquired a distinctly unsavory reputation. Although the State Police did accomplish some good, in most instances the criticism heaped upon it by Conservative Republicans and Democrats seemed justified. Furthermore, there will always remain a doubt about the necessity for its creation.

As mentioned, Governor Davis, in his 1870 inaugural address, stated that for the welfare of the state certain laws were necessary to enable him to control lawlessness and to provide for the punishment of crime. He then recommended the enactment of appropriate measures, the most important of which were laws creating a state militia and a state police system.[1] Acting upon the Governor's suggestion, the Twelfth Legislature passed the State Police bill, which became law on July 1, 1870.[2] This act provided that the State Police be composed of a chief, 4 captains, 8 lieutenants, 20 sergeants, and 225 privates. The adjutant general was to act as chief of the State Police, but the governor, as chief executive, was to be commander in chief. The act made all sheriffs, constables, marshals, and city police potential members of the State Police, to be used when necessity demanded. This new organization was given the responsibility of suppressing crime openly and of acting as a detective force in ferreting it out.[3]

[1] Austin *Daily Republican*, May 2, 1870, II, 230; *House Journal, 12th Legislature*, 1870, p. 18.

[2] *Daily State Journal*, July 2, 1870, I, 133.

[3] H. P. N. Gammel, *Laws of Texas*, VI, 193–195.

THE FIRST YEAR

James Davidson, appointed adjutant general on June 24, 1870, undertook the added obligations of acting as chief of the State Police. The official organ of the administration declared: "We predict that General Davidson will make his office anything but a sinecure, and we advise felons, assassins, desperadoes, and *their* abettors, to act, if they are wise, upon the theory that if peace is not thoroughly kept, somebody will get hurt."[4]

The chief of State Police apparently encountered recruiting difficulties. Although the act provided for 225 privates, Davidson had only 172 at the end of December.[5]

However, the State Police had been in existence scarcely a month when, on August 9, its officers reported having apprehended thirty-nine murderers and felons. Five others had been killed resisting arrest. At this time only a third of the force was in the field, and the leading Radical Republican newspaper was moved to comment, "When the force is complete, the rascals running loose had better seek a cooler region than Texas. This is the best measure ever adopted to secure the enforcement of law in our state."[6]

The original appropriation for the force was $200,000 a year, but the Legislature soon increased this amount by $75,000.[7] Still, Davidson felt that the State Police salaries were insufficient,[8] and he stated in his annual report of 1870:

The present pay of the police force is inadequate. This fact is apparent to every one who considers the expenses a policeman must necessarily incur in traveling from one point to another; paying board for himself and horse, and keeping himself mounted for instant and arduous services, and I would therefore recommend that twenty-five dollars a month additional be allowed

[4] *Daily State Journal,* June 26, 1870, I, 128.
[5] *Report of the Adjutant General of Texas, for 1870,* p. 10.
[6] *Daily State Journal,* August 21, 1870, I, 174.
[7] *Ibid.,* September 10, 1870, I, 191.
[8] By the provisions of the State Police act of 1870, the privates were paid sixty dollars a month; the sergeants, seventy-five dollars; and the lieutenants, a hundred dollars. The chief of State Police received no further compensation for his work than that which the law provided for the office of adjutant general. Gammel, *Laws of Texas,* VI, 193–195.

44

each policeman for the services of his horse, thus enabling him to keep himself properly and efficiently mounted.[9]

The small salaries probably were responsible for the great number of resignations during the fall of 1870. Several members of the force also were discharged during the same period.[10]

In a circular issued by Davidson on July 1, sheriffs were asked to furnish the names of unapprehended criminals, the nature of their crimes, and when and where the crimes had been committed. These reports, when consolidated and filed in the adjutant general's office, showed that 2,790 criminals were evading arrest in 108 counties—and 29 counties had not been heard from. Of the criminals—and also those who committed crimes after July 1—978 had been arrested by the State Police and turned over to civil authorities by the time the Adjutant General issued his report on December 31, 1870.[11]

Although some actions of the State Police show that the organization was capable of accomplishing good, many of the 1870 cases in which its members had an active role illustrate the manifold abuses which its wide and unrestricted powers made possible and the extremely irresponsible or even criminal character of certain individuals on the force.

In De Witt County, near the end of August, 1870, two men— Henry and William Kelly—were arrested by members of Captain Jack Helm's company of State Police. Although both men were unarmed, they were brutally murdered by the officers. A sworn statement describing the outrage was filed by Amanda Kelly, wife of Henry Kelly.

About the rising of the sun on the morning of the 26th of August, A. D. 1870, I saw sitting on their horses near the yard gate three men, viz:————— White, alias Doc White. John Meader and a stranger, whose name I afterwards learned was ———— Simmons. Doc White and John Meader had their hats down over their faces as if to conceal their identity. I remarked to my husband, Henry Kelly, who was then in the house, that there were three men at the fence near the gate. He at once walked to the door, and one of the men spoke to him, saying, "step out here a few minutes, we want to see you." Mr. Kelly instantly went to them, when White said to him "we want you

---

[9] *Report of the Adjutant General of Texas for 1870*, p. 12.
[10] Austin *Daily Republican,* November 5, 1870, III, 133.
[11] *Report of the Adjutant General of Texas for 1870*, p. 12.

45

to go with us to Hallettsville," distant about thirty-five miles. Henry Kelly replied, "well, I will go; but my horse is out—let me have one of your horses to drive mine up." White said, "take my mule," and to John Meader, "you go and help him." Mr. Kelly then came into the house and got his hat and six shooter and started out where the men were; they seeing the six shooter, scabbard, and belt in his hand, said to him that he need not take the six shooter along; that he must consider himself a prisoner; that Mr. Simmons was a policeman and lived in the town of Hallettsville and had been sent for him. To which Mr. Kelly replied, "all right, I did not know it," and laid the pistol and scabbard on a block about half way between the house and the gate. Henry Kelly then got on White's mule, and in company with John Meader went after his horse, which he found, and drove up in a very short time. Mr. Kelly tied his horse near the gate and came in the house to change his clothes, when I asked him if I might go with him as far as Sweet Home, a place near where his mother lived. He then asked the men if they, after leaving Sutton's, would go by where William Day lived. The reply was, "yes, we will go right by his house." Then said Mr. Kelly, "I have no time to get your buggy horse up for you; but you can get your father to drive him up for you, and you can go the main road to William Day's and meet us."

The men then in charge of Mr. Kelly left, and went in the direction of the house of William Kelly, distant about one quarter of a mile.

My father, after the lapse of some short time, drove up my horse and hitched him to the buggy and I drove rapidly to the house of William Day, where I found the mother and sister of Henry and William Kelly, and proceeded to tell them what had taken place.

Mr. Day remarked that "there is no telling what they will do with the boys; the men are along who are in the habit of killing prisoners, and I would not be a bit surprised if they kill Henry and Bill," meaning Henry and William Kelly. In a few moments we heard the report of two guns on the road we were expecting them to come. I at once became alarmed and asked Mrs. Delilah Kelly to get in the buggy with me and we would go and see if they were killed. We proceeded on the road in the direction of the firing we had heard, where we met the party in charge of Henry and William Kelly. William Sutton, who had gone to the house of William Kelly and arrested him, having joined the party that arrested Henry Kelly.

On meeting the party of men, Mr. Henry Kelly expressed some surprise at our action in coming to meet them, and inquired our reason for so doing. I replied by saying that I had got uneasy about them and had come to see what was the matter.

When we met the party, Doc White, John Meader, and the stranger

(Simmons) were riding with Mr. Henry Kelly, and about one hundred yards in advance of William Sutton, who had charge of William Kelly. In a few minutes Doc White fell back to where John Meader was with the hindermost party and got from Meader a double barrel shot gun, and then galloped his horse and joined the front party again. At this action of Mr. White, I and my mother-in-law, who was with me in the buggy, expressed to each other dissatisfaction and distrust as to what was meant. Soon we came to an untraveled and out of the way trail, that led through the black-jacks and brush timber into the country back of William Day's house. At the turning off of this trail my husband, Henry Kelly, turned his horse on the main road that led by William Day's house, which was the main traveled road and an open way for buggies, wagons, etc., and Mr. White said to him (Henry Kelly), [*sic*] "we are not going that way; we are going through this way; it is the nearest to go by the house, and you promised me to go by the house; my wife wants to go with us, and her child is at the house; come go by so she can get the child." "No," said White, "it is the nearest way to go through here." Mr. Kelly then said to me, "go by the house and get the child and meet us up in the flat above William Day's."

I and my mother-in-law proceeded a little distance towards the house, when the party in charge of the prisoners disappeared in the brush and timber along the trail way. I then said to Mrs. Delilah Kelly, the mother of the prisoners, and who was in the buggy with me. "I will go no further with you after the child; I think from the looks and actions of the men, that they are after doing something wrong, and I mean to see them if they do it; so I will get out here and go up on the hill where I can see them and look after them, and you go up to the house and get the child and come back here, and follow after us and overtake us." I got out of the buggy and proceeded up the hill until I reached the top, where I was in sight of the party, about forty or fifty yards from me. They had halted in an open place surrounded by thick bushes and trees, and engaged in conversation.

Henry Kelly was sitting on his horse near Doc White and the stranger (Simmons), and William Kelly was sitting on his horse also near William Sutton and engaged in cutting up some tobacco to fill his pipe. After preparing his pipe, he dismounted from his horse and took a match, and was squatting down with one knee on the ground, and engaged in striking a match on the bottom of the boot of the other leg, when William Sutton shot him. William Sutton was sitting on his horse at the time, and I saw him as he suddenly raised his gun, and pointing it downward in the direction of William Kelly fired it off. William Kelly in his doubled up position instantly sank to the ground. In an instant another gun fired and I saw Doc White with his gun to his face, pointed in the direction of Henry Kelly and smoke between them, and Henry Kelly instantly fell from his horse. A general firing at the bodies on the ground by the parties then ensued, and the ground where the bodies lay and the vicinity was so enveloped in smoke as to completely hide the men and bodies, too, from my vision. After the firing ceased and when I was screaming and making toward the bodies, I saw the men escape in the brush. John Meader was not with the party when the killing took place. When I reached the bodies, Henry Kelly was lifeless and motionless. William Kelly showed signs of life, but did not speak. William Kelly's clothes were on fire and continued to burn until his mother arrived and put them out. . . . I was uneasy about the fate of my husband when they turned off in the trail, from the actions of the party before they turned off and from the fact that they were in charge of men (two of whom, viz: William Sutton and Doc White) were notorious for killing prisoners, and there was an improper feeling existing between Henry Kelly and those two men, White and Sutton . . .[12]

Helm, as captain of the fourth district of State Police, was directly responsible for the behavior of his men, and for that reason was accountable for the crime. That he openly sanctioned the death of these men cannot be proved, but even before this time he was said to have been a killer. In fact, he and his men were accused of having committed as many as twenty murders.[13] Before his appointment to the State Police, Helm and C. S. Bell, a man with an unsavory reputation, had killed John Choate and his nephew Crockett Choate in San Patricio County.[14] Later, while Helm was captain of the State Police, he was alleged to have taken it upon himself to levy a tax of twenty-five cents on each citizen of Sweet Home and vicinity for the purpose of defraying his hotel expenses while there.[15]

[12] Austin *Daily Republican,* November 1, 1870, III, 129.
[13] *Ibid.,* November 18, 1870, III, 144. B. J. Pridgen, a member of the Twelfth Legislature, stated that Helm and his party had murdered the following men: Bell, Moore, Pool, Purcell, Stapp, John Choate, and Crockett Choate, and a number of other persons whose names Pridgen did not know. Pridgen stated that Helm was likewise guilty of stealing $500 from a man named Turner in Western Texas. The full names of the alleged victims of Helm could be obtained in only two cases.
[14] *Ibid.,* November 3, 1870, III, 131.
[15] *Ibid.,* December 1, 1870, III, 154.

As for the slaying of William and Henry Kelly, there is no evidence of any indictment of the murderers. Helm was removed from the State Police, but not until nearly four months after the crimes had been committed.[16] The only bill of indictment issued against him during this period came from Bee County—for robbery, and the Austin *Daily Republican* declared that although a copy of this bill was forwarded to the authorities at the capital, the warrant was not served upon Helm, even though he was known to have been in Austin when the bill of indictment was received.[17]

Another unfortunate affair concerning the State Police occurred in Waco on the night of August 6, 1870. A barkeeper at Jim Johnson's saloon, accompanied by one or two other young men,[18] visited a grocery store operated by a Negro named Fuller. They took a melon without paying for it, but soon returned it and demanded another. Fuller refused their request, but the men took one anyway. A quarrel ensued, and a policeman named Shaffer arrived on the scene. He quieted them, then accompanied the white men to Johnson's saloon. Meanwhile, the Negroes began gathering an armed force at Fuller's store.

The price of the melon was fifty cents, but the white men, it developed, had not paid for the second one either. They decided to return and give Fuller his money, and they assured Policeman Shaffer that they would create no disturbance. Jim Johnson, the saloon proprietor, returned with them, in shirt sleeves and unarmed.

As soon as the group reached the corner near Fuller's store, they were suddenly fired upon by Bill Mason, a colored state policeman. Other Negroes also started firing, and the white men fired back. Jim Johnson was mortally wounded during the battle; State Policeman Mason and a man named Rousseau received serious injuries.

Soon the Sheriff appeared at the scene, and he immediately dispatched a courier for United States troops. Then he and two companions went to the hotel where the three wounded men had been taken. The Sheriff's party had just arrived when a crowd of about thirty armed Negroes began to force their way into the entrance of

[16] *Daily State Journal,* December 4, 1870, I, 263.

[17] Austin *Daily Republican,* November 5, 1870, III, 133.

[18] Neither the name of the barkeeper nor the names of the young men could be found in the sources.

the hotel. Their purpose, it was later claimed, was to get the wounded men. The Sheriff halted them and ordered them to surrender, but they ignored him and commenced firing again.

With only five men to help, the Sheriff withstood the attack. One Negro was wounded, and even more unpleasantness would likely have followed had not the Sheriff been successful in forcing the Negroes to stop firing. The Sheriff arrested four persons, two of them Negroes, who had participated in the gun battle.[19]

The State Police had meanwhile done nothing to restore order, although M. P. Hunicutt, the district captain, was in Waco at the time. Hunicutt and his men apparently ignored the disturbance, although one of their fellow members had been involved.[20] A Conservative newspaper said:

In the recent Waco riot, we have another striking illustration of the evils of radical legislation. Having lived in that town for some length of time, we are able to say that the Negroes have ever been with some few exceptions, peaceable and well disposed. One bad man, however, in the State Police, acting under authority from a partizan legislature, changes the condition of affairs by his influence and example and a reign of terror is at once instituted. We wonder, knowing the people as we do, that they submit to this gross outrage so patiently.

If we are to have bad laws fixed upon us, for the sake of justice and right, let those laws be administered by men who will confine themselves to the letter of their instructions, and not oppress a people who have suffered sufficiently already.[21]

Another incident showing the irresponsible character of many state policemen occurred near Caldwell, in Burleson County, in the fall of 1870. A number of freedmen had gathered on the premises of a Thomas Hudson for the purpose of forming a State Guard company. While they waited, they partook freely of whiskey distributed by opponents of a plan to divide Burleson County—persons who were evidently trying to influence the Negroes to vote against division. After much drinking, the freedmen set out for the residence of John Gee, a former Burleson County registrar who had been recently re-

[19] *Flake's Daily Bulletin*, August 14, 1870, VI, 44. This paper quotes the Waco *Examiner* of August 10, 1870, in presenting the account of the story.

[20] *Flake's Daily Bulletin*, August 25, 1870, VI, 52.

[21] *Tri-Weekly State Gazette*, August 15, 1870, II, 85.

PLATE 3. The Badge of the State Police. From *The Texas Rangers* by Walter Prescott Webb. Courtesy Dr. Webb.

PLATE 4. The Travis County Jail at Austin, in use during the carpetbag era. From the Walter E. Long Collection.

placed by a friend of Thomas Hudson's. They fired several shots into Gee's house; then Sim King, a member of the State Police, delivered a vicious blow to the head of Gee's nephew. King was later arrested and pleaded guilty to a charge of assault with intent to kill. He was released under a bond of $250 to appear at the next district court in December.

Yet another incident which pictured an unpleasant side of the State Police was described in *Flake's Daily Bulletin*. In Tyler, in December, 1871, two lawyers, F. A. Godley and R. E. House, were murdered by a Negro state policeman. The trouble began when Ran Johnson, the Negro state policeman, meeting Sheriff Williams of Wood County in front of a saloon, stopped him and demanded his pistol. The Sheriff, however, convinced the policeman that he was an officer and had the right to carry a pistol, though he had none at the time. Godley and House were with the Sheriff when this occurred, and the Negro then ordered House to give up his pistol, only to be told that the lawyer was also unarmed.

House went directly to the City Hotel, but there encountering several men from Wood County, he returned with them to Scott's saloon where he found Godley still in conversation with the policeman Ran Johnson and perhaps others. At this time, there was a crowd of Negroes collected about the saloon and upon the street in front, all of them apparently much excited. Godley and House, with the men from Wood County, soon left the saloon and started back to the hotel. On their way it was discovered that one of their number was missing. Several proposed to return to the saloon for him, but Deputy United States Marshal Griffin told them to remain where they were, and that he would bring him. He found the missing man, and as they returned to the waiting group, a large crowd of Negroes and policemen followed them.

One of these freedmen declared, "There are more pistols in this crowd." Upon this remark, House was called for by another of them. When the lawyer answered, one of the Negroes exclaimed, "He's got a pistol—shoot him! Damn him! Shoot him!" Upon hearing this demand, Ran Johnson raised his gun to fire at House, when Godley caught hold of it and told him not to shoot, as there was no necessity for it. Johnson, however, jerked the gun away, and fired upon Godley, shooting him in three different places and fatally wounding him. Then turning in the direction of House, the Negro shot and killed him also.

51

Promiscuous firing into the crowd by the freedmen followed. But there was no evidence of shooting on the part of the white men, as none of them were armed. In the melee, one white man was shot in the thigh and another in the foot, while two or three Negroes were slightly wounded. Immediately following the shooting, the Negroes fled in all directions, and only one arrest was made that night. For several hours after the killing, excitement in the town ran high, but there was no outward demonstration or further trouble.[22]

Incidents such as these show the irresponsibility with which many members of the State Police wielded the power vested in them. On the other hand, they sometimes were able to make a real contribution to the safety and security of their fellow citizens. In a Hill County battle that occurred in September of 1870, the State Police exhibited a certain amount of heroism. Lieutenant Thomas Williams, two sergeants, and thirteen privates of the State Police, all mounted, had entered Hill County to arrest the Kinch West gang, an outlaw group that infested the area. There were some fifteen desperadoes in the band, and Williams had about the same number of policemen. Only a part of his force, however, were armed with long-range rifles, the effective weapons for the running battle he anticipated.

Williams scoured the country in search of the gang and finally encountered five members of it. Unfortunately, his force was divided at the time, and he also had only five men present. Nevertheless, Williams demanded surrender. The outlaws answered with oaths and bullets and a running fight over a distance of some five miles followed. Then the desperadoes reached a timbered area and were lost to sight.[23] Although Williams was thus unsuccessful, the Austin *Daily Republican,* mouthpiece of Conservative Republicans, observed that he proved himself an accomplished and efficient officer and added that it was well satisfied with his Hill County effort.[24]

[22] *Flake's Daily Bulletin,* December 17, 1871, VII, 93. The account is completed by the *Daily Democratic Statesman,* April 23, 1873, II, 61, which declared that not long after, the Negro, Johnson, was captured and imprisoned without bail; later owing to the assistance of the writ of *habeas corpus* and the aid of an able counsel, he was brought again before the judge, but he was treated as before by the court and refused bail. Following this second experience, a short time later, he escaped from jail and was not recaptured.

[23] *Daily State Journal,* October 7, 1870, I, 183.

[24] Austin *Daily Republican,* October 3, 1870, III, 105.

In many cases the reports of State Police activities described in the highly partisan *Daily State Journal* are obviously unreliable. Even if allowance is made for this paper's strong bias, however, some incidents which it describes would appear to show the members of the force performing most creditably their duty to maintain the peace. In August of 1870, the newspaper found that the State Police, with the aid of a militia company, were successful in quieting a disturbance at Burton. The facts of the incident were that Adjutant General Davidson upon returning from Cedar Bayou, where he had supposedly put a number of lawbreakers to flight, turned his attention to the little town of Burton, where he found a lively quarrel in progress and firearms being freely used. He suppressed the difficulty, and then, as the town had no civil officers, he ordered all persons within the place to lay aside their deadly weapons. This order was indignantly resisted, and at least forty men paraded the streets that night discharging their revolvers and bidding defiance to law and authority. But Sheriff Smith, having been dispatched for aid, soon arrived with a detachment of police and Captain Lusk's militia company, who promptly dispersed and disarmed the rioters. The leaders were arrested and fined.

The citizens of Hempstead and Brenham, as well as those of Burton, gave Davidson satisfactory assurance of their determination to support the officers of the law in their suppression of desperadoism. And in concluding the discussion, the official newspaper of the Davis administration declared:

A great moral revolution is in progress and the people, irrespective of party, evince a settled determination to do their part in securing peace and enforcing law. The State Police is fast becoming the most useful and popular institution in Texas.[25]

Governor Davis' lawmen thus frequently proved their value, but the very act under which they operated led to abuses and to inefficiency. The Governor, allowed excessive authority over his forces, occasionally acted without thoroughly investigating a situation and was known to have sent into an area both state police and militiamen in significant numbers when only a few would have sufficed to produce order.

One such instance occurred in the autumn of 1870. During the first week of November Davis was informed that a gang of desperadoes

[25] *Daily State Journal,* September 1, 1870, I, 183.

had gone to Madisonville to kill State Police Captain Patrick, who at that time was en route home from Austin. Instead of Patrick the gang had found a man named Tinsley, whom they believed to be a member of the State Police. They reportedly took him into a yard, tied him to a tree, and shot him to death. They then, still according to report, met and killed two other state policemen.

Captain Patrick's wife sent a messenger to warn her husband away, for the desperadoes were said to have sworn that they intended to "kill every G—— d——d Radical in Madison County and then go down and clean out Grimes County."[26]

Governor Davis, after receiving these alarming reports, ordered 50 state policemen and 300 state guardsmen to the area.[27] Adjutant General Davidson also hurried there to direct the activity.

But the reports from Madison County had been exaggerated. The disturbance had been created by only seven men: S. Baston, Elisha Baston, John Jamison, Jack Rogers, Seeley Singleton, Tider McIver, and Mat Burney, who were seen pursuing Tinsley across the prairie on November 4. Whether Tinsley escaped is not known, but no reports of his death at that time have been found. However, his pursuers returned the next morning, found John Copeland and four other freedmen standing in front of Captain Patrick's house, and fired on them. The Negroes fled into the house, and Jack Rogers demanded that they come out. Mrs. Patrick begged Rogers not to fire into the house among her children, and Rogers and his companions apparently complied with her plea. A short time later, however, Copeland leaped out the door, attempted to flee, and was riddled with bullets. The four other freedmen were more fortunate; they escaped.[28]

After this, conditions became quiet once more in Madisonville. Most residents were peaceful, law-abiding people, and they had not participated in the disturbance. Discovering that the town was quiet, Governor Davis recalled the troops.[29]

POLITICS AND MURDER IN 1871

Davis told the Legislature on January 18, 1871, that the State Police had not been fully organized, that more money was

---

[26] *Ibid.,* November 12, 1870, I, 245.
[27] *Flake's Daily Bulletin,* November 18, 1870, VI, 85.
[28] *Ibid.*   [29] *Ibid.,* December 7, 1870, VI, 99.

necessary to provide for a larger force. Illustrating the efficiency of the State Police, he pointed out that with only half of the strength allowed by law the force had made 978 arrests in six months and had recovered $30,000 worth of stolen property. Davis declared that with a larger force than currently available greater accomplishments were possible. He recommended for each county an addition of a maximum of two captains, four lieutenants, and twenty special policemen, to be paid by the county when in actual service.[30]

Acting on the Governor's suggestion, legislators introduced a bill to amend the State Police act. With the backing of a majority of Radicals, it became law on May 2, 1871.[31] This act provided for 6 captains, 12 lieutenants, 30 sergeants, and 210 privates. Policemen's salaries were increased, and they were allowed the same compensation given sheriffs. The size of the total force remained virtually the same as in the previous law. There was a slight decrease in the number of privates, but this was counterbalanced by a proportionate addition to the total number of officers enrolled. Such an increase was felt to be needed.

The act further provided that the governor could add as many as twenty special policemen whenever necessary and could appoint baggage masters and conductors on railroads as acting special policemen.[32]

By an appropriation act providing for deficiencies incurred during the fiscal year ending August 31, 1871, and providing for the fiscal year beginning September 1, 1871, the State Police received $370,000. Of this $100,000 was to be used for 1870–1871 deficiencies.[33] During 1871, $200,978.78 was spent upon the system; amounts still unpaid at the end of December, 1871, totaled $3,564.[34]

Some Texans believed that the taxation to provide for temporary maintenance of special police, amounting to $187,200 for the whole state, was unjust. They felt that the sole purpose of this provision was to carry the election for the Radicals. Whether this was the only reason for the creation of the special police cannot be ascertained, but it was true that in the congressional election of 1871 special policemen were put on duty to see that "order" was preserved. They went into service on registration day and continued on duty for twenty-four days, com-

[30] *Ibid.*, January 19, 1871, VI, 134.
[31] *Daily State Journal*, May 11, 1871, II, 90.
[32] Gammel, *Laws of Texas*, VI, 972–974.
[33] *Daily State Journal*, July 19, 1871, II, 147.
[34] *Report of the Adjutant General of Texas for 1872*, p. 11.

pleting their work on October 6, at the end of a three-day election period. They were paid three dollars a day.[35]

Twenty, or fewer, special policemen were employed in each county. Every man was under the supervision of an officer of the State Police, under a special officer named by the Governor, or under the direct supervision of the registrar, who was allowed to appoint special policemen himself. Both special and state policemen were responsible for seeing that voters were not intimidated or in any way hindered from registering or voting.

During this twenty-four–day period armed Negro special policemen were in evidence at the political meetings held by the opponents of the Davis party. This prompted even the Navasota *Ranger,* an extreme Radical organ and a supporter of the administration, to observe:

The colored policemen were in the procession with guns, which we consider altogether unnecessary. Perhaps there was no harm or intimidation intended, but while there is a revolutionary party in our midst, we are ready to misconstrue and torture everything to inflame the people, for the purpose of inaugurating another civil war, peaceably disposed citizens cannot be too cautious in trying to avoid anything that is calculated to give the enemies of the Union an opportunity to again raise the flag of secession.[36]

The political activities of the State Police in the 1871 congressional compaign should not be underestimated. In Galveston a telegram was received on July 30 by Chief of City Police Hobbs from Governor Davis stating that Davis had assumed command of Galveston city police. Chief Hobbs and his force were directed to hold themselves subject to the orders of State Police Captain George Farrow, who would act as he felt necessary to preserve order at a Radical mass meeting to be held in the city that night to nominate candiates for the convention at Houston. The effect of this can be imagined. Many freedmen in Galveston had been commissioned as special policemen, apparently in a move to gain Negro support for the nomination of the Radical congressional candidate, William T. Clark. The prospect of city government thus being in the hands of the State Police for the

[35] Gammel, *Laws of Texas,* VI, 972–974.

[36] *Flake's Daily Bulletin,* September 12, 1871, VII, 21. This paper quoted the account from the Navasota *Ranger,* and in commenting upon it, wondered where the rights of free speech had gone of which the governor, in some of his addresses of the recent past, had so eloquently boasted.

night was hardly a pleasant one for the supporters of Clark's opponents, Conservative Republicans, Stevenson and Nelson. This situation evoked the following comment from *Flake's Daily Bulletin,* an opposition newspaper:

What think Stevenson men of this? What say 240 men pledged to Nelson? Does your Radical governor intend to give you any show or does he treat you as cattle to be driven to such places as he has prepared for you?

Had Governor Davis treated Mayor Summerville, or Judge Sabin or Judge Dodge with the least respect, he would have inquired of these peace conservators before he issued the order, if it were necessary and if the peace of the city was threatened to any degree, and the answer would have been that while the political contest was spirited, yet there was no earthly need of this outrageous, illegal, and ill-judged order.

That night a large number of Galvestonians—a few whites and many Negroes—assembled in Sylvestor's Hall for the Radical meeting. The crowd created an incessant din and confusion which seemed to be increased rather than controlled by most of the officers. State Police Sergeant Haynes, a freedman, did try to bring order but was unsuccessful. Then, amid pandemonium,[37] State Senator George T. Ruby and Norris Wright Cuney, both Radical Negroes, were selected as delegates to the convention.

Clark's opponent, Nelson, was hustled off the speaker's stand several times, but finally he was permitted to speak. Nelson declared that the meeting had not been run to his satisfaction, and he asserted that it was a "put up job."[38] His supporters gave him hearty applause, but at that juncture the State Police turned off the gas lights and drove the audience out of the building.

Meanwhile, the Stevenson wing, which had walked out of the hall when Cuney and Ruby were elected, assembled on the courthouse portico and held its own meeting, selecting Sam Dodge and G. T. Nichols, delegates of a more conservative character, to go to the Houston convention. Then that group adjourned, and Nelson and his friends, after being unceremoniously forced out of the meeting hall, assembled on the portico. There Nelson spoke in behalf of his own candidacy. He was followed by a Negro named Washington. But Washington was soon interrupted by a city police officer named

[37] *Flake's Daily Bulletin,* July 30, 1871, VI, 297.
[38] *Daily State Journal,* February 17, 1870, I, 17.

McCormick and a posse of white policemen, who ordered the meeting dispersed. McCormick declared that he had no discretion in the matter, that he was acting under orders from State Police Captain Farrow, who was, in fact, present. Nelson's friends were reluctant to leave, but to avoid trouble Nelson stated that under duress he was ordering the meeting adjourned. The crowd then quietly disbanded.[39]

At the Radical convention in Houston, however, the State Police played an unimportant role.[40] Not until the elections were held did further indiscretions become obvious. At that time, in Corsicana, occurred a flagrant case of ballot-box corruption. There it was discovered that A. Hanson, Navarro County registrar, and G. W. Smith, a State Police lieutenant, had destroyed three hundred ballots. A grand jury indicted both men but, through the clemency of the district judge, Smith's case was continued. Hanson escaped when an attempt was made to arrest him.[41]

The Democrats, as mentioned, won this congressional election by majorities ranging from 3,000 to 15,000.[42] As for attempts by special police to intimidate voters, the *Tri-Weekly Statesman* had an acid observation. It quoted the Radical Houston *Union* as saying, "Every armed ruffian known to have menaced the quietude of the polls or the freedom of the voter will be brought to condign punishment." Then the *Statesman* added, "This effectually disposes of the entire State Police. What a relief when these scoundrels are safely caged in the penitentiary."[43]

A study of the records, however, discloses some beneficial work in this period by the State Police. During the fourteen months ending September 17, 1871, that organization arrested 3,475 persons. Of these, 638 were jailed for murder or attempts to murder.[44] During the entire year of 1871 eight state policemen were killed and four were wounded in active service.[45]

[39] *Flake's Daily Bulletin,* July 30, 1871, VI, 297. Where the full name or initials of persons mentioned in the above account are not given, they were unobtainable.

[40] *Ibid.,* p. 300.

[41] *Tri-Weekly Democratic Statesman,* May 2, 1872, I, 120.

[42] Louis J. Wortham, *A History of Texas from Wilderness to Commonwealth,* V, 77.

[43] *Tri-Weekly Democratic Statesman,* October 14, 1871, I, 35.

[44] *Daily State Journal,* September 17, 1871, II, 199.

[45] *Report of the Adjutant General of Texas for 1872,* p. 12.

This more heroic side was also evident in the actions of certain in-dividual members. State policeman John Hunter, whose honesty, ac-cording to the *Tri-Weekly State Gazette* of Austin, was not above question,[46] was nevertheless a man of obvious courage. A problem fac-ing Hunter concerned a band of thieves near Circleville, in Williamson County. Citizens had lost more than two hundred head of horses and cattle to them. These outlaws were said to be murderers as well, but the inhabitants of that area were afraid to betray them.

Hunter, with the aid of six freedmen—all members of the State Militia—went after the outlaws. He searched through the woods and located their headquarters. Then, on a May night in 1871, he and the six Negroes attacked the band. After a short struggle the outlaws—all six of them—surrendered. Among them was their chief, William Beard.[47]

Concerning another band of desperadoes, in Brown County, widely divergent stories were told by the *Daily State Journal* and the *Tri-Weekly Democratic Statesman.*

The conditions described by the *Journal* were bad indeed. This publication found Brown County in 1871 to be the "haunt of a gang of ferocious desperadoes" and told of a district clerk in Brownwood, Irving Moore, being assaulted by these outlaws. Moore, in defending himself, had slain one of his assailants.

A short time later, said the *Journal,* J. Ruel Glasscock, a man of questionable reputation, rode up to State Police quarters and profanely challenged the occupants to come out and fight. He was ignored, how-ever, and rode off. About three weeks later he returned to town with

---

[46] *Tri-Weekly State Gazette,* April 19, 1871, IV, 34.

[47] *Daily State Journal,* May 23, 1871, II, 100. This account was written by one who styled himself as a "changed Democrat," and he said: "I am a strong Democrat and opposed to the Republican party, but I am convinced that we could not have a better institution than the state police. I shall in the future support it, if I have to vote the Republican ticket, and I am not alone in my county, for this affair has made a great many open their eyes to the good of the police bill."

Sam Easley, a resident of Circleville at the time, later moved to Georgetown and resided there until the time of his death in 1933. Mr. Easley declared that none of these men were murderers, and William Beard was the only one who was known to have been a bad man; as a band, they were horse thieves but nothing worse. Mr. Easley recalled the visit of the State Police but could re-member no captures having been made by them at the time.

Statement of Sam Easley.

a gang of heavily armed men, among whom was Sheriff George Lee, a reputed scoundrel. They went to Irving Moore's house, found him and his deputy as well as a state policeman and four specials outside, and drove them into the house with curses and gunfire. The policemen and Moore then returned the fire, killed the "leader" of the gang —Scott J. Adams—and repulsed the others. When quiet returned, the state men counted their casualties. Moore had been shot through the arm; his deputy, J. H. McMillion, had been severely wounded in the hip; and one of the policemen had suffered a slight wound.

McMillion traveled to Austin for medical aid, and while there he recounted the particulars of the incident to the *Daily State Journal*. The *Journal*, concluded its discussion:

These high handed crimes are directly and solely political in their character. The actors and abettors are Democrats, ferocious with vile whiskey and mad with hate of the State administration, and especially of the repressive[48] measure the police bill, against which all ruffianism and scoundreldom of Texas chafes as the hyena does against its bars. The registrar reports that in the present condition of affairs no fair election can be held in Brown County as Republicans do not dare to speak or avow their sentiments and are in daily peril of their lives. We expect to hear, at any moment, of the murder of the District Clerk, against whom as the leading Republican, the deadly malice of those villains is specially leveled.[49]

The highly colored nature of this story makes one hesitate to believe it. It might have been written purely for political reasons, for the primary purpose of getting further aid from the governor to carry the coming election for the Radical Republicans. What seems to have been a more accurate account appeared in a letter written by Greenleaf Fisk,[50] a Brown County citizen. Fisk was known to have been a man of good repute, and Brownwood was built on land he donated. He was the first chief justice of Brown County, a former member of the state House of Representatives, and a veteran of the

[48] The term "repressive" here is used to apply to the State Police act, because as the above editorial implied, its purpose was to restrict the activities of scoundrels, ruffians, and lawless Democrats.

[49] *Daily State Journal*, August 31, 1871, II, 84.

[50] According to the minutes of the commissioner's court of Williamson County, Fisk was at one time county judge there.

Texas Revolution and the Mexican War. His letter occasioned an editorial in the *Tri-Weekly Democratic Statesman*.

Fisk declared that the statement published in the *Journal* was false in every way. He asserted that he lived within a hundred yards of Moore's house and did not doubt that Moore himself was the origi-nator of the many slanderous charges made against citizens of the county. Fisk said that he had lived in Brown County for eleven years, that he believed its citizens were as loyal and as peaceful as any in the state, and that he felt the same could be said of the people residing in Comanche, San Saba, and Coleman counties.

Shortly before the Brown County incident, Fisk said, Moore had become involved in a gambling quarrel with George Lee. The next day Moore armed himself with a double-barrelled shotgun and fol-lowed Lee into a store. Here another quarrel ensued, and Lee fired at Moore, but missed. Moore leaped upon a counter and fired back at Lee, who fell, fatally wounded. But before Lee died he fired again, wounding Moore in the arm. Fisk stated that this accounted for Moore's broken arm and for the false story—told by Moore, said Fisk, in order to obtain police protection.

Fisk added that on August 19, 1871, Moore and six policemen fired without warning on five or six persons who were departing for home from Brownwood after a day of trading. One man was fatally wounded. Scott J. Adams (described by Moore as a gang leader) heard the firing, quickly left a stream where he was bathing, dressed, grabbed his rifle, and hurried toward the scene. As he approached, Moore and his policemen fired at him from behind a picket fence. Adams fired back, driving the men into Moore's house, from where they renewed the one-sided battle. Adams soon fell dead—near the store in which Moore had killed George Lee. The policemen forbade the citizens to touch Adams' body, saying that they intended to scalp him and send the grisly trophy to Governor Davis and Adjutant Gen-eral Davidson.

Fisk's version of the shooting brought this comment from the *Democratic Statesman:*

It would seem that the only organized band of desperadoes terrorizing over Brown county consists of Moore and his policemen. They have shame-fully beaten and wounded several citizens, among others, John Mullins, Green Davis, the two Gibsons, Daniel Jenkins, and William Perry.

Moore, who appears to be a hired tool of the Chief of Police, alone asked for these policemen, the citizens of the county had nothing to do with it—and he is affording the citizens such protection as vultures give to lambs.

Since the occurrence of the 19th ult., no one visits Brownwood, some are trying to get away and give up the county to this organized band of policemen, leaving them to reign supreme rather than commit a breach of the peace . . .[51]

The criminal actions of certain other state policemen—in Lynn Flatt, Nacogdoches County—had tragic consequences. On December 14, 1871, G. Dawson, justice of the peace for the Lynn Flatt precinct, was holding his court in that town, and State Policemen Columbus Hazlett and William Grayson were listening. Becoming in some way dissatisfied with what they heard, the policemen threatened to break up the proceedings and to shoot an attorney, an old man by the name of Clute who was speaking in behalf of his clients. This contempt of court caused the Justice of the Peace to issue a warrant for their arrest, and the job of executing it was given to Constable John Birdwell, who immediately summoned a man named David Harvell to assist him.

Locating Hazlett, Birdwell informed him that he had a warrant for his arrest. The policeman, apparently compliant, answered, "I surrender." Birdwell then asked where Grayson was, and Hazlett answered that he was at a nearby store. The Constable instructed his prisoner to call him, and when Grayson arrived Hazlett said to him, "I am a prisoner."

"The hell you are," Grayson replied. "Die before you surrender."

Harvell, standing near Hazlett in the doorway of another store, asked for his gun.

"Do you demand my gun?" Hazlett answered. "I will give you the contents of it!" He raised his weapon and shot Harvell in the chest. But Harvell was able to step back into the store, stagger to a counter, seize a double-barrelled shotgun lying there, and empty one of the barrels, loaded with birdshot, into Hazlett's face. Then he fired the other barrel at Grayson, hitting him in the head. Harvell, who had by this time been struck by two more bullets, walked behind the counter, collapsed, and died.

Despite their painful wounds, the two state policemen mounted their horses and left Lynn Flatt. About three miles north of town they

[51] *Tri-Weekly Democratic Statesman*, September 19, 1871, I, 24.

stopped at Grayson's house and assembled a force of thirty or forty Negroes. Openly defying the law, they declared themselves immune from arrest.

At Nacogdoches, Sheriff R. D. Orton heard about the trouble, summoned a posse of ten or fifteen men, and hurried to Lynn Flatt, arriving there two days after the murder. He found many people panic-stricken.

No warrants had been issued for the state policemen, and Orton had this done immediately. Then, with his posse, he started for Grayson's house. While en route there he encountered twenty or thirty well-armed Negroes, compelled them to surrender, and sent them under guard to Nacogdoches, seventeen miles distant.

Orton found Grayson's house empty. The surrounding territory, including Rusk and Cherokee counties, was searched but no trace could be found of the two state policemen. Opinion was voiced by the residents that they had left the country. Orton returned to Nacogdoches, released the captured Negroes, and disbanded his posse.

Then, on the night of December 19—five days after the murder—Constable John Birdwell was called to the door of his Lynn Flatt home and was killed. Virtually everybody blamed Hazlett and Grayson, and the people again became panicky, fearing especially the consequences of the friendship between the Negroes and the two state policemen.

When news of Birdwell's murder reached Sheriff Orton the next day, he again raised a posse and hurried to Lynn Flatt. At the dead man's home he found the body, lying where it had fallen. That night, at an inquest, it was decided that the Constable had received his death at the hands of "unknown" parties, but warrants were issued for the arrest of Hazlett and Grayson and five of their friends. The Sheriff called an additional hundred men for the posse and searched the surrounding country, including neighboring counties. Once again his efforts were unsuccessful. Concluding that the fugitives had fled to Austin, Orton dispatched a group of men to that place.

Rumors soon became prevalent that the murderers were still in the community, however, and that they were instigating the Negroes to violence. So great had become the fears of the white population in regard to the Negroes that Sheriff Orton disarmed all suspicious colored men. This helped to calm the people.

A few days after the Sheriff disbanded his posse Lieutenant Thomas Williams of the State Police, who had performed efficiently in the

Hill County incident described earlier, arrived at Lynn Flatt, bringing with him two prisoners—William Grayson and Columbus Hazlett. The Lieutenant offered to turn them over to Orton, on two conditions: that guards for the prisoners were to be members of the State Police, selected by Williams, and that the sheriff was to give a receipt for the prisoners. Orton refused to accept these conditions on the grounds that they reflected on his good faith and that they were not in accordance with the law, which delegated to the sheriff legal custody of all prisoners. Williams would agree to no other arrangements.

Orton hurried to Rusk and returned with M. Priest,[52] judge of the Fourth Judicial District,[53] who did all in his power to induce the Lieutenant to turn over the prisoners. Still Williams refused. After three days of vain effort Priest issued warrants for the arrest of the Lieutenant, the prisoners, and their guards, and he gave the warrants to the Sheriff. Because of the late hour, the number of the men to be arrested, and the absence of a posse the arrests were deferred. The policemen fled and made their way to Austin, taking Hazlett and Grayson with them.

Soon after this Adjutant General Davidson and some twenty-five officers arrived at Lynn Flatt, returning Grayson and Hazlett. Davidson released the two prisoners to the civil authorities, and after an examining trial before Justice of Peace Dawson they were jailed at Nacogdoches, without bail. Civil law had been allowed to triumph, and peace was again restored to the county.[54]

Although citizens did thus suffer, occasionally, at the hands of the State Police, from time to time the policemen themselves suffered from the actions of desperadoes. Such an instance occurred in Gonzales County, where two Negro state policemen were victims of John Wesley Hardin. Later, when writing his biography, Hardin recounted the story:

[52] Richard W. Haltom, *History and Description of Nacogdoches County*, pp. 39–43.

[53] *Tri-Weekly State Gazette*, February 5, 1872, IV, 179.

[54] Haltom, *History and Description of Nacogdoches County*, pp. 43–44. The part the State Police played in three instances in which martial law was declared in 1871 is narrated in detail in a later chapter. In two of these cases, in Hill County and in Freestone and Limestone counties, certain state policemen were largely instrumental in bringing about the humiliating condition which these localities had to bear.

. . . We all knew that many members of this State Police outfit were members of some secret vigilant band, especially in DeWitt and Gonzales Counties. We were all opposed to mob law and so soon became enemies. The consequence was that a lot of negro police made a raid on me without lawful authority. They went from house to house looking for me and threatening to kill me, and frightening the women and children to death.

They found me at a grocery store in the southern portion of Gonzales county. I really did not know they were there until I heard some one say:

"Throw up your hands or die."

I said "all right," and turning around saw a big black negro with his pistol cocked and presented. I said:

"Look out, you will let that pistol go off, and I don't want to be killed accidently."

He said: "Give me those pistols."

I said "all right," and handed him the pistols, handle foremost. One of the pistols turned a somerset in my hand and went off. Down came the negro, with his pistol cocked, and as I looked outside, I saw another negro on a white mule firing into the house at me. I told him to hold up, but he kept on, so I turned my Colts 45 on him and knocked him off his mule the first shot. I turned around then to see what had become of No. 1 and saw him sprawling on the floor with a bullet through his head, quivering in blood. I walked out of the back door to get on my horse and when I got back to take in the situation, the big negro on the white mule was making for the bottom at a 2:40 gait. I tried to head him off but he dodged and ran into a lake. I afterwards learned that he stayed in there with his nose out of water until I left. The negro I killed was named Green Paramoor and the one on the white mule was a blacksmith from Gonzales named John Lackey—in fact, they were both from that town.

News of this, of course, spread like wild fire, and myself and friends declared openly against negro or Yankee mob rule and misrule in general. In the meantime, the negroes in Gonzales and adjoining counties had begun to congregate at Gonzales and were threatening to come out to the Sandies with torch and knife and depopulate the entire county. We at once got together about twenty-five men, good and true, and sent for these negroes to come along, that we would not leave enough of them to tell the tale. They had actually started, but some old men from Gonzales talked to them and made them return to their homes. From that time on we had no negro police in Gonzales. This happened in September, 1871.[55]

[55] John W. Hardin, *Life of John Wesley Hardin*, p. 25.

65

Although Hardin was scarcely a reputable character, a good many men of honor shared his dislike of the State Police. One of them was J. W. Williams, a former member of the force, who wrote a letter to the Austin *Democratic Statesman* in September of 1871. It stated in part:

> . . . I do not call upon discharged policemen alone to attest the truth of my statements, but upon all good and true men who have been or are now connected with that department . . .

We have been speculated upon by General Davidson and been made tools of to defraud and bankrupt the State of Texas. He has furnished you with horses unfit for the service and law required of you, at four or five times their real value, with arms, clothing and badges, at a large advance on the cost of the state. He has exacted receipts for money not only in advance of payment, but in advance of service; and when you have spent your last dollar in defraying the expenses incidental to the performance of your duty, he has discharged you without a dollar and cursed you from his office like dogs.[56]

The *Democratic Statesman,* as quoted by the *Daily State Journal,* continued in an editorial comment,

The way the thing is done is this: Our Adjutant General picks out some poor devil in the street who has not a dime in the world and tells him he would like to make a policeman of him and furnish him with his outfit for service. The man, glad of even the ghost of a chance to earn an honest penny, of course, accepts.

Our Adjutant General then takes up the happy fellow to his office, and he is furnished with an old condemned saddle and bridle, and an old broken down horse unfit for service, worth from $10. to $20., for which he is charged from $50. to $115.; a uniform suit of shoddy clothes, cost $12., for which he is charged $20.; a Winchester carbine, cost $30., for which he is charged $40.; a policeman's badge worth $1., for which he is charged $3. And now we have a new made policeman, fully equipped for the service of the holy work of reducing Texas to a sublime state of peace and order—but we don't have him long. And as soon as his term of service has been sufficient to pay for his outfit, he is entirely forgotten and ignored by his honored chief. He applies again and again for his pay for services rendered, and is coolly told that there is no money in the Treasury, and there is no telling when there will be any. He suffers long with hope de-

[56] Austin *Democratic Statesman,* September 26, 1871, I, 27.

ferred, and finally throws off his commission in disgust, and tells the world how he has been treated . . .

The *Journal,* denounced both the letter and the editorial, and declared:

General Davidson has furnished horses occasionally to policemen. In every instance, however, they were furnished to men who formerly belonged to his company in the United States army, and the price that was charged against them was much lower than the market price for horses of the same kind when bought from outside parties. As regards the shoddy uniform, General Davidson offered the contract to several merchant tailors in the city of Austin. They declined to take the contract except at prices utterly beyond what he could have the same goods made up for in the North. The offer (from the lowest bidder) was $26.50 here in Austin. The uniforms were made in Boston at $14.65 each. Add the freight for a small amount of uniforms, the exchange, and the other small expenses, and $20. will cover the expense for the uniforms.

Then there is the badge. No policeman on the force can say a badge has ever been charged to him. Stoppages to the amount of three dollars have been made against every policeman to cover the cost of the badge, but as soon as his connection with the force ceases, either by resignation or otherwise, the amount stopped against him has been placed to the credit of his account upon the return of the badge of the office. . . .[57]

THE LAST MONTHS OF THE STATE POLICE

The climax of State Police activities, both good and bad, seemed to have been reached in 1871. During the following year little mention was made of it. There were no cases of martial law, few instances of murder by the State Police—and scarcely an account of any work against the numerous outlaws infesting the state.

Perhaps the most startling incident of the year 1872 was the flight, that November, of James Davidson, chief of the State Police and adjutant general of Texas.[58] After his departure it was discovered that he had taken $34,434.67 of state money with him.[59]

Many Texans speculated on Davidson's sudden disappearance, and

[57] *Daily State Journal,* October 1, 1871, II, 211.

[58] C. P. Denman, "The Office of the Adjutant General in Texas, 1835–1881," *Southwestern Historical Quarterly,* XXVIII, 317.

[59] *Report of the Adjutant General of Texas for 1872,* p. 5.

for some time there was doubt about the real reason for it. Some persons believed that he had resigned his post to occupy a position in the state Senate, to which the citizens of Bell County had reportedly elected him.[60] Others knew this to be false, for he had resigned before the election. But since he had earlier announced himself as a senatorial candidate, some persons presumed he had freed himself from his office to give more time to the race. Although Davidson's state policemen were generally despised by Conservatives, the chief himself, however little admired, had not borne the brunt of this hatred. The news of the theft must therefore have come as a great surprise.[61]

Davidson's property was immediately attached by the state for the amount he had taken.[62] He himself fled to Belgium and remained there,[63] never returning to Texas. To fill the vacant office of adjutant general, Governor Davis selected his own nephew, Frank L. Britton, who occupied the position for the rest of Davis' term.[64]

During the 1872 elections the State Police were again aided by special policemen appointed for that purpose. Once more officers appeared at the polling places, ostensibly to keep order and to prevent fraud, and their mere presence was usually sufficient to accomplish this. The people feared any conflict with the State Police, assuming that a disturbance would result in a proclamation of martial law.[65]

Two incidents which deal with the activities of the police at conservative political meetings in the fall of 1872 throw light on the character of the organization. The first of these, as described by the *Democratic Statesman,* occurred in September, at Austin, where a crowd had gathered to view the raising of a mammoth Greeley hat which was being hoisted above one of the local saloons. The proprietor of the establishment had provided a band to entertain the audience, and at the same time, had invited a Mr. Schultze, a Horace Greeley enthusiast, to deliver a speech in behalf of that Liberal Republican presidential candidate. Greeley was not only the nominee for this new national party for reform—which would draw the Conservative Republican

---

[60] *Tri-Weekly State Gazette,* December 18, 1872, VI, 3.
[61] *Ibid.*
[62] *Ibid.,* November 25, 1872, V, 149.
[63] William D. Wood, *Reminiscences of Reconstruction in Texas and Reminiscences of Texas and Texans Fifty Years Ago,* p. 19.
[64] *Report of the Adjutant General of Texas for 1873,* p. 3.
[65] Wood, *Reminiscences of Reconstruction in Texas,* p. 19.

votes in Texas—but he also received the nomination of the Democratic party for the nation. The address was made and upon its completion the Radicals, although aware that this was a Greeley meeting, procured a speaker from their own party, a Mr. Quick, to reply to Mr. Schultze. After the Radical speaker had been respectfully listened to and had at length retired, Henry Dickerson, one of the most respected colored men of Travis County, began to speak to the crowd in behalf of Greeley. In the midst of his speech, he was approached by an armed band of police, headed by City Marshal Evans who struck him upon his arm with a cowhide whip and ordered him to leave the stand. At this action, the crowd became incensed, and a more serious disturbance seemed imminent. Disaster probably would have followed had the crowd chosen to vent its anger upon Evans, for a group of armed policemen stood on the outskirts of the crowd ready to take any action which might be necessary to protect the city marshal.

At this moment, however, John Cardwell, editor of the *Democratic Statesman*, mounted the stand beside the speaker and begged the audience to remain quiet and influenced them to such an extent that an outbreak was avoided. Henry Dickerson was sent away under guard to his friends, but a large number of the crowd still lingered around the speaker's stand. Among those remaining were Cardwell and a group of armed police. City Marshal Evans, evidently angry at Cardwell for frustrating his plans, went down the street and in a short time returned with Ratcliff Platt, chairman of the Radical county executive committee. Evans had given Platt a pistol, and Cardwell could hardly have been prepared for the attack which was now made upon him. Platt approached Cardwell, exclaiming: "Damn you, you are the one we want." But before the Radical could use his pistol, it was wrested from him by those standing near. Platt was then taken down the street, closely guarded by his friends, and turned loose.

The *Democratic Statesman,* in concluding a discussion of the incident, said:

It is well known that it has been the zealous purpose of Davis to declare martial law at the capital on the least pretext, and no doubt this devilish plan was for the purpose of raising serious difficulties, which would give an excuse for suspending, especially at this point, the civil law. . . . The circumstance is an insult to the citizens not only of Travis county and Texas, but of the whole United States. It is the suppression of free speech, heretofore one of the dearest rights of the American people.

The police mentioned in this account and in the description which follows were not specifically designated as State Police, but they undoubtedly were members of the organization, for all city police, by the provisions of the State Police act, were made members of it, and they were to be used when necessity demanded. The actions of the police in each of these instances were so similar to political activities of the State Police in 1871 that it is to be presumed they were actually hired members of the organization.[66]

The other affair, as narrated by the Dallas *Herald,* occurred in Galveston at a Democratic political meeting. A Negro orator, L. D. Miller, speaking in behalf of the Democratic party, had begun an address, which was temperate in nature and should have been offensive to no one, but he could hardly be heard for the demoniac yells of a mob of drunken Negroes who had congregated around the stand for the purpose of making a disturbance. When at last he gave up in despair, they crowded around him yelling: "Kill the d——n dog!" "Hang the d——n orator!" "Shoot the d——n hypocrite!" "Tear the d——n Democrat to pieces!" and many other threatening exclamations of like nature. A few white Democrats went to his relief, and surrounding him to prevent his injury, they marched him to the Exchange Hotel. At his door in the hotel, the drunken mob made a rush at Miller, some with knives, others with razors and pistols. Upon their approach, Joseph Atkins, who assisted in protecting Miller, felled the first man with his cane, and at the same time, Sheriff Owens and acting deputy John Price presented their pistols, which gave the others an opportunity to get Miller into the hotel. By this time, at least two hundred Negroes were crowded around the door, and for about fifteen minutes, they rent the air with loud oaths and obscene expressions; then realizing that they could not get their man, slowly retired.

The most remarkable feature of the whole episode was that only one policeman was present during the entire proceeding. His only action was to arrest deputy John Price for drawing a pistol to prevent the Negroes from taking Miller, who had placed himself in Price's charge.[67]

By the first day of January, 1873, the State Police was made up of

[66] *Democratic Statesman,* September 3, 1872, II, 18.
[67] Dallas *Herald,* November 2, 1872, XX, 8.

5 captains, 8 lieutenants, 15 sergeants, and 156 privates. The force seems to have functioned effectively during early 1873; from January 1 through March 31, 403 arrests for crimes were reported. Adjutant General Britton weeded out his incompetent officers, discharging thirty-five men, and he kept the rest busy. Four state policemen were killed in the execution of their duties[68]—attempting to arrest a band of desperadoes at Lampasas.[69]

In the majority of instances of conflict arising between the State Police and the citizens of Texas which have been discussed in this chapter, the state policemen were at fault, but in this affair at Lampasas, the opposite condition was true.

Five justices of the peace of Lampasas County, unable to cope with the lawless conditions existing there, and evidently reflecting the attitude of the citizens, petitioned the governor in January, 1873, to send them a State Police force strong enough to handle the situation. Perhaps in response to this petition, the chief of State Police ordered Captain Thomas Williams, whose Hill County activities have already been discussed, with a force of seven men to aid the local authorities in quelling the disturbed condition. Upon Captain Williams' arrival early in March, he learned of the presence in town of a number of armed men, and on March 19, he observed one of these, an outlaw named Bill Bowen, wearing a pistol. Bowen entered a barroom, and Williams, evidently believing this a decoy, sent three of his men to different points nearby to await developments, and then with three of his other state policemen, Privates Wesley Cherry, T. M. Daniells, and Andrew Melville, he followed the outlaw into the saloon to arrest him for carrying arms. Williams instructed his men not to draw their pistols because he wanted to make a peaceable arrest. Upon entering the room, Williams saw Bill Bowen, and approaching him, demanded his surrender, but the outlaw refused to give himself up. Standing with their backs to the bar, a group of men observed Williams as he now attempted to wrest the weapon from his adversary. At this juncture, a volley was fired upon the state policemen by at least eight or ten of these men. Captain Williams and State Policemen Cherry and Daniells were all killed, while Andrew Melville was mortally wounded. Martin and Thomas Horrell, two of the perpetrators of the

[68] *Report of the Adjutant General of Texas for 1873*, p. 5.
[69] *Norton's Union Intelligencer*, February 15, 1873, IX, 492, and March 29, 1873, IX, 498; *Daily Democratic Statesman*, March 20, 1873, II, 132.

71

tragedy, were both wounded in the head. Regardless of his condition, however, Thomas Horrell made his escape, leaving Martin to be arrested with Allen Whilicraft and James Grizell, two other members of the party.

The responsibility for this crime rested upon a lawless set of men who frequented Lampasas and were highly condemned by the citizens of the town. The bodies of the policemen were buried in honor by the people, and the dying officer was given the best possible attention.

At about this same time however, at Paris and Marshall, two persons were killed by state policemen without justification. On January 2, 1873, in Paris, a young man by the name of Ebenezer Davis was murdered by James Wheat, a state policeman. Davis had been indicted before the grand jury of Lamar County at the previous term of the district court for carrying a pistol. However, he had not been arrested for this offense. Wheat had arrived in Paris on the evening previous to the murder, and upon hearing of the indictment against Davis, went at once to the boy's home. The state policeman was accompanied by Ed Musgrove, another member of the force. The two men found Davis sitting by the fire with his mother and family. The policemen were asked to be seated, but they declined, stating that they had come to arrest the young man. Davis willingly consented to go with the officers and walked out in the yard, where he was followed and fatally shot in the back by Wheat. No resistance had been offered by the boy, nor had he attempted to escape. His murderer, known to be a notorious character, was at the time under the influence of whiskey. It was reported that Mrs. Davis, the young man's widowed mother, holding her dying son in her arms, said to Wheat in her agony, "You have killed my son, my only dependence for support; now kill me." Whereupon the state policeman only laughed at her. Wheat and Musgrove returned to town from the scene of the murder and reported the crime to Lieutenant Halbert of the State Police. Wheat then made his escape, but Musgrove was placed in custody.[70]

The affair at Marshall, in April, concerned a young man by the name of James D. Flanagan, who having been drinking, had some words with and drew a pistol on a hostler at a livery stable where he had put his horse. Louis White, a Negro state policeman, went to arrest him, but when he took hold of the youth by his coat, Flanagan

[70] *Daily Democratic Statesman,* January 26, 1873, II, 87.

slipped out of the garment and left it in the policeman's hands. White drew a pistol and presented it at the breast of Flanagan, who although now unarmed, had his hand in his pocket. The Negro then threatened: "Don't you draw anything on me, or I'll blow your brains out," and told the boy to "come on." Instead of "coming" Flanagan commenced backing away from the policeman, who continued to hold his pistol leveled at him. When Flanagan had walked about two-thirds of the way across the room, White, without saying another word or moving any closer to his victim, fired, killing the boy almost instantly.[71]

With a Democratic majority in the Legislature in 1873 the State Police organization was doomed. Foreseeing this eventuality, the Governor urged legislators to continue the support. He said:

The State Police has relieved the State of multitudes of bad characters, but I decidedly do not think their services can yet be dispensed with. Since their organization, two years and six months ago, the total cost of the police (up to the first instant) has been $408,274.12, or an average annual cost of $163,309.64. They have so far as reported, during that time, arrested 581 persons charged with murder, 760 charged with attempts to kill, 1,748 charged with other felonies, and several thousands charged with lesser offenses. They have also recovered and returned to the owners a large amount of property, of which no account has been kept since the first six months, when about $30,000 was so recovered.

In the execution of their duty, eight policemen have on different occasions lost their lives and a number have been wounded. Of necessity the efficiency of the police has been impaired of late by the depreciation of state warrants, in which they are paid, amounting generally to near half their pay.[72]

Bills were nevertheless introduced in both the House[73] and Senate[74] to repeal the State Police act. They were consolidated as House Bill 236, and by April 12 the measure had passed both legislative bodies. The bill was vetoed by the Governor, however, and in an address to the Legislature on April 19 he argued strongly for continuing the system. Despite his pleas, the House of Representatives voted 58 to 7 to override the veto.[75] The Senate also passed the repeal over Davis'

[71] *Tri-Weekly Civilian,* April 14, 1873, XXV, 287.
[72] *Norton's Union Intelligencer,* February 1, 1873, IX, 490.
[73] *Daily Democratic Statesman*, January 22, 1873, II, 84.
[74] *Ibid.,* January 21, 1873, II, 83.
[75] *Ibid.,* April 20, 1873, II, 159.

veto—by a vote of 18 to 7. Voting for it were three Republican senators—Flanagan, Franks, and Saylor—who thus disregarded party affiliations.[76] To the relief of most Texans the hated organization passed from the scene.

Still the State Police had proved beneficial in some ways other than those already mentioned. Local peace officers could not pursue an offender beyond the boundaries of their jurisdiction, but state policemen were empowered to cross county lines and thus could bring more criminals to justice. Occasionally, too, they captured or drove from Texas certain outlaws whom local officers were afraid to antagonize.

But the despotic character of the organization was obvious. In addition to the faults already mentioned the system had other obvious disadvantages. (1) Members received their appointments from the governor and were responsible solely to him, leaving citizens no voice in the matter. (2) Local peace officers, obligated to guarantee rights of the citizens by whom they were elected, were liable to be incorporated into the organization at any time and thus to fall under the governor's sole authority. (3) State policemen, limited only by the Texas border, could arrest an individual in one district and try him in another, in violation of the state Constitution which stipulated that a crime be tried in the district where committed. (4) Members were allowed to enter and search private homes and to seize the occupants without a warrant. (5) Members were also permitted to act as secret agents, sometimes maliciously gaining the confidence of citizens for the purpose of betraying them.

It was no wonder, then, that most Texans were glad to see the organization go. When word of the repeal was received State Police Lieutenant J. M. Redman was in Denton. In a letter to Adjutant General Britton he described the reaction of the citizens there:

. . . I reached Denton on the 29th inst. where I find great rejoicing over the repeal of the Police Law, by the Ku Klucks, murderers and thieves. When the news was received here the people of this place fired anvils from 2 o'clock in the evening till 3 or 4 o'clock. I am told by Sergt. Davis that the citizens of this place threaten to mob Capt. Hill[77] on his return from Austin,

---

[76] *Ibid.,* April 23, 1873, II, 161.

[77] The Captain Hill mentioned here was evidently A. C. Hill, an officer in the State Police, whose name is mentioned on the Muster Roll of the State Police (MS.) found in the office of the adjutant general of Texas.

though while I fully believe they (some of them) have it in their hearts to do so, I think they will be afraid to do it. Yet I do believe there is men in this county, if they had the power and it would not be found out on them would murder every Republican in it, but thank God they are afraid to do the crime they so much desire.[78]

[78] Transcripts from the office of the adjutant general of Texas (1870–1876). Letters of the State Police, Reserve Militia and State Guard, MS.

THE DECLARATIONS OF MARTIAL LAW

ON THREE OCCASIONS IN 1871 Governor Davis declared martial law. Evidence shows that in two instances—in Walker County in February[1] and in Freestone and Limestone counties in October[2]—such a step was unnecessary. There was a question too of whether martial law was necessary in Hill County in January. But in Walker County and in Freestone and Limestone counties residents were forced to pay for the maintenance. In the other instance the offenders themselves were taxed.[3]

THE HILL COUNTY TROUBLES

Events leading to a declaration of martial law in Hill County, as related by Adjutant General Davidson in his report to the Governor, began with the murder of a freedman and his wife near Clifton, in Bosque County, on December 26, 1870. At an inquest on the following day two Hill County residents, Sollola Nicholson and James J. Gathings, Jr., were blamed for the slayings.

Present at the inquest was State Police Lieutenant W. T. Pritchett. With a portion of his command he hurried to the Hill County home of Colonel James J. Gathings, where the alleged murderers were said to be hiding.[4] Pritchett had no search warrant,[5] and Colonel Gathings refused to admit him, declaring, "You cannot search my house with

[1] *Tri-Weekly State Gazette,* March 3, 1871, III, 169.
[2] *Daily State Journal,* October 11, 1871, II, 219.
[3] *Senate Journal, 12th Legislature,* 1870, p. 283; *Daily State Journal,* February 10, 1871, II, 13.
[4] *Daily State Journal,* February 10, 1871, II, 13.
[5] *Tri-Weekly State Gazette,* January 27, 1871, III, 54.

your damned Negro police." Gathings threatened to kill the Lieutenant if he insisted on entering, but Pritchett was undeterred. He went in and thoroughly ransacked the house. The Lieutenant's efforts proved fruitless, however, as the men had escaped.[6]

Pritchett and his men left and, after breakfasting about a mile from the Gathing's residence, continued the search. Pritchett sent four men on ahead, and he had scarcely renewed his journey when a group of twelve or fifteen persons claiming to be law officers appeared from behind brush along the road, levelled their guns at Pritchett and the two state policemen he now had with him, and demanded their surrender. Against such odds, Pritchett and the policemen gave up, and they were detained for two hours until a magistrate arrived. When he reached the scene he issued a warrant for the arrest of the state policemen.

In his report to the Governor, Davidson quoted Pritchett as saying:

By this time myself and men were thoroughly convinced that we were in the possession of an infuriated *mob,* and were arrested by irresponsible persons who were neither officers of the law and without authority or writ for our arrest. Upon this conviction, I made an affidavit that justice could not be done me in that precinct. They then made the writ returnable before Justice Booth of Hillsboro. We were carried to Hillsboro under guard of some twenty men. On reaching Hillsboro, my four men sent ahead were there overtaken and arrested also. We then proceeded to the trial under charge that myself and men had forcibly entered the premises of J. J. Gathings without a search warrant. It seemed that the news had spread throughout the country while our trial was going on. During the trial, the court room was filled with men armed with *shot-guns* and *six-shooters.* There was intense excitement during the whole trial. At the conclusion of the trial, the justice placed my bond at five hundred dollars for my appearance one week hence. When this was announced, J. J. Gathings, the leader of the mob, being armed, walked up to the justice's stand and with anger and clenched fist, swore to the court that "by God if the bond is not made strong and substantial, I will re-arrest him and hold him until that date of his trial."

Lieutenant Pritchett and his men were released, but subsequently other warrants were issued on the same charges for his recapture, although they evidently did not include his men. Davidson, again quot-

[6] *Daily State Journal,* February 10, 1871, II, 13.

ing, said that Pritchett declared, "Affairs were becoming still more serious, as more armed men were coming in; whiskey freely drank, and myself and men threatened and insulted."

Pritchett attempted to leave the county, was again arrested, but escaped. His own impression, stated later, was that he and his detachment were detained the first time in order to give the criminals, Sollola Nicholson and James Gathings, an opportunity to escape, as he believed that they were but a short distance ahead of him.

In his report to the Governor, Adjutant General Davidson continued the story in his own words:

This outrage taken in connection with the previous disregard of law evinced by the citizens of Hill County, as shown by the correspondence held with this office, copies of which accompany this report, and to which your Excellency's attention has been previously invited, induced me to represent the state of affairs in that section as totally beyond the control of the civil officers of the law.

Pursuant to special orders No. 3 current series, and instructions from your Excellency, I started for Hill county on the morning of January 12, 1871. I was detained *en route* by a very severe norther, accompanied by a terrible storm of snow and hail and consequently did not reach Hillsboro until Sunday, the fifteenth of January.

By orders from this office, Captain E. H. Napier and his company of state guards, numbering fifty (50) men were directed to proceed to Hill County, and reached that point some time after I had arrived.

I found affairs in confusion, officers intimidated, authority resisted, and a spirit of defiance to law extant, which the civil officers were powerless to control.

In accordance with my instructions and your Excellency's proclamation, martial law was declared; Colonel J. M. Gibbs, Reserve Militia, placed in command and a provost marshal appointed. Orders were issued for the arrest of James J. Gathings, James Gathings Jr., Philip Gathings, James Denmember, William L. Turner, David Gathings, and Dr. A. M. Douglas, as leaders in the outrage against Lieutenant Pritchett and his men, which was promptly effected.

These men were brought before me, acknowledged their participation in the outrage, and the amount of three thousand ($3,000.00) dollars was assessed upon them. Of this amount, twenty-seven hundred and sixty-five ($2,765.00) dollars (one thousand of which was in gold) was paid over promptly by the parties assessed, and it is estimated as sufficient to cover all expenses incident to the declaration of martial law in that county.

All disbursements made from this fund to the present time have been upon vouchers properly certified to, and on file in this office. Some payments have yet to be made on this account.

I deemed this matter of procedure more equitable and just to the inhabitants of Hill county generally, than an assessment upon the people at large, and my views were concurred in by the parties themselves as stated to me.

The presiding justice of the county informed me that his decision in Lieutenant Pritchett's case was rendered upon January 11, 1871. The presiding justice of the county informed me that his decision was rendered upon fear of murder by the infuriated mob in the court room at the trial. Subsequently, he made affidavit that he had acted under fear of his life, which I left with Justice Lawrence of Hill county.

The county remained under martial law for two days, when it was sufficiently quiet to turn over to the civil authorities, which was done and the troops ordered to their homes.

This application of martial law, I am happy to say, has had the effect of rendering that county as peaceable and subservient to the laws as any other portion of the State.[7]

The statement presented the administration's attitude toward the difficulty in Hill County. But the Waco *Examiner,* published in neighboring McLennan County, probably came nearer to expressing the opinion held by most citizens. This editorial, reprinted in the *Tri-Weekly State Gazette* of Austin, stated:

We have never known in the history of America, such flagrant abuse of power—such an open and bold violation of the rights of liberty and property of citizens by a constituted authority as that which we are now about to relate. Our readers are familiar with the facts connected with the arrest of the State Police in Hill county a few weeks ago by Colonel Gathings and others.

. . . Davidson, Adjutant General of the State, with a number of State Guard (we believed about 80) passed through Waco a few days since on his way to Hill county to investigate the affairs of that county.

. . . The acts and doings of this all powerful functionary, as we have received from credible sources, are these:

[7] *Daily State Journal,* February 10, 1871, II, 13.

Upon his arrival, he sent first an orderly and subsequently the sheriff for Colonel Gathings, Dr. Douglas, and others. They were taken to the courthouse, from which all persons were excluded except the officers and the accused, and the courthouse surrounded by the troops. Then the Adjutant General informed them that no court martial would be formed if they would pay the expenses of the troops, which were about $500.00 a day. Colonel Gathings said he was unable to pay that amount, when General Davidson told him that $3,000.00 in currency would satisfy him, to which Gathings consented; they were turned over to the civil authority, and Gathings was required to give a bond in the sum of $2,000.00 and others in the sum of $1,000.00 . We learn further that Gathings was informed that on failure of his compliance, the troops would be quartered upon the people, and that he would be tried and sent to the penitentiary, before he could appeal to any other tribunal. He was refused permission to consult a lawyer, and required to make his decision in fifteen minutes. The bond given by Lieutenant Pritchett for appearance to answer for a violation of law was called for and given by the sheriff.

. . . The Militia law empowers the Governor, under certain circumstances, to declare martial law in any county, and he "shall call out such part of the State Guard, Reserve Militia or State Police as may be in his opinion necessary to the suppression of disorder. The expense of maintaining the State Guard, Reserve Militia, or State Police called into active service under this section, may in whole or in part be assessed upon the *people* of the county or counties where the laws are suspended (General Laws, p. 16). . . . And if martial law had been necessary, Davidson had no right to accept a reward for *having it decided.* But even had Hill county been under martial law, the act quoted authorizes a tax to be levied on the *people* of the county and not supposed *offenders.* So that it may be seen that the action of Davidson has no foundation in the laws which give him authority. . . .[8]

MARTIAL LAW IN WALKER COUNTY

Far more serious were the disturbances in Walker County, and they resulted in more drastic punishment inflicted upon the people. The trouble began during a district court session in January, 1871, when a colored man by the name of Jenkins, who had been badly beaten, appeared before the grand jury to make a statement. A few days later his body was found near Huntsville, the county seat, and it presented unmistakable proof that he had been murdered.

[8] *Tri-Weekly State Gazette,* January 25, 1871, III, 153.

State Police Captain L. H. McNelly and a small force of policemen were ordered to the county to investigate, and he soon acquired information that led to the arrest of four persons: Nat Outlaw, John McParrish, Fred Parks, and Jo Wright. These men were brought before District Court Judge J. R. Burnett for a hearing. Subsequent events were reported in a letter written to the Governor on January 25[9] by W. H. Horne, a Radical Republican who was district attorney of the Thirtieth Judicial District.

Messrs. Baker, Maxey, and Hightower were the attorneys for the defendants. I represented the State. During the trial which lasted three days, in the examination of the witnesses for the State and for the defendants, there was much excitement manifested by the friends of the prisoners and threats were made that the prisoners should not go to jail if committed. All the evidence was reduced to writing and after argument of counsel the court in a written opinion, after reflecting upon the threats and warnings of assassination and intimidations of the court, declared it to be the opinion of the court that three of the prisoners, Jo. Wright, John McParish, and Nat Outlaw were guilty of the offense charged. The prisoner Parks was discharged from custody, and Captain McNelly was ordered by the court to take the other prisoners to jail there to await the next term of the District Court.

The prisoners in the meantime, who through the aid of their friends outside and inside the court room, had concealed upon their persons at least two six shooters each, and immediately began to fire upon the officers. Captain McNelly was shot down; one of his policemen, Tom Kesee, was also wounded, the ball taking effect in the face and passing around the neck. Both of these officers, however, continued to fire upon the prisoners until two of them succeeded in making their escape from the court room, both, however, wounded. On the street, the two prisoners who escaped were met by their confederates who armed with shot guns were in such force as to prevent any further attempt to arrest them. Mounted upon horses, shooting off their pistols and yelling like savages, the prisoners followed by their friends made their escape from town. Captain McNelly ordered the Sheriff to summon a posse to pursue the prisoners, but he made a written report that only two citizens could be found who were willing to aid in their capture. Two policemen who were at the base of the stairs leading up into the court room when the first shot was fired, were prevented from giving any assistance by confederates of the prisoners who with pistols presented and cocked

[9] *Daily State Journal,* February 10, 1871, II, 13.

were threatened with immediate death if they attempted to move. Thirty or forty shots were fired in the court room and several shots in the street.

Judge Burnett and District Attorney Horne were both shot at, and the night after an attempt was made to assassinate the Judge. The party to this attempt was one Steward, ex-sheriff and an active aider and abettor in the conspiracy to murder the officers of the court and secure the escape of the prisoners.

It is impossible at this writing to give you the names of all those who are liable to arrest. When you give such protection as will make the witness feel secure, then I will take pleasure in prosecuting if you will also protect the court from assassination.

At the time of my leaving Huntsville, I had information that the prisoners were guarded by thirty or forty well armed friends who defied arrest and threatened death to Captain McNelly at all hazards. There were so many sympathizers and aiders in the escape that I prefer stating who were not, in justice to the few who did not in any way give them aid or comfort: Judge J. H. Benton, Colonel Abercrombie, Sanford Gibbs, Dr. Rawlings, Mr. Bush of Rawlings and Company, and Mr. Kelly, county commissioner.

There was no excuse for the first act—a cold blooded murder and assassination of a poor old freedman and certainly nothing in extenuation of the last attempt to shoot down the officers of the court, for no advantage was taken of the prisoners by the State. They had able counsel and many friends who were willing witnesses. Yet the evidence against Outlaw, McParish, and Jo Wright after an impartial trial was of such a character as to warrant their commitment by the court without bail and despite the efforts of their learned, zealous and over active counsel to create the impression that a great judicial wrong was perpetrated. Even now public opinion slowly forming, points to McParish, Wright, and Outlaw as the murderers and assassins of Sam Jenkins.[10]

One newspaper declared that the disturbance in the courtroom occurred because at the conclusion of the hearing Judge Burnett immediately drew from his pocket a written opinion, indicating that the accused had been prejudged. The same newspaper stated further that although the behavior of the defendants merited punishment, their actions were not sufficient evidence to show that the civil government in the county was powerless to suppress crime.[11]

[10] W. E. Horne to E. J. Davis, January 25, 1871, State Police Letters of 1871, MS.; *Daily State Journal,* February 10, 1871, II, 13.

[11] *Daily State Journal,* February 10, 1871, II, 13.

On February 7 the state Senate passed a resolution asking the Governor to bare any information he might have regarding the acts of lawlessness reported from Hill and Walker counties. Along with other evidence he submitted the letter from W. H. Horne, and he enclosed a statement giving his own attitude regarding the trouble:

... I am not aware that the history of the United States or in fact, any country where the English language is spoken, presents a parallel to this Walker county affair for overbearing lawlessness. While doubtless many of the citizens of that county deprecate the act, they all stood by supinely, or actively aided the attack upon the judge and officers of the law while engaged in the exercise of their legitimate authority and sworn duty.

In conclusion, I have to state that I am preparing to send troops into Walker county, and that martial law will be proclaimed therein, the guilty parties arrested and punished, if they be found, and the cost assessed upon the people of the county.[12]

Martial law was indeed declared in Walker County—on February 15, 1871. Then on February 27 Adjutant General Davidson convened a military commission which apprehended for trial about twenty persons.[13] Most were arraigned for failing to answer the Sheriff's summons to aid in the recapture of the prisoners. Some were convicted, and regarding this, one observer, N. G. Kittrell, said:

He [Davidson] then proceeded to organize a military commission composed of State Militia officers and tried four young men who had been schoolmates of mine and fined three of them one hundred dollars, and sentenced one to the penitentiary for five years, and actually put him into convict stripes. That was nearly a year after the Constitution of 1869 had been approved by Congress and the State fully restored to the Union.[14]

Outlaw, who was alleged to have been one of the murderers, was tried by the court martial in Walker County and drew a five-year penitentiary sentence. Davidson censured the decision, declaring that the court martial had been neglectful in its duty and that the man should have been hanged. Governor Davis examined the case, however, pardoned Outlaw, and rebuked Davidson severely for the adjutant

[12] *Tri-Weekly State Gazette,* March 3, 1871, II, 169.
[13] State Police Letters of 1871, MS.
[14] Norman G. Kittrell, *Governors Who Have Been and Other Public Men of Texas,* p. 53.

general's condemnation of the "leniency."[15] The following year Outlaw sued Governor Davis, Adjutant General Davidson, and others, alleging false imprisonment. The defendants pleaded justification on the grounds of Governor Davis' martial law proclamation, but a district judge held that this was insufficient, declaring that the martial law proclamation was both illegal and unconstitutional. A verdict was rendered in favor of Outlaw, who received as compensation twenty thousand dollars.[16]

To pay for martial law expenses in Walker County a tax of fifty cents on one hundred dollars was levied on the taxpayers.[17] This evoked protests, but the people submitted peacefully. Kittrell, writing much later, explained their attitude:

The people of Texas, in common with all the people of the South, had been for more than five years subjected to the domination of the scalawag, the carpet-bagger, and the Negro, and were to such a large extent deprived of the right of suffrage, that they were somewhat cowed and broken in spirit.

In no other way can I account for the people of Huntsville submitting to the outrage inflicted upon them. As I look back upon the day when I, but a little more than a youth, went with a committee of citizens to protest against the tax levy and martial law, and explain that they had done nothing to merit such a treatment, I recall how contemptuously the petty tyrant Davidson treated the committee. I wonder that the people had not risen in a body and wiped him and his roving band of buccaneers off the earth. I have always regretted that they did not.[18]

[15] *Flake's Daily Bulletin,* March 21, 1871, VI, 186. Flake says:
In the proceeding the Governor has clearly shown himself an unjust ruler. In the first place by having a citizen tried in time of peace by a court martial, and in the second place in pardoning a man after conviction who was guilty of the crime charged, if the court which tried him was a proper court to hear and determine the matter.
The truth is Davis became alarmed for the consequence of his unlawful action as exposed, in a legal point of view in *Flake's bulletin,* and sneaks out of the results by pardoning a man he knew to have been illegally condemned.
[16] *Daily State Journal,* April 9, 1872, III, 63. A new trial was granted in this case. The second trial was not investigated by the author since Adjutant General Davidson absconded from the state in the latter part of 1872 and Davis, as evidence shows, was never wealthy; therefore, the second case, even if decided in Outlaw's favor, could have gained him little financially. The political significance of the first decision was the important thing.
[17] *Tri-Weekly State Gazette,* March 3, 1871, III, 169.
[18] Kittrell, *Governors Who Have Been,* p. 53.

Soon after the disturbance had occurred in Walker County, Captain L. H. McNelly of the State Police, who had played a rather prominent part in the event, was interviewed by a reporter of the Galveston *News* on the subject. This interview, which was uncomplimentary to the administration's policy in that section, was republished in the *Daily State Journal.*

Reporter: Captain, I have called to say that we cannot find any report of yours among the published documents of the Walker county matter. You must from your position have made one. Why is it not published?

Captain: I made two: the first by telegraph from Navasota, the second by mail, some eight or ten days after the occurrence. I do not know why they were not published.

Reporter: Did you recommend the declaration of martial law in Walker county?

Captain: No sir. There was no occasion for it.

Reporter: On whom does the blame for the disturbance rest?

Captain: On the sheriff. It was his business to have disarmed the prisoners when they came into his custody, and I supposed he had done it, or I would have acted differently. Had he done so, I could have taken the prisoners to jail without firing a shot. I would have been stopped outside, but I could have overcome the friends of the young men by fair expostulation and reason. After their escape, I could, had it not been for my wound, have got a hundred citizens to volunteer for the pursuit.

Reporter: I ask you again, Captain, was there any necessity for martial law?

Captain: No sir; not a bit. The evidence is that General Davidson, with eight or ten men—and he has not more—is collecting that tax. If the people of Walker county were lawless, they would show it now.

Reporter: Did you ever see or know anybody else who ever saw a Ku Klux?

Captain: No Sir. There is no such thing in my district. In the year 1867, some of the most respectable Texans were alarmed lest the Negroes would rise, rob, and murder them. They formed a society for protection. It died out in a few months. There is no secret political society in Texas but the Loyal League. There may be young men in neighborhoods who have signs and calls by which they communicate with each other, just as thieves, gamblers, and prostitutes do, but there is nothing more than this.

Reporter: Why was martial law declared?

Captain: I do not know.

Reporter: Was it for money?

Captain: Possibly.

The *Daily State Journal,* the official organ of the Davis administration, said of the above interview:

Here we find the broad and plain assertions made, as coming from the police captain, that there was no need for martial law; that there are no Ku Klux in the disturbed district; that martial law was declared by the State Executive "possibly" for money, while it is more than insinuated that the highest authorities of the State are seeking to disturb the public peace, "in order to force the people into resistance." In other words, a sworn official is published as charging his superiors with the blackest and most unmitigated villainy. On the publication of the conversation in the *News,* McNelly telegraphed to General Davidson that his words had been garbled and that the proper correction should be made.

We append what he called his "correction." It is lame, evasive, and inadequate. Either Captain McNelly did or did not make the charges impugning the honesty, and honor and political morality of his superiors that were published in the *News.* His reply is neither an admission nor a denial, and fails to meet the case so entirely as to leave the impression on the reader of the substantial correctness of the conversation given to the public in the columns of the *News.*

The contents of McNelly's "correction" letter were as follows:

Houston, Texas
March 8, 1871

Editors *News:*

In today's issue of the *News,* I find a report of a conversation I had with your reporter. Not anticipating at the time a publication of the conversation, I was perhaps less guarded in my statements than I should have been, that is, I should have guarded against the possibility of the reporter misunderstanding me, as it is evident he has done.

. . . I stated that I could and intended to have, all parties that refused to obey the order of the sheriff, indicted.

The reporter states that I when asked, "was martial law declared for the purpose of getting money?" answered, "Possibly." The reporter misunderstood the sense I used the word in, if I used it at all. I did not intend saying that Governor Davis or General Davidson should have been guilty of such a crime. Had I thought so, I should have been the first to denounce them. And as for the last question, I have this to say, that I only know the intention of the authorities at Austin by the instructions that I have received by orders, and from personal interviews with Governor Davis and General Davidson, and they have ever cautioned me to be prudent and courteous in the discharge of my duties as a policeman, and have promptly dismissed all officers that I have reported for doing otherwise.[19]

[19] *Daily State Journal,* March 17, 1871, II, 43.

THE CALAMITY IN LIMESTONE COUNTY

Perhaps the most distressing experience any group of Texans had to undergo during the regime of E. J. Davis occurred in Freestone and Limestone counties in a period of a few weeks following September 30, 1871. On that date D. C. Applewhite was killed by Mitchell Cotton, one of four Negro state policemen who attacked him in the town of Groesbeck.[20] Details of the murder were given by an eyewitness, J. D. Parish, in a sworn statement to J. H. Lofland, justice of the peace of the Limestone County First Precinct.

My place of business is immediately opposite Clark's saloon, where the shooting of D. C. Applewhite on the thirtieth of September occurred. I saw Dan Galagher and D. C. Applewhite enter Clark's saloon just before the shooting commenced. They were closely followed by three colored policemen,[21] two of whom commenced drawing their six shooters before they got to the door, or in sight of where Applewhite was standing, with his back towards the door. As they entered the door, Galagher and Applewhite turned with their faces towards the door. Immediately afterwards, I heard some one say. "Don't shoot!" but the policemen almost instantly opened fire on Applewhite. Applewhite then ran out of the door and crossed Navasota street, followed by the policemen who continued firing at him. I saw the policemen as they were retiring from the dead body and going in the direction of the mayor's office. One of them had a six-shooter, flourishing it over his head. *I heard him say, in a loud and excited tone of voice, "There is another white livered son of a b—— that I want to kill. I will have this town flowing with white blood before morning."* On the following morning I heard A. Zadek Jr., mayor of Groesbeck, say that he had ordered the citizens to arm themselves and arrest the murderers of Applewhite. On Sunday morning, October 1, the report was current that the colored people were rallying for the purpose of attacking the town. At about five o'clock Sunday evening, news reached Groesbeck that two of the murderers of Applewhite had been arrested and placed in jail. The citizens seemed to be at once satisfied *and since that time the town has never been so quiet and orderly.*[22]

Corroborating this testimony was a formal remonstrance presented to the Legislature by Limestone County citizens, who hoped thus to

[20] *House Journal, 12th Legislature,* Adjourned Session, 1871, p. 218; *Daily State Journal,* October 17, 1871, II, 24.

[21] Other evidence indicates that there were four Negro state policemen.

[22] *House Journal, 12th Legislature,* Adjourned Session, 1871, p. 223; *Daily State Journal,* October 17, 1871, II, 24.

give a true picture of conditions in the county and to avoid the martial law that seemed likely to come. Seventy-four citizens signed the paper. According to them, A. Zadek, Jr., mayor of Groesbeck, approached a crowd who had gathered around the body of Applewhite, while the policemen were fleeing. Zadek summoned all persons present to aid him in keeping the peace. A short time later he made a similar statement to another crowd. Soon the mayor had a large group of armed men, ready to follow his orders.

Meanwhile, the four state policemen had fled to the Mayor's office, where they barricaded themselves. From this location they dared authorities to arrest them. Flourishing their pistols, they shouted threats and fired two or three shots at persons passing on the opposite side of the street. About an hour later the policemen were reinforced by some twenty associates, who had come, armed and mounted, from the direction of Springfield. After consultation they all retreated from Groesbeck as night fell, shouting threats against the whites and firing a number of shots. Later, persons coming in from the country declared that the Negroes were being reinforced and that they intended to return and burn the town.

The Mayor appointed A. H. Stegall, a respected Groesbeck citizen, to act as town marshal and to organize a special police force to patrol the streets. Two forces, one on foot and one mounted, were organized and instructed to follow the state policemen.

At midnight, before the special force had departed, Sheriff Young and Deputy Newton of Limestone County came to Groesbeck. Affidavits were sworn out against the murderers of Applewhite, and warrants for their arrest were issued. The Sheriff called on Dr. J. J. Robertson, who had been given command of the mounted force of thirty-five men, to accompany him, and the posse—now under leadership of the Sheriff—hurried to a position half a mile from a place known as "Merrick's Quarters," where it was believed that the policemen were hiding. There the Sheriff and his deputy left the posse in command of Dr. Robertson and went on to the "Quarters." They returned in a short time; the Sheriff said that he had talked to Merrick and Giles Trammel, leader of the colored police, and that they declared that Mitchell Cotton, one of the men for whom the warrants were issued, had been sent away, but that Jones, another whom the posse sought, was nearby. The Sheriff, determining to return for Jones, took one man with him and ordered the rest of the posse to stay behind.

Some time later Sheriff Young and his assistant returned to the waiting posse. Young, reporting that Giles Trammel had gone on a mile and a half further to arrest Jones, ordered the posse to return to Groesbeck, foreseeing no further need for it. Young said he would go back to "Merrick's Quarters," and as soon as the arrest was made he would take the prisoner to Springfield.

Dr. Robertson returned with his posse to Groesbeck. When he arrived it was nearly daylight, and all was quiet. Complying with the Sheriff's orders, Robertson dispersed the posse.

Later that day—Sunday, October 1—citizens from all over the county flocked to Groesbeck, having heard that the colored policemen were threatening to attack the town. The mayor calmed them, but he ordered Dr. Robertson to reassemble his men. Robertson, himself, was given a warrant for the arrest of Applewhite's murderers and told to execute it, but after he and his men had traveled only a short distance from town the order was revoked, and the posse again dispersed. Apparently the reason for the revocation of the order was the arrival of a State Guard company, a stronger force, which made Robertson's posse unnecessary.

About ten o'clock that morning the Sheriff returned to Groesbeck, with this State Guard company under the command of Captain W. H. Richardson. After consulting with certain leading citizens he decided to proceed immediately with Richardson's men to arrest Applewhite's murderers, for the sheriff had been unsuccessful in his attempt to arrest Jones. Cotton too had not been apprehended. By that time the Negroes had been reinforced by 100 or 200 armed supporters.

Late in the afternoon, however, word of the arrest of Cotton and Jones reached Groesbeck. Upon the receipt of this information quiet was restored. The news of these arrests, however, proved to be false.

Three days later, on October 4, Judge J. W. Oliver arrived in Groesbeck and at a called meeting that day he told citizens that martial law had been threatened. If they would organize themselves into a special police force, Judge Oliver declared, he would bestow on them authority to execute orders according to the law, and martial law might thus be avoided. Accordingly, about fifty leading citizens organized themselves into a special police force, were sworn in by Judge Oliver, and were placed under the command of Colonel Mitchell, a well known resident.[23] Mitchell then placed himself and his men at the disposal of State Police Captain George W. Farrow. They performed their duties "to his entire satisfaction."[24] In pursuance of their duties these special policemen made a number of arrests.

The two Negro state policemen wanted for Applewhite's murder, however, remained at large. Concerning them, the *Memorial of the Citizens of Limestone County to the Legislature,* dated October 11, declared:

Indeed, the only arrests which have not been made, when ordered, of any party implicated in this tragedy or the alleged riot, are that of the two colored policemen, against whom warrants were issued more than a week ago for the killing of Applewhite. But they are permitted by the authorities to go at large, and while this memorial is being prepared, are walking the streets of Groesbeck, unmolested by the officers of the law or anyone else.

Further increasing the tension was the murder on Saturday night, October 7, of a Negro named Lee. Charged with the murder was Anthony Simms, who was arrested and jailed. He was later declared insane.

During all this excitement Groesbeck held its congressional election.[25] The registrar placed Captain Richardson's State Guard company on duty at the polls, and the voting proceeded quietly. Leading citizens pledged protection to every colored man who came to vote, but local Radical Republican officials, evidently believing that the Negroes would not be duly protected, ordered them to remain away from the polls, saying this was not the time for the colored men to vote. A number of Negroes who had come to cast their ballots were ordered to leave.

Concluding their *Memorial,* Limestone County citizens declared:

We respectfully submit this report with our accompanying proofs to your honorable body, and earnestly invite the calm and dispassionate attention of every member of the Legislature of Texas thereto. We respectfully insist that we have violated no laws as a people. Everything done by us was at the command of the officers of the law and for our own protection from the threats and menaces of a mob of infuriated men.

[23] *House Journal, 12th Legislature,* Adjourned Session, 1871, pp. 218–221.
[24] *Daily State Journal,* October 17, 1871, II, 224.
[25] *Tri-Weekly Democratic Statesman,* October 10, 1871, I, 33.

We would therefore appeal to you as the representative of a free, enlightened, and law abiding people, to stand by us in this the darkest hour of our history, and avert the evils and calamitous consequences which would be visited upon us by a declaration of martial law and a suspension of the writ of *habeas corpus* and right of trial by jury.[26]

The Governor, however, was swayed by letters received from Radical Republicans residing in Limestone and Freestone counties and by other matters. On his own initiative, and without the consent of the Legislature, he proclaimed martial law in both counties on October 9, 1871. He stated his reasons:

Whereas it has been officially made known to me, and the official reports have been corroborated by the verbal statements of individuals of good repute personally cognizant of the facts by them stated that there exists in the counties of Limestone and Freestone in said State a combination of lawless men, claiming themselves to consist of several thousand persons organized as an insurrectionary force, too strong for the control of the civil authorities of said counties, which has murdered an unarmed and unoffending citizen in his own house; the individuals composing which, carry pistols and other weapons prohibited to be worn on the person by law, have discharged firearms in public places, and have by threats, violence, and organized force intimidated and controlled the civil officers of Limestone county, so as to prevent them from discharging their respective duties, who have precluded the holding of a fair election in said last named county and even presume to place picket guards upon the public highways, arrest and detain as prisoners, citizens of the State, and stop the coaches carrying the United States mails, and interrogate in an inquisitorial and menacing manner the passengers therein, and to cut the telegraph wires to prevent communication with the seat of government, which insurrectionary force exists as an armed and organized mob contrary to law, and is too numerous to be arrested and held by the civil authorities and to be tried by the district courts.[27]

For a month martial law was forced on the citizens of Limestone and Freestone counties, until it was removed on November 10.[28] To pay the costs, a penalty of $50,000 was levied on residents, at a rate of 3 per cent on all taxable property. Civil law was superseded and the writ of *habeas corpus* was suspended,[29] but the citizens evidently re-

[26] *House Journal, 12th Legislature,* Adjourned Session, 1871, pp. 221–222.
[27] *House Journal, 12th Legislature,* Adjourned Session, 1871, p. 179.
[28] *Daily State Journal,* November 23, 1871, II, 256.
[29] *Tri-Weekly Democratic Statesman,* October 12, 1871, I, 34; *House Journal, 12th Legislature,* Adjourned Session, 1871, p. 180.

mained quiet. State Police Sergeant B. F. Baldridge, who was stationed in Limestone County, described conditions to Adjutant General Davidson:

Everything is comparatively quiet here at present. But much bitter feeling exists against the General and State government and especially are they hostile toward the administration of Texas and heads of all departments. And their opposition to the Police is extreme, but at present somewhat smothered down.[30]

The House of Representatives, although its members were Radical Republican, denounced the Governor's action. On November 6, 1871, it adopted by a vote of 44 to 33 a resolution stating:

The action of his Excellency E. J. Davis, in declaring martial law in the manner aforesaid, in the counties of Freestone and Limestone, be and the same is hereby disapproved as being unnecessary to the ends of public justice and uncalled for, as the counties were in the unobstructed exercise of their proper jurisdiction and illegal as the Legislature was then in session.
Resolved further that the Governor be and is hereby requested and instructed to restore civil authority in said counties and to withdraw all armed forces therefrom and disband the same.[31]

Three days later martial law ended in Limestone and Freestone counties.[32]

[30] B. F. Baldridge to James Davidson, October 21, 1871, State Police Letters of 1871, MS.
[31] *Tri-Weekly State Gazette,* November 6, 1871, IV, 140; C. Appleton (ed.), *American Annual Cyclopaedia,* 1871, XI, 732.
[32] *Daily State Journal,* November 23, 1871, II, 256.

TEXAS POLITICS IN 1871 AND 1872

THE TAXPAYERS' CONVENTION

DURING THE SUMMER OF 1871 a group of prominent Texas citizens, including E. M. Pease, Morgan C. Hamilton, George Hancock, M. H. Bowers, R. M. Lane, and others, called upon fellow Texans to hold meetings at the county level for the dual purpose of discussing heavy state taxation and of electing delegates to a state taxpayers' convention to be held at Austin in September.[1]

As a result, ninety-four counties sent delegates to the convention held on September 22, 23, and 25.[2] The meeting represented a unified effort by Conservative Republicans and Democrats to undermine the Davis party, using as tools the heavy state expenditures, the high taxes, and the likelihood of continued extravagance by the Radical legislature.[3]

The temporary chairman of the convention was Major George B. Erath of McLennan County; E. M. Pease was given the permanent chairmanship.[4] After taking his seat ex-Governor Pease addressed the convention, describing the critical financial condition of the state.

. . . Now, little more than a year and a half has elapsed since the present civil government was established in our State. The government commenced operations with a large balance in the Treasury, but by improvidence and extravagance we are now reduced to the humiliating position of seeing the

[1] *Democratic Statesman*, August 12, 1871, I, 8.
[2] John Henry Brown, *History of Texas from 1685 to 1892*, II, 456.
[3] Charles W. Ramsdell, *Reconstruction in Texas*, p. 308.
[4] Frank Brown, "Annals of Travis County and the City of Austin," Ch. III, p. 51, MS.

warrants of the State hawked about the streets of Austin at six bits on the dollar, and sold with difficulty even at that rate. And now the people are startled with the statement that upwards of six millions of dollars are to be collected from the people the current year, when $800,000.00 would furnish an ample amount for the legitimate purpose of the government. . . . It is evident to every reflecting mind that our State government is bankrupt; and you see no recommendation made by those in power for a reduction of the expenditures. We might entertain some hope of remedy for these evils if the lawmaking power had provided for an election for State officers during the present year, but we are denied that hope by the enactment of a law which postpones this election for twelve months.

A committee of seven was appointed to confer with Governor Davis about reducing state expenditures and to hold conferences on that subject with such committees as might be appointed by the Legislature. This committee was unsuccessful in attempting to confer with the governor, for Davis refused to recognize the convention in any way. The committee also met little immediate response from the Legislature, but some favorable action, the result of the work of the convention as a whole, would later be taken by the legislative body. Other committees were also appointed: one to prepare a "general business" agenda for the meeting, another to prepare a statistical report on the condition of finances and taxation, and another to obtain information from the adjutant general concerning his administration, as chief of State Police, of the unpopular State Police law. There is no evidence that Adjutant General Davidson personally cooperated in furnishing this information.[5]

The committee on general business, composed of twenty-one members, was divided into three subcommittees, which on Monday night, September 25, submitted three lengthy reports against the Administration. The first presented a catalogue of Administration infractions of the state Constitution and of existing state laws. The other two dealt with alleged inequities arising from the State Police act and the public school act. The reports suggested methods of remedying these various wrongs.

The report of the committee on statistics, in explaining the con-

[5] *Democratic Statesman,* September 23, 1871, I, 26; Ramsdell, *Reconstruction in Texas,* p. 309; *Tri-Weekly Democratic Statesman,* November 23, 1871, I, 52; E. W. Winkler, *Platforms of Political Parties in Texas,* "Proceedings of The Taxpayers Convention, 1871," pp. 128–140.

dition of state finances and taxes, gave conclusive evidence of the enormous increase of expenditures and taxation under the Davis Administration and suggested ways of correcting those evils. The committee declared the 1 per cent school tax to be unconstitutional and recommended that the people resist it, paying instead only the one-eighth of 1 per cent levied by the Legislature. To suggest proper resistance methods an advisory committee was appointed.[6]

The chairman of the committee on statistics, A. J. Hamilton, explained that the tax rate for the state had risen from $0.15 on the $100 in 1866 to $2.175 on the $100 under the Davis administration, and this did not include occupation and city taxes or the $2 annual poll tax. Neither did it include the levy to pay interest on the bonds promised the International, the Southern Pacific, and the Trans-Continental railroads. The state had obligated itself to pay approximately 14 million dollars to the three railroads, and this would mean an additional increase of $0.60 on the $100. The resolutions presented by the committee on statistics, and adopted by the convention, went into great detail as to the matters of taxation.[7]

[6] *Democratic Statesman,* September 23, 1871, I, 26.
[7] Winkler, *Platforms of Political Parties,* pp. 128–140. The resolutions of the committee on statistics were as follows:
1. That the present rates of taxation are greatly in excess of the legitimate and necessary wants of the government. 2. That the legislature now in session, be and they are hereby requested by this Convention, as the Representatives of the Taxpayers and citizens of the State, to revise and remodel the tax laws, so as to levy in lieu of all other direct ad valorem taxes, only one-third of one per cent, on all real and personal property, not exempt from taxation, for State purposes and not exceeding one-half that rate for county purposes. The constitutional rate for school purposes to be taken from the amount thus levied for state purposes.

The estimated value of property subject to taxation in 1871, as found by the committee on statistics, was $212,000,000.00, and in order to give a concrete estimate of the amount of taxes levied that year, it presented the following figures:

One-half of 1 per cent on the estimated value of taxable property as ad valorem state tax	$1,060,000.00
One-quarter of 1 per cent, ad valorem county tax . .	530,000.00
One-quarter of 1 per cent, ad valorem bridge tax . .	530,000.00
One-eighth of 1 per cent, as per one-quarter of state tax for school purposes	265,000.00
One-half of 1 per cent as tax to pay frontier bonds	106,000.00
A 1 per cent tax for schoolhouse purposes, etc. . .	2,120,000.00
Poll tax for roads and bridges estimated . . .	150,000.00

The convention declared that the ordinary annual expenses of the government should not exceed $695,000. It stated that an ad valorem property tax of one-third of 1 per cent for the state and one-sixth of 1 per cent for the counties should be sufficient, instead of the one-half of 1 per cent and one-quarter of 1 per cent then being levied. These suggested ad valorem property taxes plus poll taxes, license taxes, and occupation taxes were calculated to produce revenue ample to meet all necessary expenses, afford a liberal amount for public schools, and still leave a surplus in the treasury.

The convention further resolved that if the Legislature failed to provide for a general election in 1871 a committee was to be appointed to memorialize Congress and ask its intervention.[8]

Governor Davis quite naturally opposed the taxpayers' convention. On the night of September 23, 1871, he led a spectacular demonstration against it, marching up Congress Avenue to the Capitol at the head of a band of turbulent Negroes. At the Capitol he addressed the crowd. His speech and the incidents which followed were described by an Austin Democratic newspaper:

"Fellow citizens: In ancient times, it was the custom of the people to purify their temples when defiled by burning and sprinkling incense round the same. This temple, our capitol, has been polluted by the presence of the taxpayers of the State, and therefore, it devolves upon you, my colored brethren, to purify the place. As we have no incense, I would suggest that you form in double ranks and march around this building, singing those glorious hymns of freedom, with which you all are so familiar."

Thereupon, this squad of one hundred Negroes—the most ignorant, superstitious, and servile representatives of the race that could well be selected out of our colored male population of some 600—marched around the building, at the hour of midnight, singing, "John Brown's Soul Is Marching On," and "Rally Round the Flag, Boys." This duty performed, the Governor, so-called, but on this solemn occasion priest and prophet, retired to his mansion, amid the shouts of a delighted populace. . . .

The mob, for it can be called nothing less, organized at Buaas Hall, where they had been harangued by Davis and others for several hours. In marching

Poll tax for schools estimated	150,000.00
License and occupation tax for state estimated . .	300,000.00
License and occupation tax for county estimated . .	150,000.00
Total	$5,361,000.00

[8] F. Brown, "Annals of Travis County," Ch. XXX, p. 51, MS.

through the streets they filled the air with tumultuous shouts. Men leaped from their beds, thinking a riot had broken out in our usually quiet city. The yelling and singing was heard in the remote sections of Austin, and created no little excitement and wonder. And such rabble was countenanced, led by the Governor of the State of Texas![9]

On September 30, after the convention proper had adjourned, the advisory committee submitted its suggestions for avoiding payment of excessive taxes. It paid particular attention to the 1 per cent ad valorem tax[10] which the directors of each school district could levy for the construction of buildings and maintenance of schools, as provided in section five of the public school act of 1871.[11] The committee contended that when an effort was made to collect the 1 per cent tax an application for injunction would be granted—provided the judge was honest.

The taxpayers' convention evidently had some effect on the people, judging by results of the congressional elections held the very next month.[12]

THE ELECTION OF 1871

As mentioned, the state Constitution provided that a general election be held in 1871, but the law passed in August, 1870, prohibited a general election before November, 1872. Terms of the Texas representatives in Congress were expiring, however, and vacancies had occurred both in the state Legislature and in other state and local offices. Consequently even the Radicals realized the necessity of a special election, to be held in the fall of 1871. The election was proclaimed by the Governor on May 24, 1871, to take place October 3–6.

In the meantime the Twelfth Legislature had removed the speaker of the House, Ira H. Evans, and elected William Sinclair of Galveston to be his successor. This removal took place on May 10, 1871, because Evans opposed the Radical Republican proposal to postpone the gen-

[9] *Democratic Statesman,* September 26, 1871, I, 27.

[10] *Ibid.,* October 3, 1871, I, 30.

[11] Gammel, *Laws of Texas,* VI, 959–962. This tax was separate from the taxes and other means used to create the available school fund. The available school fund was obtained from one-fourth of all the ad valorem and occupation taxes assessed since March, 1870, and the accruing interest from railroads since that date.

[12] J. H. Brown, *History of Texas,* II, 456.

eral election twelve months beyond the time fixed by the state constitution, as well as certain other measures the extremists supported. Evans was reported to have been an excellent presiding officer.[13]

Conservative Republicans and Democrats were heartened by their prospects. In special elections held during the last week of November, 1870, to fill vacancies in the Legislature, the two groups had been able to capture several districts that in the 1869 election went to the Radicals. The Radicals were perturbed over this attack upon their strength, and Governor Davis threatened to declare martial law in two of these counties, Cherokee[14] and Houston, because of evidence of intimidation.[15]

Also working for the benefit of the more moderate elements was the fact that in some districts Democrats and Conservative Republicans had been able to fuse in policy, thus increasing their chances of success. At a fusion convention at Seguin on December 9, 1870, the Democrats, in the majority, were able to effect their plans for an outright Democratic organization in the Fourth District, and they nominated John Hancock for Congress.

A Democratic state convention, called on November 22, 1870, for the last week of January, 1871,[16] assembled in Austin on January 24[17] and was in session for four days.[18] Nat Terry was elected president of the convention; Ashbel Smith was named chairman of the platform committee, and the platform declared allegiance to the principles of the national Democratic party.

The platform likewise accepted the abolition of slavery as an established fact and promised to guarantee through state legislation the security of all men, white or black. It also expressed a desire to en-

[13] F. Brown, "Annals of Travis County," XXX–XXXI, pp. 11–16, MS.; C. Appleton (ed.), *American Annual Cyclopaedia*, 1871, XI, 721.

[14] Thomas Sheriff to E. J. Davis, January 21, 1871, Executive Letters of E. J. Davis, January, 1871, MS. Thomas Sheriff, a lieutenant of the State Police, informed the Governor that during the November election in Rusk, Cherokee County, freedmen were threatened with being waylaid and shot or driven from their homes, while the white Radicals were "insulted and abused." He concluded that an American Flag was torn down and trampled upon by Davis opponents, but that a Confederate flag was in evidence.

[15] Ramsdell, *Reconstruction in Texas*, p. 305.

[16] *Ibid.*, p. 306; Austin *Daily Republican*, November 28, 1870, III, 153.

[17] Austin *Daily Republican*, January 26, 1871, III, 200.

[18] Appleton, *American Annual Cyclopaedia*, 1871, XI, 734.

PLATE 5. Anne Britton Davis, the wife of Governor E. J. Davis. From the University of Texas Archives.

PLATE 6. The Governor's Mansion in Austin in the early 1870's.

courage immigration, condemned the acts of the Radical Republican administration, noted each violation of state and national constitutions, and denounced the suspension of the writ of habeas corpus, the State Police act, and the printing act. The platform concluded with an invitation to "all good men," regardless of what their past political preferences might have been, "to unite with the conservative party" to remove the Radical Administration from power and to release the people from oppressive taxation.[19]

Democratic candidates for Congress, in addition to John Hancock in the Fourth District, were these: First District, W. S. Herndon; Second District, John C. Connor; Third District, D. C. Giddings.[20] They were opposed by the following Republican nominees: First District, G. W. Whitmore; Second District, A. M. Bryant; Third District, W. T. Clark; and Fourth District, Edward Degener.[21]

The election order issued on August 9, 1871, by the Adjutant General, at the command of Governor Davis, was an arbitrary instrument intended to aid the Radicals in the election. It declared that peace officers and members of the State Guard and State Militia acting under the Governor's command should be placed at registration and polling places to supervise the conduct of the voters.[22]

A Conservative newspaper commented:

Of all the Governor's infamies, his "election order" is the most infamous. It is impossible for us to express the indignation which it has aroused. But of one thing certain, there is a point beyond which forbearance ceases to be a virtue, and Governor Davis and his satraps may learn to their cost, that the People of Texas cannot and will not always submit to their arbitrary usurpations and tyrannical edicts.[23]

Upon learning of the election order ex-Governor A. J. Hamilton entered actively into the campaign for the Democrats. His influence probably brought many Conservative Republicans with him.[24] Another influential factor was a new publication; in July the Statesman Publishing Company of Austin received party authorization to publish an

[19] Austin *Daily Republican,* January 26, 1871, III, 200.
[20] *Tri-Weekly State Gazette,* July 14, 1871, IV, 71.
[21] *Daily State Journal,* August 24, 1871, II, 178.
[22] *Ibid.,* August 13, 1871, II, 169.
[23] *Tri-Weekly State Gazette,* August 18, 1871, IV, 86.
[24] *Democratic Statesman,* August 1, 2, and 3, 1871, I, 3, 4, and 5; Seth S. McKay, "Texas under the Regime of E. J. Davis," p. 134, MS.

official newspaper known as the *Democratic Statesman*.[25] This paper, aided by the San Antonio *Herald,* led the fight for the Democrats.[26] The two newspapers doubtless accomplished a great deal toward overcoming the influence of the official administrative organ, the *Daily State Journal,* and of the various judicial district newspapers provided for by the Radicals in the printing act.[27]

All over the state the Democrats held mass meetings. Early in September the *Democratic Statesman* declared that the Radicals were hopelessly divided into three factions and implied that unification would be impossible. The newspaper asserted that the Administration, composed of plunderers and office holders, was the first and most numerous faction. Then there was the Morgan Hamilton group, a minority of good repute. The railroad subsidy faction represented the third wing, opposed to Davis. Because of this split, the Governor had become anxious about the outcome of the election, the newspaper asserted, and was canvassing the state in behalf of his faction—the first wing.[28]

Long before the election was held the Democrats anticipated fraud. John Hancock suggested that in every county a private box be prepared for holding duplicates of all Democratic votes. Davis, learning of this proposal, ordered the arrest of anybody who attempted to put it into effect.[29] Registration fraud in Harris County was discussed by the San Antonio *Herald,* which declared:

. . . Registered colored voters never die nor remove. Of 1,500 white voters registered in 1868, which was half the real number, 250 had died or removed, including a prominent merchant now living in the city. Of 2,400 Negroes registered in 1868, of whom not more than 1,000 had ever lived in the county, one had died, one moved.[30]

During the registration and the election, the polls were surrounded by armed men, in compliance with the election order, yet the Demo-

[25] *Democratic Statesman,* August 1, 1871, I, 3.

[26] *Ibid.,* August 1, 2, 3, 1871, I, 3, 4, and 5; McKay, "Texas under the Regime of E. J. Davis," p. 134, MS.

[27] Gammel, *Laws of Texas,* VI, 246–249.

[28] *Democratic Statesman,* September 5, 1871, I, 10.

[29] San Antonio *Herald,* September 10, 1871, XIV, 215.

[30] McKay, "Texas under the Regime of E. J. Davis," p. 136, MS.; San Antonio *Herald,* September 15, 1871, XIV, 220.

cratic candidates were victorious. According to the first returns, a full
Democratic delegation had been elected. These early returns showed
the following tabulations:

Democratic Vote	Republican Vote	Independent Vote
First District:		
Herndon 16,172	Whitmore 11,572	
Second District:		
Connor 18,285	Bryant 5,948	Norton (no vote reported)
Third District:		
Giddings 23,374	Clark 20,406	Stevenson 409
Fourth District:		
Hancock 17,010	Degener 12,636	

Votes of one or more counties in each district, however, were rejected by state canvassers. Consequently the result of the election was
altered, by official declarations. In the First District, the vote of Rusk
County was rejected because of alleged intimidation and fraud. Nevertheless, the result as announced by the Administration was a victory
for Herndon, who had received 14,521 votes against 10,209 for his
Republican opponent, Whitmore. In the Second District, the returns
from Bowie, Marion, and Red River counties were not acceptable to
the state canvassers, but the Democratic candidate, Connor, was declared to be elected, receiving 15,900 against 4,002 for Bryant. In the
Third District, returns from Freestone, Limestone, Bosque, and Brazos
counties were rejected, as were 2,322 Washington County ballots cast
for Giddings, the Democratic nominee. Thus the final official returns
from the Third District showed Clark, the Republican candidate, with
18,407 votes, and Giddings, who was declared to have won in the
early returns, with 17,082.[31] But Giddings contested the election, and
after persistent effort he obtained his seat in Congress in May, 1872.[32]

In the Fourth District, canvassers would not accept returns from
Bee, Brown, Concho, Fayette, and Starr counties, but regardless of this
the Democratic candidate, Hancock, won the election with 15,022
votes against Degener's 11,152.

[31] Appleton, *American Annual Cyclopaedia,* 1871, XI, 735.
[32] Ramsdell, *Reconstruction in Texas,* p. 310; *Daily State Journal,* June 13,
1872, III, 119.

The total vote in the state was 125,812, and it showed a Democratic majority of 24,279. The first step in the redemption of Texas from Radical control was successful.[33]

THE INDICTMENT AND TRIAL OF GOVERNOR DAVIS

During its winter term in Austin in 1872 the United States District Court indicted Governor Davis for issuing a fraudulent certificate of election to W. T. Clark of the Third District.[34] Then another indictment was returned against Davis, charging him and Attorney General William Alexander with being principals in the second degree for aiding and advising Secretary of State James Newcomb, principal in the first degree, to reject the whole vote of Brazos County and about half of the vote of Washington County in the contest between Clark and Giddings.[35] These offenses were in violation of the Enforcement Act.[36] The official Administration organ, *Daily State Journal,* declared that the grand jury had been bribed.

We present evidence enough to satisfy every unprejudiced person that the grand jury of the Federal Court was bribed—that it was simply a tool in the hands of disloyal tricksters to overthrow the State government, and defraud the United States Government of its legitimate revenues. We will withhold the balance in reserve until permitted by authorities to make it public. We understand that since the District Attorney has learned of the bribery of the grand jury, he has determined to apply to the court to quash all indictments found by them and ask for the impaneling of a new jury. The court in vindication of its own dignity, should at once proceed to sift the matter to the bottom and we doubt not will grant the motion of the Attorney.[37]

But in actuality the district attorney, C. T. Garland, had no intention of quashing the indictments. On the contrary, he had given an adverse opinion to the issuance of a certificate of election for W. T. Clark.

[33] Appleton, *American Annual Cyclopaedia,* 1871, XI, 736. A circular issued by the Radicals and signed by Secretary of State J. P. Newcomb, Adjutant General James Davidson, and J. C. De Gress, the state superintendent of public schools, stated that in not more than twenty-five counties was there a fair election held.

[34] *Democratic Statesman,* February 6, 1872, I, 83.

[35] *Ibid.,* June 15, 1872, I, 139.

[36] San Antonio *Herald,* February 8, 1872, XV, 34.

[37] *Daily State Journal,* February 20, 1872, III, 20.

The Radicals then censured the marshal and the judge, but to no avail.

The Waco *Register,* as quoted in the *Daily State Journal,* defended the Governor's policy in regard to the contested election as follows:

And here it is proper to allude to Governor Davis' connection with this case as the disposition to do him injustice in this, as in nearly all matters, is apparent in the so-called Democratic press.

The law makes it the privilege of county officers of election to forward to the State Board of Election officers, consisting of the Governor, Secretary of State and Attorney General, at the close of each election, any sworn testimony which they may give themselves or take from others, showing intimidation or other irregularities at the election in their respective counties. The law provides that the State Election Board aforesaid shall give the testimony forwarded to them such weight in making up the official returns as they think it entitled. At the close of the last election, considerable testimony of this sort was forwarded to the State officers of election from several counties in this Congressional district. This mass of testimony had either to be considered or ignored by the State board of return officers. They considered it and allowed it to have weight, but not full or decisive weight, for the Governor refused to give Clark a clear certificate of election. The certificate or what might as properly be called a statement, set out by declaring the Governor's doubts as to the result of the election in the third district when the testimony he had received was taken into consideration. In the certificate or statement, the Governor also explicitly declared that he ought to give the certificate and that if left to himself, he would give it to neither and would remand the question to the people for another election; but that the law compelled him to give a certificate to one or the other. The kind of certificate given by the Governor to Clark in effect left the result of the election an open question to be decided upon evidence, by Congress. Had all the testimony from the several counties been received by the Governor with no allowance and with the disposition to make the most of whatever was forwarded to him in this way, more likely a clear certificate had been given to Clark. But such, it would appear, was not the case. The governor considered all of the testimony in the spirit of giving each, part and parcel, according to character of witness and circumstances, its proper weight. To have given a certificate to Giddings would have seemed like ignoring testimony in regard to the election which the law made it his duty to receive and consider. Giving the kind of certificate he did to Clark very properly placed the whole matter before Congress for decision upon all the evidence pro and con that might be adduced before that body, by the constitution, the final judge of the election of its own members.[38]

[38] *Daily State Journal,* June 13, 1872, III, 119, quoting the Waco *Register.*

According to the *Democratic Statesman* of Austin, when news of the indictments reached the national capital, the President's official organ, the Washington *Chronicle,* declared that the object of the indictments was "to insult President Grant" and to bring his administration into disrepute. Therefore, the Democratic press in Texas asserted that Grant had determined to remove the district attorney and probably the marshal as well, because in a similar situation in Arkansas he had removed both of these officials when Governor Powell Clayton was indicted for issuing a fraudulent certificate of election to a defeated candidate for Congress. Governor Davis, Secretary Newcomb, United States Senator J. W. Flanagan, and William T. Clark all made appeals to the President to remove the district attorney, but Senator Morgan Hamilton, upon learning that Grant favored removal, called on the attorney general in Washington and warned him of the problems that might evolve from such a move, reminding him of the Arkansas incident. Hamilton declared that such action would serve as an admonition to all officers not to do their duty when men of certain political standing were prosecuted.

The warning accomplished nothing, for while Hamilton was absent from the capital, on a brief visit to Ohio, Grant appointed a new district attorney, A. J. Evans, and had him confirmed before Hamilton returned.

Evans assumed his duties at the beginning of the spring term, and time was not sufficient to make him familiar with the cases already on the dockets of the district and circuit courts. Moreover, the grand jury was already considering several hundred new cases. As could have been anticipated, the cases against the Governor, which had been remitted from the district to the circuit court, were in no condition to be tried when called.

When they were ready they offered a striking comparison to the Arkansas proceedings. In the Governor Clayton case, the demurrer to the indictment had been well argued by the best lawyers of Little Rock, but in the case against Governor Davis, former District Attorney Garland was not even asked by Evans what witnesses he had. A prominent lawyer, Charles S. West, who had agreed to assist Garland in the prosecution, withdrew from the case upon learning that Garland had been removed, assuming that Grant was determined that there should be no able prosecution.

The case in which Davis had been indicted alone was tried first.

District Attorney Evans made no attempt to prove the real charge contained in it. The principal witness for the prosecution, Attorney General Alexander, was not even introduced. Moreover, the extensive documentary evidence easily accessible was not presented. Had Alexander testified, he would undoubtedly have fastened guilt upon Davis. As it was, however, Davis was acquitted of the charge contained in the first indictment.

Initially, former District Attorney Garland expected to prove that Governor Davis had authorized the use of two ballot boxes in Washington County, and then had thrown out the votes placed in one of them for reasons that the Governor knew were false. But Evans did not introduce the evidence to bear this out. In the second trial, as in the first, Governor Davis was acquitted, and as soon as the second verdict was rendered the case against Newcomb was dismissed. Discussing the indictment and trial, the *Democratic Statesman* declared:

... The only thing gained for the cause of justice by the prosecution was the exposure of Grant's unscrupulousness in shielding his political friends from punishment for crime, and the decision of Judge Bradley that the Federal Courts do have jurisdiction over offenses committed by corrupt Governors against the purity of the ballot.[39]

THE TREASURY MUDDLE

On May 27, 1872, Governor Davis declared the office of state treasurer vacant. This was done, Davis stated, because the man who held that position, George W. Honey, had absented himself from the state without the consent of either the Legislature or the Governor and had left the control of the treasury in the hands of J. H. Burns, an unbonded officer. The Governor, feeling certain that Honey had gone for an indefinite period, asserted that he had received reliable information that both Honey and Burns had been using state funds for their own private benefit.[40] Perhaps a more important reason for Honey's removal, however, was that he and the Governor had quarreled over the issuance of the International Railroad bonds. Honey wanted to sign and issue the bonds, but Davis, although he had signed

[39] U. S. Circuit Court Minutes, Book E, pp. 530–531; *Democratic Statesman,* June 15, 1872, I, 139; San Antonio *Herald,* February 8, 1872, XV, 34; *Daily State Journal,* February 14, 1872, III, 14.

[40] *Daily State Journal,* August 12, 1872, III, 169. Testimony of Governor Davis in the Honey case.

the bonds the previous year, had now arrived at the conclusion that they were unconstitutional, and he, therefore, opposed their issuance. Comptroller A. Bledsoe had earlier refused to countersign the bonds for the same reason.[41]

The Governor filled the vacancy by appointing Dr. B. Graham of Austin, and he named a commission composed of Eugene Bremond, Clement R. Johns, James H. Raymond, Willis L. Robards, Henry W. Dodge, and J. D. Elliott to take charge of the office papers, books, and funds which were to be inventoried and turned over to Dr. Graham, after Graham had executed the required bond.[42]

The Comptroller, A. Bledsoe, ordered Burns to surrender his office and to show the exact condition of the treasury, but Burns refused. Nor would he furnish the combination of the lock to the outside safe or, in any manner, contribute to the investigation. When Davis called on him to furnish to the commission both a statement and an exhibit of the funds on hand Burns again declined to do so, declaring that he would consent only on the stipulation that he be restored to office. In the midst of this confusion the new treasurer was authorized to assume his duties, but he was instructed not to take any action until he had formally received the funds.[43] The secret of the combination locks was known only to Honey and Burns, and since Burns would not aid the commission, it was necessary to await the return of Honey, who by this time was expected back in the city.[44]

Honey telegraphed Burns from Louisville, Kentucky, on May 29, saying that he was starting that day for Austin. But when he reached the capital early in June, he too refused to allow the commission to interfere with the treasury department, declaring that the law stipulated that the treasurer and comptroller were to make quarterly settlements and that the comptroller was required to have permission to count the money. Honey said he was willing to allow this as soon as he himself was given possession of his office.

The day that Honey returned Attorney General William Alexander executed an affidavit before the mayor of Austin, charging both Honey and Burns with "misappropriation of public funds" by selling to an

---

[41] Ramsdell, *Reconstruction in Texas,* p. 311; Appleton, *American Annual Cyclopaedia,* 1872, XII, 764.

[42] *Daily State Journal,* May 30, 1872, III, 107.

[43] *Tri-Weekly State Gazette,* May 29, 1872, V, 72.

[44] *Daily State Journal,* May 31, 1872, II, 108.

Austin banker gold belonging to the available school fund. According to the report of the Comptroller, the Treasurer was then chargeable with more than $750,000, including $30,000 in gold, cash in hand, less the amount paid out on warrants during the preceding quarter.

Again Governor Davis asked Honey to open the safes and vaults in order that their contents might be inventoried, but still Honey refused. On June 20 the grand jury of Travis County and the district attorney jointly addressed District Judge J. W. Oliver, then presiding at Austin, requesting him to name a commission to visit the treasury and to open the safes and vaults, using force if necessary. This commission was then to count the funds and to ascertain the condition of the books, papers, and various records and to report their findings to the grand jury for further investigation. Judge Oliver instructed Sheriff Zimpleman to notify Davis of these proceedings and to ask the Governor for his cooperation,[45] cooperation which Davis was very willing to give. The Governor declared that Honey and Burns should be given an opportunity to surrender the combinations to protect the safes from the damage of forcing them open. Appointed as commissioners for the task were the foreman of the grand jury, A. B. Burleson, and Adjutant General Davidson, C. R. Johns, J. H. Raymond, S. M. Swisher, F. M. Moore, James P. McKinney, and Leander Brown.[46]

After Honey had been informed of this action he agreed to be present at the opening of the safes and to submit to an investigation. After a brief delay the safes were opened, and the commission conducted its inquiry. Adjutant General Davidson, Honey, Burns, and Dr. Graham were present to act as witnesses, but they were not allowed to take any part in the actual counting of money.

On June 26 the commission delivered its report, but Judge Oliver declared that it was incomplete and ordered the members to finish their work the next day by examining papers and packages that he said had not been considered.[47] The final report appeared soon afterward, and the Radical *Daily State Journal* said:

. . . The Report of the Treasury Commission, though chiefly noticeable for what it does *not* reveal only by implication, shows that the Treasurer has been loaning the funds to various parties, while at the same time refusing to

[45] F. Brown, "Annals of Travis County," Ch. III, pp. 41–45, MS.
[46] *Tri-Weekly State Gazette,* June 17, 1872, V, 80.
[47] F. Brown, "Annals of Travis County," Ch. XXX–XXXI, pp. 45–46, MS.

cash warrants when presented at the counter, on plea of no money. It shows that boasted excess of $64,000.00 claimed for the Treasury was not money but *warrants* placed there for what purpose the public can readily infer.

So far from there being any excess, there is an actual *deficit* of nearly one hundred thousand dollars. The special funds belonging of right in the Treasury aggregate about $250,000.00 while the Commission found there a total of both general and special funds amounting to $153,000.00. The difference is believed to have been used for outside speculation.

So notorious is this fact that Mr. Honey's defenders no longer allege his innocence, but admit that he had speculated and claim as his defense, as did the *Galveston News* recently, "that all Treasurers do so." It is sufficient to say in reply to this sophistry that, if all do it, the more necessity exists for making an example when one is caught in the act. . . .[48]

A year later a joint committee was appointed by the Thirteenth Legislature to investigate the treasury and to report on whether there had been any deficiency at the time Honey vacated his office and, if so, the amount. They reported that there had been indeed a deficit, but the amount was difficult to determine. After crediting Honey with all amounts claimed by him, including $153,381.37 in warrants not entered on the cash book or canceled as required by law (which might not have been paid so far as any evidence in office showed), there was still a shortage of $55,734.39 in currency and $5,700.00 in specie standing against him. To offset these amounts, the joint committee reported, Honey claimed a credit of $28,896.13 in currency for amounts of sight drafts drawn by Bremond and Company of Austin on B. A. Botts, President of the City Bank of Houston. Honey claimed that they were held by him as cash at the time of the seizure of his office, and that he also then possessed twenty-five frontier defense bonds of $1,000 each, valued at $22,500, and four United States five-per-cent bonds with coupons, equal to $2,502.50. But these transactions were extremely irregular. The report noted that there would seem to be no limit to the action of the treasurer if drafts of a private party were allowed to lie in the drawer of the treasury while the money these drafts represented was in the hands of other parties, possibly at interest for the treasurer's benefit.[49]

During the session of the Thirteenth Legislature the House of Representatives found that treasury funds during Honey's tenure had been

[48] *Daily State Journal,* July 2, 1872, III, 135.
[49] *Senate Journal, 13th Legislature,* pp. 1104–1105.

used for a time to abet private ends and that its books had fallen into "reckless disorder."[50]

In February, 1873, Honey was tried in district court on the charge of misappropriation of public funds, but the jury acquitted him. Other cases against him waited on the criminal docket, but all were dismissed.[51]

Several months earlier, in the latter part of 1872, Honey had entered suit against Graham, the Davis-appointed state treasurer, to recover his lost position. The case, appealed from the district court, went before the State Supreme Court where it was held pending for more than a year, as the justices were for a long period unable to reach an agreement on it.[52] Finally, in October, 1873, the court decided in favor of Honey, reinstating him at once.

The court declared that the issue was whether there was a vacancy in contemplation of law or not, and that there was not. Justice M. B. Walker, who delivered the majority opinion, stated that it was conceded the governor had authority to fill the office of state treasurer when it became vacant, but it could not be admitted that the governor could create a vacancy by the removal of an officer who held his office by constitutional tenure. Justice Walker added that it was clearly stated in the state Constitution that impeachment or indictment and conviction should be the means for expulsion, and that until a judgment of expulsion was rendered the officer concerned was still the incumbent. He emphasized that the court had not been asked to decide whether the Governor's action in removing Honey had served the public interest.[53]

After this decision the Attorney General on October 24, 1873, ordered that Honey be reinstated.[54] As state treasurer he had only a little more than two months left to serve; his term was to expire with the Radical administration in January, 1874.[55]

[50] *House Journal, 13th Legislature*, p. 27.
[51] F. Brown, "Annals of Travis County," Ch. XXX, p. 51, MS.
[52] *Weekly Democratic Statesman*, October 30, 1873, III, 14.
[53] *Honey* v. *Graham, Texas Supreme Court Reports*, XXXI, 18–19.
[54] F. Brown, "Annals of Travis County," Ch. XXX–XXXI, pp. 51–53, MS.
[55] *Weekly Democratic Statesman*, III, 14, October 30, 1873. Democratic reaction to the final decision of the *Honey* v. *Burns* suit may perhaps be judged by the following account:
. . . We have often before, during the heated interest in this case, expressed our opinions upon it. The removal of Mr. Honey was one of those high-handed measures

THE ELECTION OF 1872

Preparing for the fall general election, the Radical Republicans assembled at Houston in May of 1872 for their state convention. They denounced the nomination by Liberal Republicans of Horace Greeley for President of the United States, declaring that the choice was made in the interests of the Democratic party. They endorsed Grant's administration as being "just and honest" and instructed their delegates to vote for his renomination at the national Republican convention at Philadelphia in June. The state convention declared its confidence in the "personal integrity and incorruptibility of E. J. Davis," and it promised to provide free education, to protect the frontier, to encourage internal improvements without increasing taxes, to eliminate every superfluous expense of state government, and to reduce taxation. Besides naming presidential electors and delegates to the national convention, the convention nominated L. D. Evans and A. B. Norton for Congress from the state at large. Andrew J. Evans became the party nominee for Congress from the third district; W. O. Hutchison was the fourth-district choice. Democratic candidates in the other two districts evidently were unopposed.[56]

Democrats held their state convention at Corsicana in June with John H. Reagan presiding as chairman. Ashbel Smith again served as chairman of the platform committee, as he had the previous year.[57] The Democratic platform condemned the administration of President Grant and expressed satisfaction with the Liberal Republican party, but it vowed allegiance to the Democratic party, whose national plat-

---

where law, as has been his custom, was placed at defiance by Governor Davis. The constitution provided for the removal of State officers by impeachment, before a high court of the State, and by no other means: yet Governor Davis, claiming that Honey's office was vacated in consequence of his absence from the State—a charge which up to this time could have been brought against almost every other State officer—declared to this effect, and by force seized upon the office, drove out Mr. Honey's clerks and placed Dr. Graham in possession of the office. There was never a greater outrage committed upon the civil rights of any community than this extraordinary assumption of the infamous measures adopted by the lawless band of radical politicians who have controlled unfortunate Louisiana since the war. It was a continuation of that despotic rule, which incarcerated the Democratic Senators of the Twelfth Legislature to secure the passage of the infamous and tyrannical police and enabling acts, the taking away of *habeas corpus* from the inhabitants of Limestone and Walker counties and other repeated wrongs against the citizens of Texas.

56 *Daily State Journal,* May 31, 1872, II, 108.
57 *Ibid.,* October 3, 1872, III, 217.

form was soon to be drawn up at the Baltimore convention. The state Democratic convention, however, declared that regardless of who became the party nominee for President there was no reason for modifying the present plan of "putting down and removing the abuses under which our people labor" as a result of the "dishonest and unscrupulous state government of Texas."

The Democratic platform also stated its opposition to all moneyed subsidies to private corporations by the state; asserted that it was the duty of the government to provide protection for the frontier; condemned the Davis Administration for having plundered the school fund by speculation, but declared it was the duty of the state to establish common schools so that every child might enjoy the benefits of education.[58]

The convention nominated A. H. Willie of Galveston and Roger Q. Mills of Navarro County for congressmen at large.[59] The ticket also included the names of the Democratic congressmen victorious in the special election of 1871; they were reannouncing their candidacy.[60]

Governor Davis, as mentioned, had been elected to serve a term of four years. He took the oath of office and began serving as provisional governor on January 17, 1870, and was formally inaugurated on April 28, 1870, shortly after Congress recognized the state government. Davis claimed that his term of office began with his formal inauguration, but the Democrats contended that his administration commenced with his oath as provisional governor on January 17, 1870.

The Democratic side of the argument was presented by John D. Elliott of Austin, editor of the *State Gazette.* In answer to him Governor Davis wrote:

It is my understanding of the tenure of office of the Legislature to be elected in November next, that it expires on the 2nd day of December of the year 1873, being two years from the 2nd day of December, on which last mentioned day according to the opinion of the Attorney General, and, I believe, of most lawyers of the state, the Legislature, elected in the Fall of 1869, expired. It will then, be the duty of the Legislature to be elected on the 5th day of November, to provide for the election of their successors in

[58] Houston *Daily Telegraph,* June 22, 1872, XXXIII, 190. Platform of the Democratic party.
[59] *Tri-Weekly Statesman,* October 29, 1872, II, 42; Appleton, *American Annual Cyclopaedia,* 1872, XII, 766.
[60] *Tri-Weekly Statesman,* October 29, 1872, II, 42.

November, 1873, and at the same time of Governor, Lieutenant-Governor, Comptroller, Treasurer, Commissioner of General Land Office, etc.; also of the Sheriffs, District Clerks, Justice of the Peace, and other county officers.

. . . If the Governor, Lieutenant-Governor and other State officers are to be elected, then all county officers who were elected at the same time and for the same term of office, should also be elected. Now the Governor was installed on Thursday, the 28th day of April, 1870, and his term of office will expire on that day in 1874, a year and a half after the proposed election. You will perceive (Constitution, Art. 4, Sec. 4) that he holds his office for four years "from the time of his installment."[61]

Earlier in September Governor Davis issued a proclamation calling for the general election, which would begin on November 5 and continue for four days. In addition to deciding officeholders the election was to determine the permanent location of the capital.[62] Davis circularized his order for conducting the election, and it was similar to the one issued the year before. An exception was that the State Guard, Militia, and peace officers on duty were this time to be assisted by special policemen, whose numbers were not to exceed twenty.[63]

As the election neared many Democrats expressed dissatisfaction with a decision of the national party, which had promised to support the Liberal Republican candidates, Horace Greeley and B. Gratz Brown. To publicize their stand Texas Democrats met in Austin October 17 and 18 and proclaimed their displeasure in resolutions. They instructed their chairman to appoint a committee of six to prepare and publish an address to the registered Democrats of Texas explaining objectives of the meeting. This committee was also to arrange meetings with Democratic electors to urge them to vote for Charles O'Conor and John Quincy Adams II, who had been nominated by "straight-out" Democrats at Louisville, in the event the Texas vote would not change the result of the election.

This conference had no effect on the outcome of the election, but previous Democratic party work exerted a tremendous amount of influence, for Democrats won a majority of the state offices and all con-

[61] *Tri-Weekly State Gazette,* May 27, 1872, V, 71. This newspaper printed Elliott's letter to Davis, dated May 22, 1872, and Davis' reply, dated May 24, 1872.

[62] Appleton, *American Annual Cyclopaedia,* 1872, XII, 767.

[63] *Daily State Journal,* September 27, 1872, III, 211, copy of the circular of Governor Davis.

gressional seats. As in the last election, however, not all of the ballots were acceptable to the administration. Votes from El Paso and Presidio counties were thrown out "on account of mob violence, intimidation, and undue influence being practiced during the election." Votes cast in Wilson County were not accepted because the election was not held at the county seat; those from Coleman, McMullen, Menard, and Pecos counties were not counted because they did not possess sufficient numbers of registered voters to entitle them to organization. Webb County also lost its vote "because 200 aliens were allowed to vote on declaration-of-intention papers taken out before the clerk of the district court in vacation." Still, the Democrats could celebrate a decisive victory, and they helped give Horace Greeley a state lead of 19,029 over President Grant.[64]

Austin was selected as the permanent location of the capital, and an amendment to the state Constitution was ratified prohibiting future granting of land except for internal improvement and prohibiting the sale of land certificates except to settlers on that same land, in lots not exceeding 160 acres. This same amendment stipulated that the Legislature should not grant out of the public domain, even for construction of internal improvements, more than twenty sections of land for each completed work. But a qualification stated that nothing in the amendment was to affect any rights secured by laws passed before its adoption.

[64] Appleton, *American Annual Cyclopaedia*, 1872, XII, 766–767; Ellis Paxson Oberholtzer, *A History of the United States Since the Civil War*, III, 51–52.

THE DECLINING DAYS OF RADICALISM

THE WORK OF THE THIRTEENTH LEGISLATURE

THE THIRTEENTH LEGISLATURE assembled in Austin on January 14, 1873, and continued in session for five and a half months, adjourning on June 24.[1] In the House, where there was now a Democratic majority, much opposition to Administration policies was voiced. In the Senate, half of the membership had been held over, but here too a majority—of three—opposed the Radical leadership.[2]

As early as January, 1871,[3] there had been talk of impeaching Governor Davis. Now, after the election of the new Legislature, this possibility was more widely discussed. Certain Democratic newspapers, however, believing that such a step would be a serious mistake, asked that no attempt be made and declared that Texans desired "peace, retrenchment, reduction of taxes, repeal of obnoxious and oppressive laws, and development of the material resources of the state."[4] Perhaps the fear of federal interference precluded any active steps toward impeachment of the Governor. Then, too, the conciliatory message with which Davis greeted the new Legislature may have had a soothing effect, for in it he showed a desire to cooperate with that body in the enactment of beneficial legislation.[5]

[1] Frank Brown, "Annals of Travis County and the City of Austin," Ch. XXXII, p. 7, MS.
[2] Seth S. McKay, "Texas under the Regime of E. J. Davis," p. 140, MS.; Houston *Telegraph,* January 12, 1873, XXXIV, 55.
[3] *Flake's Daily Bulletin,* January 31, 1871, VI, 1705.
[4] Houston *Telegraph,* January 12, 1873; McKay, "Texas under the Regime of E. J. Davis," p. 141, MS.
[5] *Daily State Gazette,* January 18, 1873, VI, 19, declared of Governor Davis' message at the opening of the Thirteenth Legislature:

PLATE 7. The State Capitol at Austin at the time of the Coke-Davis Imbroglio. Ellison Photo Company.

PLATE 8. The Texas Senate in session in the State Capitol, taken from *Frank Leslie's Illustrated Newspaper*. From the Walter E. Long Collection.

In that message Davis allowed the subject of state finances to assume a prominent position. He complained of the delinquencies existing in the assessment and collection of taxes and expressed the opinion that if these delinquencies could be removed through some remedial action by the Legislature a tax of 1 per cent or less would care for all state government expenses. Davis also outlined the disposition made of the state bonds,[6] and of this particular statement the *State Gazette,* ordinarily unsympathetic with the Administration, declared:

The system of Radical legislation, placing in the hands of the Executive the bonds of the State, independent of the checks contemplated by the constitution, was altogether at fault, and it is astounding that it should become necessary for the Chief Magistrate to render a financial exhibition of his department of the government. But it is believed he sought to maintain the public credit. It is certainly apparent that he has not been made a party to any species of peculation in public securities, and has sought to realize their highest value without extortionary diminution.[7]

Davis commended the work of the State Police and observed that the State Militia act was a necessary one, but he declared his willingness to modify both the school law and the election law. Concerning the election law, he recommended that it be amended to allow polls to be opened in justice precincts rather than county seats and that the number of election days be reduced from four to one. He maintained that his term of office should expire on April 28, 1874; therefore, the election law should be changed, he said, so as to authorize a general election of state officers at some date before then. With this statement he virtually admitted the unconstitutionality of the then-existing election law—the passage of which he had advocated—that provided members of the Twelfth Legislature House of Representatives be allowed to serve for three years instead of the two that the state Constitution permitted.[8]

The message of Governor Davis, published by us on yesterday, will be read with as much interest as sincere satisfaction everywhere in our State. It is an earnest effort on the part of the Executive to co-operate with the Legislature in the enactment of wise and salutary laws; and certainly this is all the country can require of the Chief Magistrate of the State. Our political antipathies do not go to the extent of refusing a recognition of honest purpose in the Chief Magistrate to do right, and we are at all times prepared to assume full measure of responsibility of dealing justly and fairly by our political opponents.

[6] *House Journal, 13th Legislature,* pp. 17–25.

[7] *Daily State Gazette,* January 18, 1873, VI, 19.

[8] *House Journal, 13th Legislature,* p. 41.

The work of the new Legislature was begun in earnest at once. The two houses immediately passed a new printing act repealing the objectionable features of the existing measure, and by thus putting an end to official patronage virtually put out of existence the official Radical organ and all other partially state-supported partisan newspapers.[9] The next law to be removed from the statute books was the State Police act, long hated by the Democrats.[10] The Militia act was greatly altered by repealing that portion of the law that provided for the organization of the State Guards and by depriving the governor of the power to declare martial law.[11]

Removal of arbitrary provisions in other measures followed. Certain appointive powers of the Governor as stipulated in the "enabling" act were eliminated, and these offices were now filled by election as the Constitution had provided.[12] The character of the election act was also changed, providing for precinct election, and the voting only at county seats was thus eliminated. Moreover, it was provided that the election should be held on one day instead of four. Election managers were to count ballots in the presence of two reputable registered voters, who were to be of different political parties,[13] if such representatives could be found.

Two school acts deserving attention were passed during the session of the Thirteenth Legislature. The first of these measures to become law provided that one-half of the public domain was to be set apart for the support and maintenance of public schools.[14] The other drastically changed the Radical school laws, taking away from the state superintendent his extensive powers over teachers, officers, and funds and making his office elective. The arbitrary state board of education ceased to exist; in its place appeared an elective administrative board of five school directors for each county. This board was to name an ex officio county superintendent of public instruction from among its own members. The work of school organization was to a great extent left

[9] H. P. N. Gammel, *Laws of Texas,* VII, 456–461.

[10] *Ibid.,* VII, 493.

[11] *Ibid.,* VII, 468–470. By the new measure, no longer could the county or counties where martial law might be declared, be assessed the cost of its maintenance at the discretion of the governor.

[12] *Ibid.,* VII, 482.

[13] *Ibid.*

[14] *Ibid.,* VII, 467–468.

to the state superintendent, but his policies were made subject to the will of the people.[15]

On April 24 an act was passed reapportioning the state into new senatorial and representative districts and providing for a general election of all state officers and members of the Legislature to take place on the first Tuesday in December, 1873.[16]

The *Democratic Statesman* praised the Thirteenth Legislature and declared that it deserved the commendation of the people. The editor thought that the lawmaking body had made but one mistake: it had not settled the matter of the bonds with the International Railroad, instead it left the issue dangling. He also declared that the Legislature had unwisely supported Comptroller Bledsoe in his refusal to sign these bonds.[17] (As mentioned, Bledsoe believed that the law providing a tax to obtain subsidies for the International Railroad was illegal. In 1872 pressure was exerted on the Comptroller, and he asked Attorney General William Alexander for an opinion. In his decision he sustained Bledsoe.[18])

THE ELECTION OF 1873

In the spring of 1873 the Thirteenth Legislature had provided, of course, that a general election for all elective state and county officials be held—on the first Tuesday in December, 1873. First to begin planning a campaign were the Republicans, who assembled in their state convention in Dallas on April 20[19] with General Mallory as chairman. The ticket included these men: for governor, Edmund J. Davis; lieutenant governor, R. H. Taylor; state comptroller, J. E. Thomas; state treasurer, A. T. Monroe; land commissioner, Jacob Kuechler; and superintendent of public instruction, A. B. Norton.[20] The platform affirmed support of the national Republican Administration, expressed disapproval of the work of the Thirteenth Legisla-

[15] *Ibid.*, VII, 536–546. The county superintendent of public instruction was also to serve as president of the board of five county school directors, each of whom represented a precinct.

[16] *House Journal, 13th Legislature,* p. 915.

[17] *Democratic Statesman,* June 4, 1873, II, 195.

[18] Brown, "Annals of Travis County," Ch. XXX, p. 27, MS.

[19] C. Appleton (ed.), *American Annual Cyclopaedia,* 1873, XIII, 737.

[20] *Ibid.*, p. 738.

ture, declared opposition to any race discriminatory laws, and asserted a stand favoring railway construction and immigration.[21]

The Democrats, strongly hopeful of another victory, assembled in Austin on September 5. Among those present at the well-attended convention were ex-Governor Throckmorton, Congressman George W. Clark,[22] and the platform chairman, John H. Reagan, former postmaster general of the Confederacy.[23] Some of the younger members, who had just entered politics but would later be party leaders, were Joseph D. Sayers, George C. Pendleton, and Seth Shepard.[24]

Richard Coke was nominated for governor on the fifth ballot, and R. B. Hubbard was unanimously chosen for lieutenant governor. The party then selected the following candidates for the remaining offices: Stephen H. Darden, state comptroller; A. H. Dorn, state treasurer; J. J. Groos, commissioner of the general land office; and O. M. Hollingsworth, superintendent of public instruction.

The platform congratulated the Thirteenth Legislature for repealing the Militia law, the State Police act, the enabling law, the Radical registration and election laws, and the school law passed by the Twelfth Legislature and commended it for having replaced these objectionable measures by just enactments. The platform favored frontier protection, railroad construction increased by land grants rather than by money subsidies, and a new constitutional convention. A resolution was passed criticizing Democratic members of Congress who cooperated with the Republican majority in the passage of the "back salary bill." Another declaration expressed support of the Ohio State Democratic Convention, which had condemned as unconstitutional Grant's action in Louisiana setting up by force a government with no legal title to rule.[25]

Both Democrats and Republicans conducted vigorous campaigns. Radicals and freedmen declared that the Democrats were planning to re-enslave the Negro. Davis delivered frequent speeches in densely populated East Texas before often-disorderly crowds of whites and Negroes. Democrats worked hard to overthrow the Radical administration, and Richard Coke, the gubernatorial nominee, conducted a hard-hitting campaign.

[21] E. W. Winkler, *Platforms of Political Parties in Texas,* pp. 154–157.
[22] McKay, "Texas under the Regime of E. J. Davis," p. 156, MS.
[23] Dudley G. Wooten, *A Comprehensive History of Texas,* II, 364, 402.
[24] McKay, "Texas under the Regime of E. J. Davis," p. 156, MS.
[25] *Weekly Democratic Statesman,* September 11, 1873, III, 7.

In the election, held on December 2, there was undoubtedly fraud and intimidation on both sides. Loyal League members threatened Negro Democrats, and some ardent Democrats also intimidated Negro Republicans. Under-age whites on both sides were known to have voted.[26]

The election resulted in an overwhelming victory for the Democrats. Coke received 85,549 votes, Davis only 42,663. For lieutenant governor, Hubbard received 86,825 votes, Taylor 42,812. Democrats were elected to fill all of the state and most of the county offices and won a majority in the state Legislature.[27]

THE SEMICOLON CASE

Radical leaders were not willing to accept defeat quietly, and they suddenly developed doubts about the constitutionality of the election law. This was paradoxical, since Governor Davis himself had recommended its passage and had signed the bill.[28] However, a case was prepared by the Republicans for the purpose of obtaining a decision from the State Supreme Court. They had already arranged for a Houston man, Joseph Rodriguez, to vote twice and to be arrested for so doing. The case was taken to the State Supreme Court on an application for a writ of habeas corpus.[29]

In view of the assumptions of the Radical party, it is necessary to examine the section of the state Constitution and the pertinent clause of the election law to see if their argument was soundly based. Section six, article three of the state Constitution read,

All elections for State, District, and County officers shall be held at the county seats of the several counties, until otherwise provided by law; and the polls shall be opened for four days, from 8 o'clock, A.M. until 4 o'clock P.M. of each day.[30]

[26] Charles W. Ramsdell, *Reconstruction in Texas,* p. 315; McKay, "Texas under the Regime of E. J. Davis," p. 158, MS.

[27] Appleton, *American Annual Cyclopaedia,* 1873, XIII, 739.

[28] *House Journal, 13th Legislature,* p. 41.

[29] *Daily Democratic Statesman,* December 27, 1873, III, 128. Appleton, *American Annual Cyclopaedia,* 1873, XIII, 739; *Texas Supreme Court Reports,* XXXIX, 708–709.

[30] Gammel, *Laws of Texas,* VII, 395–427; *Daily Democratic Statesman,* January 6, 1874, III, 135; *Texas Supreme Court, Reports,* XXXIX, 706–707.

Section one of the recent election law provided that each precinct should constitute an election district and that the county courts could divide their justice precincts into as many election units as they might deem expedient. Section twelve provided that all state elections should be held for one day only and that the polls should be open on that day from eight o'clock in the morning to six o'clock in the afternoon.[31]

The point raised by Radicals was that section twelve was unconstitutional. They admitted that all of the first clause of the original section—to the semicolon after the word "law"—was legally abrogated by the new election law. The Radicals insisted, however, that the second clause, because of the semicolon preceding it, was distinct from the first and not subject to change by the Legislature. They contended then that the election was illegal because it had not been held for four days.

The Democrats were apprehensive over the possible outcome of the pending *Ex-parte Rodriguez* case but were determined not to lose the victory. Their reaction was indicated by the following editorial in the San Antonio *Daily Herald:*

If the Supreme Court chooses to make itself a party to this conspiracy, let the Supreme Court abide the fate which awaits its co-conspirators . . . The whole people of Texas have endorsed the election law by the same act which makes Constitutions, and the Constitution itself cannot stand in the way of the whole body of the people, thus expressed in regular form and so emphatic a manner. The people have the right to alter, reform, or abolish that Constitution in such manner as to them may seem fit, and by the individual act of every citizen and in the manner prescribed by law, they have done so. Let Richard Coke be installed and let the Legislature just elected meet. If the usurper and his backers can put Coke out, over the power of the State, let them do it. If Texas is a State, and if her citizens are men, Coke will be inaugurated and the Fourteenth Legislature will sit.[32]

On January 5, 1874, the State Supreme Court announced its decision, declaring the election unconstitutional, since section twelve of the election act of March 31, 1873, was in violation of section six of article three of the state constitution.[33]

[31] *Daily Democratic Statesman,* January 6, 1874, III, 135; Gammel, *Laws of Texas,* VII, 472–482; *Texas Supreme Court Reports,* XXXIX, 706–707.

[32] San Antonio *Daily Herald,* January 2, 1874, XVI,132.

[33] *Ex parte Rodriguez, Texas Supreme Court Reports,* XXXIX, 706; Appleton, *American Annual Cyclopaedia,* 1873, XIII, 739.

The attitude of the Democrats to the decision of the *Ex-parte Rodriguez* case may be judged by the following account taken from their leading party newspaper:

After going through the farce of a protracted investigation of a fictitious case, gotten up for the purpose, the Radical Supreme Court of this State, on Monday, usurped the province of declaring the election law and the late election under it illegal, null and void. We do not feel disposed to multiply words about it, and we could hardly express our feelings fully if we attempted it. It is now evident that the whole matter, from the beginning, was a conspiracy to defraud the people of Texas of the right of self government, and continue the radical rule over them indefinitely, with all its attendant curses. By this act, the judges of the Supreme Court of this State have covered themselves with infamy as with a garment. While we earnestly implore our fellow citizens to receive this blow calmly, and commit no act of violence, which is the very thing desired by our enemies, let them show by their conduct the opinion which all honest men are bound to entertain of judges who will prejudge and lend a hand to destroy the liberties of an unoffending people.[34]

Supreme court members who heard this case were Wesley Ogden, presiding judge, and Moses B. Walker and J. D. McAdoo, associate justices.[35] Had the decision been enforced, it would have led to endless confusion, for by it all state, county, and precinct officers chosen in 1873 were illegally elected. But it was disregarded throughout the state; the elected officials qualified and began discharging their duties as officers as if no decision had been rendered.[36]

THE COKE-DAVIS IMBROGLIO

As a result of the *Ex-parte Rodriguez* decision Governor Davis was determined to prevent the newly elected officials from assuming their respective duties. He therefore issued a proclamation on January 12 citing the findings of the court and declaring:

Whereas, great public injury and further complications of public affairs are likely to result from any attempt on the part of those claiming to have been chosen as members of the legislature and other officers at said elec-

[34] *Daily Democratic Statesman,* January 6, 1874, III, 135.

[35] J. H. Davenport, *The History of the Supreme Court of the State of Texas,* pp. 95–97.

[36] Brown, "Annals of Travis County," Ch. XXXII, p. 6, MS.; *Daily Democratic Statesman,* January 13, 1874, III, 141.

tion, to assume the positions they claim; therefore, for these and other reasons which it is not necessary to incorporate herein, it is deemed advisable, and it is so ordered, that those who have been chosen as legislators and other officers shall not attempt to assume the position they claim unless by further action of adequate authority, such elections may hereafter be validated.[37]

When the proclamation was issued the newly-elected members of the Fourteenth Legislature were assembling in Austin, as the session was to begin the next day. They ignored the Governor's order.[38] Davis, fearing that despite his proclamation the Legislature would meet and that Coke would be inaugurated, called on President Grant for help.[39]

In Washington, Texas representatives of both the Radical Republicans and the Democrats held consultations with the President. The Democratic congressmen, Hancock and Giddings, visited Grant first, presented copies of the state Constitution and the election law, and explained in detail the history of the trouble. The President listened with interest and replied that the proper time to declare the election law unconstitutional had been before the election. He assured the Texans that if Davis should call for aid to prevent the inauguration he would not grant it.

On the morning of January 12 Senator Flanagan visited Grant and urged him to support Governor Davis, but the President told him with obvious irritation that since the Governor himself had signed the election law, had been a candidate under it, and had been decisively defeated, the time had come for him to get out of the way. Grant added that he did not wish to see the Louisiana muddle duplicated in Texas. The President had political reasons for not interfering: he hoped for a Republican victory in the congressional elections of 1874 and did not want to risk weakening his position.

Flanagan immediately telegraphed advice to friends in Austin to withdraw all opposition both to the meeting of the Legislature and to the inauguration of the new governor.[40] On the same day Grant sent

[37] *Daily Democratic Statesman,* January 13, 1874, III, 41; Appleton, *American Annual Cyclopaedia,* 1873, XIII, 739.

[38] *Daily Democratic Statesman,* January 13, 1874, III, 141.

[39] Appleton, *American Annual Cyclopaedia,* 1873, XIII, 740.

[40] George W. Paschal, *A Digest of the Laws of Texas,* II, 1893; Brown, "Annals of Travis County," Ch. XXXII–XXXIV, pp. 7–8, MS.

Davis a dispatch in which he repeated most of what he had told Flanagan. He declared:

Your dispatches and letters reciting the action of the supreme court of Texas, in declaring the late election unconstitutional, and asking the use of the troops to prevent apprehended violence, are received. The call is not made in accordance with the Constitution of the United States and the acts of Congress under it, and cannot, therefore, be granted. The acts of the legislature of Texas providing for the recent election having received your approval, and both political parties having made nominations, and having conducted a political campaign under its provisions, would it not be prudent, as well as right, to yield to the verdict of the people as expressed by their ballots?[41]

The newly elected Democratic senators, representatives, and state officers held an informal meeting at the Austin City Hall on January 12. The public was not admitted. John Ireland was elected president and T. J. Bell secretary of this party gathering.

The Democrats in their meeting decided to proceed with the organization of the Fourteenth Legislature on the next day, providing the two houses of the old legislature approved at a meeting that night. Radical members of the Thirteenth Legislature declared that they would assemble the next day and send for absentees. Such action did not presage cooperative action.

Both Richard Coke and R. B. Hubbard were in the city, and each consulted party members on January 12. At that time they determined to avoid any illegal action if they were opposed by force, as they expected to be. They also anticipated that Governor Davis would rely on help from Grant should fighting flare up; at that time they were unaware of the President's refusal. Travis County Sheriff George B. Zimpleman, General Henry E. McCulloch, Colonel John S. Ford, and General William P. Hardeman were present at the consultations and were to be available the following day, for quieting the angry crowd that was expected. Fear was expressed that Governor Davis' friends would seize the capitol before morning and prevent the newly elected legislators from occupying the chambers. To thwart such a move the legislators determined to take possession at once.

[41] *Daily Democratic Statesman,* January 18, 1874, III, 146; Appleton, *American Annual Cyclopaedia,* 1873, XIII, 740; Brown, "Annals of Travis County," Ch. XXXII, pp. 8–9. MS.; Paschal's *Digest of the Laws of Texas,* II, 1893.

In the evening of that same day an Austin man, William A. Pitts, en route to a Democratic meeting, found that the lower floor of the capitol was already filled with armed men. Arriving at the meeting, he explained these facts to the assemblage and said he would try to get the key to the two second-story legislative chambers from the custodian, a Mr. Nelson, and to keep possession by barring the doors.

With the aid of H. C. Surghnor, Pitts accomplished this task and held the halls until the Fourteenth Legislature took possession the next day. But before the new members appeared these two men had to withstand an attempt by armed opponents to force an entrance.

On January 13 the Fourteenth Legislature organized without opposition, and a committee informed Governor Davis of this fact. Davis replied that he would not recognize the new body and gave in writing the following reasons:

In reply to your verbal communication made to me to-day, I have to state that I do not think it advisable, or for the public good, that I should disregard the decision of the Supreme Court made recently, touching upon the late election, by officially recognizing the gentlemen you represent as being the constitutionally elected Fourteenth Legislature.

It seems to me that there is some better solution of this present difficulty than that the Governor and those claiming to be the elected Legislature should jointly combine to override the judiciary and disregard their construction of the constitution. I must believe that such course will leave the door open for dangerous uncertainty in the future, both in the matter of authority to enact the legislation that may be proposed by the gentlemen you represent, and the matter of the constitutional existence of the highest tribunal of our State. There may be found two Supreme Courts, and even two legislatures claiming authority. It is even now claimed by some that the Thirteenth Legislature is at present the only legally existing Legislature, and that it only can constitutionally convene and provide for this emergency. It will then be only, after all, a settlement brought about by a species of revolution or violence as against the court making the decision.

. . . I will be happy to join you and the gentlemen you represent in applying the promptest and most feasible remedy in this difficulty. It has been repeatedly held that the recognition of Congress and the Executive of the United States will settle the question of what body of men constitute the Legislature, and which is the proper State government. This may afford a solution to be accepted by all.

I am more free to act with independence in securing, with you or those gentlemen, that sort of solution, because I feel myself entirely disinterested herein. I accept the election, whether constitutional or not, as conclusive against myself, and will in no event continue to exercise the functions of the office I hold beyond my constitutional term of four years.[42]

At the same time that the Fourteenth Legislature assembled in session upstairs the Thirteenth Legislature met in the basement of the capitol. Neither one had a quorum.[43]

On Thursday, January 15, a committee of the Fourteenth Legislature informed Governor Davis that the House of Representatives had passed a resolution declaring that since the Secretary of State had refused to deliver to the Speaker of the House the election returns for the offices of governor, and lieutenant governor, and for the constitutional amendments, the Speaker had appointed a committee of seven to determine the results of the election by any means the committee might deem best. Davis was then requested to direct the Secretary of State to deliver the election returns to either the Speaker or the committee.

The Governor replied that although the Legislature was not entitled to the election returns, the committeemen might go to the Secretary of State's office and take them, and no resistance would be offered. The returns were obtained this way.[44]

That same day, during a short recess of the Fourteenth Legislature, a parade of armed men—white and Negro Radicals—took place in the basement of the capitol. The Democrats believed the purpose was to provoke violence while Davis was still governor, thereby preventing the installation of Coke. After the recess the Fourteenth Legislature returned to counting the votes while Davis' Adjutant General, F. L. Britton, and a squad of men patrolled the basement, as the Davis supporters had done since the night William Pitts discovered them. Throughout the rest of that day and the following night the force remained there, and it was supplemented by Negroes arriving from the country. If they did not come armed the Adjutant General supplied them with weapons from the state arsenal.

When Coke and Hubbard were inaugurated Thursday night Austin

[42] Appleton, *American Annual Cyclopaedia,* 1873, XIII, 740; *Daily Democratic Statesman,* January 15, 1874, III, 14.

[43] Appleton, *American Annual Cyclopaedia,* 1873, XIII, 740.

[44] Brown, "Annals of Travis County," Ch. XXXII–XXXIV, pp. 22–28, MS.; Appleton, *American Annual Cyclopaedia,* 1873, XIII, 740–741; Paschal's *Digest of the Laws of Texas,* II, 1893.

was blanketed with snow, but the two men were warmly received by the Legislature and an enthusiastic crowd.[45] Immediately after the inauguration Governor Coke, directing his attention to Britton's armed crowd, named Henry E. McCulloch adjutant general, thus to assume authority over the area that included the capitol and nearby public buildings.[46]

Also on Thursday night Britton had ordered Captain M. D. Mather of the Travis Rifles to report to the capitol immediately with his company fully armed. Mather relayed the order to Lieutenant A. S. Roberts, who called his men. Roberts marched his company to the capitol, but they were met by Sheriff Zimpleman, who used his authority to summon a posse to assume control of them. Zimpleman delivered them to Coke, and the Governor placed them under the command of General McCulloch, who in turn put them under the authority of the two legislative charmbers.[47] The Marshal and city police were then free to aid in preserving order by preventing traffic between the two floors.

Democrats were especially anxious to maintain peace, for they had heard that Major Russell, from the staff of General Augur, commander of the Department of Texas, had arrived in Austin to observe the situation. Major Russell declared that President Grant had ordered General Augur to take charge of the state government and to appoint a military governor if fighting occurred. With this forbidding development in mind Judge J. P. Richardson of the 27th Judicial District, a Coke advocate, had arranged a meeting with two other men—Democratic Adjutant General McCulloch and Colonel J. C. De Gress, a Radical leader—and suggested that a truce be agreed upon to continue throughout the night. A truce was arranged and continued until the following morning.

[45] John Ireland to General H. E. McCulloch, April 16, 1892. Volume of Miscellaneous Correspondence, MS.

[46] Guy M. Bryan to General W. P. Hardeman, March 2, 1891. Volume of Miscellaneous Correspondence, MS.

[47] Brown, "Annals of Travis County," Chapter XXXII, p. 37, MS. The Travis Rifles marched up the stairs to the hall, where they stacked arms and posted sentinels. Their purpose of course was to guard the legislative halls, but they spent the night in the Senate chamber. Lieutenant Roberts, their commander, stayed in the ante chamber of the Senate with General Henry E. McCulloch and Colonel John S. Ford until morning.

A. S. Roberts to General Henry E. McCulloch, April 22, 1892, Volume of Miscellaneous Correspondence, MS.

That was the evening Coke was inaugurated, and the danger of battle had seemed imminent. T. B. Wheeler, Mayor of Austin, gave a detailed account of two different incidents occurring on the night of January 15, which came very near causing bloodshed.

During the day the Coke followers had been permitted to go down the inside steps which led to the north of the building. After dark, the mayor and a friend of his, Joe Denton, who resided north of the Capitol, thinking they would still be permitted to go out this way, started down the steps. Before they had gone far they were ordered to halt. They continued to descend until they were told that if they came farther they would be killed. They then observed by the dim light that it was Major Degress speaking, and that a white man and two Negroes held guns leveled at them. The mayor insisted on going out that way, when Major Degress said, "Mayor, I have nothing against you; but I am ordered to let no person come down these steps tonight, and if you take another step these men will shoot you." The mayor replied, "Major Degress, you have the advantage of me now, but I will see you again," and then he and Denton went back up the steps. When the crowd heard and saw what had happened, they made a rush to go down the steps. Excited voices came from the crowd, asking the mayor, "Didn't they say they would shoot you?" He replied, "It makes no difference what they said to me. Keep them back, keep them back." Hearing this, the crowd made another rush to go down, and were checked only by the use of guns and clubs in the hands of the Travis Rifles and police.

Another incident which occurred that night, and which came near bringing on a collision was when an armed squad of Davis followers advanced toward a cannon, which young Haralson, one of the Travis Rifles, was guarding. Haralson, who knew no fear, brought his gun down on them and ordered them to halt. They did so, and retreated at once to the Capitol.[48]

In line with his attempt to prevent fighting Richardson took steps to have the cannon on the capitol grounds spiked, and the Democratic guard removed from it.[49] The Davis forces then posted a sentinel at the gun, and throughout the cold night he walked his post, tramping a path.

The truce ended with the night, and De Gress, the Radical, appeared on the grounds early the next day with a squad of men who proceeded to the cannon and tried to load it. The Democrats, watching from the

[48] T. B. Wheeler, "Reminiscences of Reconstruction in Texas," *The Southwestern Historical Quarterly*, XI, (1908), 56–58.
[49] J. P. Richardson to General Henry E. McCulloch, May 5, 1892, Volume of the Miscellaneous Correspondence, MS.

second floor, believed he intended to turn it upon them to force their surrender or retreat from the building. When De Gress and his men found the gun spiked they returned disgustedly to the basement of the capitol while the Democrats jeered gleefully.[50]

The state of Texas possessed a modest supply of arms and ammunition which were stored in the state arsenal a short distance from the capitol. The Democrats resolved to make an attempt to gain control of this equipment. Thus shortly after the noon hour on Friday, the Travis Rifles left the capitol and marched to the arsenal on West Avenue with the object of taking possession of it for Coke. At the request of Governor Coke, Mayor T. B. Wheeler accompanied them for the purpose of preventing bloodshed. Some of the Davis men had arrived at the arsenal first and were in armed occupancy, when the Travis Rifles arrived. Wheeler anticipated trouble and asked Lieutenant Roberts to withdraw the Travis Rifles. This was done, and Wheeler faced the arsenal alone. The mayor then asked Hamp Cox, a radical who was in command of the building, to surrender it to him at once, but this Cox refused to do, declaring that he was acting under the command of Governor Davis. Lieutenant Roberts had returned during the conversation, and the three agreed that Cox should surrender the building, but the arms and ammunition would be placed where neither party could use them. A receipt was to be made to Cox in the name of the Coke government for these materials. The mayor had begun to write the receipt, when he was interrupted by the approach of Captain Hill, a white man, leading a group of twenty or thirty Negroes, who were running with arms presented. At this time, Lieutenant Roberts had already rejoined the Travis Rifles who were a short distance away but were out of sight. Hill arrested Wheeler at once, but explained to the mayor that the act was done under the authority of Governor Davis. Wheeler feared a battle would occur should the Travis Rifles attempt to rescue him, and upon seeing them come in sight, he vigorously motioned them to withdraw. Although the Negroes were thick around the mayor, he was able to convey his signal to the Travis Rifles who once more retired. Hill and his Negro guard then led Wheeler into an enclosure which surrounded the arsenal. Here the mayor attempted to

[50] Wheeler, "Reminiscences of Reconstruction in Texas," pp. 50–62; *Tri-Weekly State Gazette,* January 17, 1874, VII, 14; Brown, "Annals of Travis County," Ch. XXXII, p. 41, MS.; unsigned account in Volume of Miscellaneous Correspondence, MS.

convince the freedmen that the Coke party was right in its stand, and that President Grant, realizing this, had refused to interfere. He told the Negroes that they were being led by a few bad men who, when they got the freedmen into a fight with the white people, would run away and let the white men kill them. Some of the Negroes now began to take Wheeler's part, and immediately after, compelled his release.

The mayor then hastened to town, where news of his arrest had preceded him, and a crowd of armed citizens was preparing to go to his rescue. He addressed these people and begged them not to cause any trouble, as federal interference would probably result, and a recurrence of military rule in the state would follow. In concluding his speech, Wheeler requested the barkeepers of the town to close their saloons until the following day at twelve o'clock. The saloon men of Austin complied. The crowd, now thoroughly quieted, slowly dispersed.

Shortly after the release of the mayor, Adjutant General William Steele, Coke's new appointee who occupied the position briefly held by Henry McCulloch, sent a detachment of troops under the command of Captain Dave Wilson to take the arsenal. Wilson had the arms and ammunition removed from the arsenal and stored in a house in town.[51]

On the afternoon of January 16 the four acting sergeants-at-arms of the Fourteenth Legislature—General W. P. Hardeman, Sheriff Zimpleman, Colonel Timmons, and McLemore—held a conference with Governor Davis in the basement of the capitol. They proposed to the Governor that all manifestation of force cease and that both parties disperse their armed men. If this were done, they promised, no effort would be made by the Coke party to eject Governor Davis and his officials. They also offered to return the arsenal to the bonded officer who ordinarily was responsible for it.

Davis accepted their proposal and immediately dismissed his militia. Within fifteen minutes all armed men in the vicinity of the capitol had disappeared.

On the following day, January 17, Governor Davis wrote Governor Coke that he neither regarded Coke as the chief executive nor felt that he was entitled to any of the official records. Davis asserted that he himself was governor until April 28, 1874, at which time his constitutional term of four years would end. He added that it was a mutual re-

---

[51] Unsigned account in Volume of Miscellaneous Correspondence, MS.

sponsibility of theirs, as citizens striving to maintain peace, to decide immediately upon some plan for settling the governorship question, and he proposed that they submit it either to President Grant or to Congress for final settlement. But under the federal Constitution, Davis maintained, sustainment of state government against domestic violence was a Presidential duty, and thus it was proper for Grant to decide which of the two was the rightful administration. Davis again proposed that he and Coke join in taking such steps as would be appropriate to obtain a prompt decision and stated that he trusted Coke and would meet his offer in a proper spirit.

Coke replied the same day, declaring that the people had decided at the polls that he was the constitutional governor. He stated that he had been properly installed and had accepted such action as final, and he declined to consider the proposal.

Then, soon after Coke's reply had reached Davis, a telegram arrived from Washington settling the question. Not satisfied with Grant's answer to his first dispatch, Davis had wired him once more, again asking for military assistance. But Grant still refused. United States Attorney General George H. Williams answered Davis' second request as follows:

Your telegram that according to the Constitution of Texas you were Governor until the 28th of April, and that Hon. Richard Coke has been inaugurated and will attempt to seize the Governor's office and building, and calling upon the President for military assistance, has been referred by him to me for answer. I am instructed to say that, after considering the fourteenth section of Article 4 of the Constitution of Texas, providing that the Governor shall hold his office for the term of four years from the time of his instalment under which you claim, and section 3 of the Election Declaration attached to such Constitution under which you were chosen and which provides that the State and other officers elected there under shall hold their respective offices for the term of years provided by the Constitution, beginning from the day of their election, under which the Governor elect claims the office, more than four years having expired since your election, he is of the opinion that your right to the office of the Governor at this time is at least so doubtful, that he does not feel warranted in furnishing United States troops to aid you in holding further possession of it, and therefore declines to comply with your request.[52]

[52] Brown, "Annals of Travis County," Ch. XXXII, pp. 43–46, MS.; George

Davis accepted the decision as final. A Conservative newspaper reported that his private secretary notified Coke that the office would be ready for the new governor to occupy at twelve o'clock Monday, January 19, but that Davis would leave a written protest.

Coke assumed that the keys would be delivered to him. He waited in vain until four o'clock, when he went to the executive office, accompanied by his sergeant at arms and several other persons. The door was locked, but a man broke it open.[53]

In its version of the incident the Radical *Daily State Journal* said nothing about the notification Coke was alleged to have received from Davis' secretary. It reported that the new governor went to the locked executive office, where an unidentified East Texas senator ordered the door broken open with an axe. Coke and his followers took possession of the room. Then they visited the state department, where they found Newcomb at his desk. He surrendered his keys and left.[54]

That same day Governor Davis issued an address to the people of Texas in which he recounted the events that preceded his ouster and presented reasons and documentary evidence to justify the course he had pursued. Davis declared that since Grant had refused aid there had been two alternatives left to him: either to yield or to use what force he had available. He said he had chosen the lesser evil and had given way to a new government, which he condemned as one founded upon usurpation.

On January 20 the Fourteenth Legislature passed a resolution expressing thanks to President Grant for sustaining the new government. Two days later, in celebration, the Travis Rifles paraded with music to the capitol, where they fired a salute of 102 guns. Governor Coke and Lieutenant Governor Hubbard appeared on the steps of the capitol and delivered addresses that reflected the happiness felt by most Texans.[55]

H. Williams to E. J. Davis, January 17, 1874, Volume of Miscellaneous Correspondence, MS.

[53] *Ibid.; Tri-Weekly State Gazette,* January 20, 1874, VII, 15.

[54] Brown, "Annals of Travis County," Ch. XXXII, p. 47, MS.; *Daily State Journal,* January 20, 1874, IV, 18.

[55] Brown, "Annals of Travis County," Ch. XXXII, pp. 48–49, MS.; *Daily State Journal,* January 20, 1874, IV, 18. The Radicals, of course, were not happy. Their attitude toward Grant's action in not sustaining Davis may be indicated by the following account from the *Daily State Journal,* January 20, 1874:

A difficult crisis in the history of Texas was thus passed. Had an armed collision occurred, military government with all the humiliation incident to it would have been reimposed.

It is here understood that the President had disregarded the decision of our Supreme Court, and had gone even further than the Democrats themselves expected to go—recognizing the election declaration which was never adopted by the people, or recognized by Congress, as paramount to the Constitution of the State, and virtually ordering the Governor to surrender his office to the usurpers even before the expiration of his constitutional term. The courts are powerless; the government of the State has been forcibly usurped, and President Grant has backed the usurpation. If he intended to leave the question involved to the courts, he should have said so.

SECTION II ECONOMICS OF THE CARPETBAG ERA

6

THE HERD, THE FARM, AND THE MINE

INTRODUCTION

AFTER THE CIVIL WAR Southern capital had vanished; bank stocks and deposits had lost all value. Many plantation owners were unable to continue their operations. In Texas, farm stock in general decreased 20 per cent from 1860 to 1866, although sheep showed a gain of about 20 per cent.[1] Land was valued at from one-tenth to one-fourth of its 1860 price. Mortgage sales were numerous, and a large percentage of East Texas land changed hands. In the cotton region labor problems proved to be critical. After a year or two of trial, planters concluded that the recently freed Negroes, having a tendency toward shiftlessness, could not be depended upon as day laborers, and they advocated increased white immigration from other states and from Europe.[2] Nevertheless, the Texas Negro population increased during the years 1860–1870 by 35 per cent,[3] for during the war thousands of slaves had been sent in from Louisiana, Arkansas, and other Southern states to keep them away from the Union army. After peace came most of them stayed in Texas.

To aid the Negro the Freedmen's Bureau, a division of the War Department, was created. Its duties were to provide for the administration of confiscated property, to distribute supplies to the poverty-stricken freedmen, and to aid in regulating their labor problems. But in Texas the work of the Freedmen's Bureau did not prove satisfactory because the organization, through its Bureau agents, interfered with

[1] *Texas Almanac and Emigrants Guide,* 1867, p. 107.
[2] *Ibid.,* 1869, p. 96.
[3] U. S. Bureau of the Census, *Ninth Census of the United States,* 1870, I, 5; Seth S. McKay, "Texas under the Regime of E. J. Davis," p. 3, MS.

relations between the employer and his Negro employees, to the detriment of the workers' dependability.[4] In 1868 the Freedmen's Bureau, an obvious failure, was abolished, and Texans were able to cope with the Negro problem a little more successfully.[5] Eventually share tenancy began to appear as planters, realizing the unreliability of Negro labor, subdivided their lands into small farms and rented them. At the same time the high price of cotton encouraged development in new sections. But the economic growth of Texas in the late sixties was hampered not only by labor problems but also by the absence of railway transportation; railroads were confined for the most part to the section immediately surrounding Houston and Galveston. Although East Texas had fewer transportation problems than the interior its recovery was greatly hampered because of the inefficiency of Negro labor.

The southern section of the state suffered less than other areas. Here there was no dependence on the Negro farm worker, since cattle and sheep raising were the chief means of livelihood.[6] South of San Antonio lay territory especially adapted to the raising of cattle. That area, diamond shaped, extended north and south from San Antonio to Brownsville and east and west from Indianola to Laredo. A natural breeding ground for cattle, it possessed a semitropical climate and sufficient water.

A few cattle drives had been made before the Civil War. During the conflict some cattle were delivered to the Confederate forces, but this trade declined when the Mississippi River fell under Union control. Then, following the war, cattle drives began on a large scale. Herds numbering 260,000 were started north in 1866, the destination usually being Sedalia, Missouri, where rail transportation to St. Louis and other cities was available. But that year many of the drivers were unable to deliver their cattle to Sedalia because of armed mobs that met them in southeastern Kansas, southern Missouri, and northern Arkansas. The excuse given for this interference was that the herds carried the Texas fever and would introduce the disease among northern cattle. The herds of 1867 and 1868 were much smaller, but they arrived safely at the new cattle town of Abilene, Kansas. The following year,

[4] *Texas Almanac,* 1869, p. 227.
[5] *Ibid.,* 1869, p. 227; McKay, "Texas under the Regime of E. J. Davis," p. 3, MS.
[6] McKay, "Texas under the Regime of E. J. Davis," p. 4, MS.

1869, the number driven to Abilene was 350,000—the largest to that time.[7]

The wheat section of the state, consisting of thirty North Texas counties centered around Dallas, experienced crop failures in the years following the Civil War. Rust, the grasshopper, and otherwise unfavorable seasons took their tolls and discouraged the wheat grower in the years between 1865 and 1870. On the other hand, the Negro labor problem was not of much concern to farmers of that district.[8]

In South Texas the Germans and other immigrants had not been materially affected by the outcome of war, for these people did not depend upon Negro labor.[9]

The agricultural decline during the decade 1860–1870 might best be indicated by the following table:

	1860	*1870*	*Per cent*
Value of farms	$88,101,320	$60,149,950	31.1
Value of farming			
implements	6,259,452	3,396,793	56.6
Farm acreage	25,343,028	18,396,523	27.4

The percentage of farmlands that were improved increased from 10.4 to 16.1. But cotton production decreased from 431,463 bales in 1859 to 350,629 in 1869. Cotton prices fluctuated greatly during the early reconstruction period; in 1865 the price was 43.2 cents per pound and in 1870 it was 17 cents.

Whereas Texas agriculture lagged, there was an increase in manufacturing, railroad building, and banking in the decade 1860–1870. Railroad mileage increased from 307 in 1860 to 711 in 1870, or 131 per cent. Manufacturing establishments numbered 983 in 1860 and valued their products at an estimated $6,577,202. In 1870 they numbered 2,399 and had an estimated product value of $11,517,302. In 1870 there were four national banks in the state—two in Galveston, one in Houston, and one in San Antonio—whose capital and surplus amounted to $575,000. The policy of prohibiting state banks, adopted by the state in 1846, was abandoned by the Constitution of 1869, and a number of them were organized. During the reconstruction period

[7] Walter Prescott Webb, *The Great Plains,* pp. 209–223.
[8] *Texas Almanac,* 1870, p. 148.
[9] McKay, "Texas under the Regime of E. J. Davis," pp. 4–5, MS.

137

credit facilities rested largely in the hands of merchants and private lenders.[10]

Thus in the years between 1865 and 1870 Texas was attempting to recover from adverse economic conditions resulting from the Civil War. These seemed to have troubled the cotton planter more than any other group. By 1870, however, he was becoming slowly adjusted to the problem of utilizing freedmen's labor. Other Texas industries generally prospered during the early years of reconstruction.

CATTLE AND OTHER LIVESTOCK

Cattle played an important role in the economic development of the state during the carpetbag era. In 1870 fully 300,000[11] head were driven to Abilene, Kansas. Texas drovers must have realized a great deal financially from their herds that year, as was indicated in the following account taken from a Topeka, Kansas newspaper.

. . . The trade mainly concentrates at Abilene—on the Kansas Pacific railway, 160 miles west of the Missouri river, 440 miles from St. Louis and 670 miles from Chicago. The cattle come principally from northern Texas. They are bought there by the herd at the following prices per head: beef cattle $11, milch cows $6, three year olds $7, one year olds $2.50. The average distance driven is about 700 miles. Time consumed in driving, two months. Cost of driving $2 per head exclusive of 29 per cent risk for stampeding, stealing, etc. Arriving in Abilene in good order, a mixed drove is held at about the following average figures: beef cattle $20., milch cows $12., three year olds $10., two year olds $7., one year olds $5. After being "grazed" through the summer, the same cattle are worth 20 per cent more. Beef cattle of average flesh, ready for market, are valued at $25.[12]

Higher prices than those just quoted were sometimes paid, and many herds sold for as much as thirty to forty dollars a head. Fifty to sixty dollars was paid for wintered herds which were, of course, fatter and in better condition than the herds which had just completed the long drive. Drovers had no difficulty locating buyers that season.[13]

[10] E. T. Miller, *A Financial History of Texas,* pp. 158–159.

[11] Webb, *The Great Plains,* p. 223; Joseph G. McCoy, *Historical Sketches of the Cattle Trade of the West and Southwest,* pp. 225–226; J. E. Haley, "A Survey of Texas Cattle Drives to the North, 1866–1895," pp. 203–205, MS.

[12] *Tri-Weekly State Gazette,* November 2, 1870, III, 119. The above account was quoted by this paper from the *Kansas State Record,* published at Topeka.

[13] McCoy, *Historical Sketches,* p. 226.

Cattlemen returning from Kansas were elated over their success and began preparing for the next year's drive. Drawing capital from financiers attracted by the promising future of the business, they were able to pay for stock as soon as it was received.[14]

The greatest drive in history was made in the spring of 1871, when 700,000 head arrived in Kansas from Texas. But the high prices offered at that time also induced other western cattlemen to send their herds to the market, which became glutted. Buyers were few.[15] To make matters worse, the eastern railway companies ceased a rate war that had prevailed in 1870 and raised prices to a level that more than repaid them for any benefits given the cattlemen the previous year. Moreover, the season was rainy, and the cattle, unable to fatten on coarse and spongy grass, brought low prices.[16] Half of the herds brought to Kansas remained unsold; they were wintered on nearby prairies at a serious loss.[17] Some drovers, however, held contracts and were able to sell. Colonel J. F. Ellison, a well-known drover, made a contract with a ranchman on Smoky River, located between Abilene and Ellsworth, to deliver a herd of 2,000 beef steers at two and one-half cents a pound.[18] Crawford Burnett contracted to sell Armour and Company of Chicago 10,000 steers; these were delivered in Texas, in Mason County, and were sold at $12 in gold.[19] Another herd of 1,200 steers brought $10 each on the range.[20] Some cattlemen were able to obtain even higher prices: George W. and C. C. Slaughter, for instance, sold 2,000 head at $33.80.[21]

Although Abilene was the chief cattle market, another Kansas town, Newton, came into prominence in 1871. That spring the Atchison, Topeka, and Santa Fe Railroad, building south of the Kansas and Pacific, reached a point about sixty-five miles south of Abilene. Here Newton was established at that time, and a large cattle shipping yard was constructed near the town. Newton did only a moderate business, however, gaining at the same time a disproportionate national reputa-

[14] Haley, "Survey of Texas Cattle Drives," p. 205, MS.; J. Marvin Hunter, *The Trail Drivers of Texas*, 22.

[15] Webb, *The Great Plains*, pp. 230–231.

[16] McCoy, *Historical Sketches*, pp. 225–227.

[17] Webb, *The Great Plains*, p. 231.

[18] Haley, "Survey of Texas Cattle Drives," p. 207, MS.

[19] Hunter, *Trail Drivers of Texas*, 43.

[20] *Ibid.*, p. 255.

[21] *Ibid.*, p. 206.

tion for disorder and bloodshed.[22] Baxter Springs, located in south-eastern Kansas at the terminus of the Kansas City and Fort Scott railroad, and Junction City, situated east of Abilene, also received a part of the cattle trade.[23]

Those cattlemen who attempted to winter their stock on the Kansas prairie were financially ruined by the experiment. The fall and winter of 1871 proved to be unusually cold, and an early-season blizzard covered the buffalo-grass ranges with a thick crust of ice. Freezing and starving, many of the cattle drifted, and almost all of them were lost. An estimated 250,000 head died in Kansas that year.[24]

As a result drovers were scarcely optimistic about 1872 prospects, and the number of cattle driven north dropped to about half that of the previous year. But in 1872 drovers found a better market—and they also discovered that a demand had arisen for a better grade of beef. Cattle from northern ranges, being in better condition, brought higher prices.

Another significant change occurred in the business at this time. The corn belt produced a large crop that year, and in consequence there developed a demand for cattle as feeders. After that cattle were raised in Texas and sent north, where they were kept on ranges for an indefinite period until ready to be rounded out and marketed.[25]

In 1872 there was greater competition among the railroads for the cattle trade than had existed the year before.[26] The stock, instead of being driven to Abilene as had been done the previous year, were delivered at Wichita and Ellsworth, Kansas. The combined number sent to the two places totaled 350,000.[27]

Generally, the cattle season of 1872 proved satisfactory to the drovers, and as a result there was a marked increase in the size of the 1873 drives. Three railways now competed for the cattle trade: the Kansas and Pacific, the Atchison, Topeka, and Santa Fe, and the Leavenworth, Lawrence, and Galveston.

The Kansas and Pacific attempted to persuade drovers to come to Ellsworth, Ellis, and Russell. The Leavenworth, Lawrence, and Gal-

---

[22] McCoy, *Historical Sketches,* p. 229.
[23] Haley, "Survey of Texas Cattle Drives," p. 209, MS.
[24] *Ibid.,* pp. 211–212.
[25] Webb, *The Great Plains,* p. 231.
[26] McCoy, *Historical Sketches,* P. 248.
[27] Webb, *The Great Plains,* p. 223.

veston was able to attract about 50,000 cattle to Coffeyville. The Santa
Fe drew great numbers to Wichita. Interested parties spent money
freely in an attempt to entice drovers and their herds.[28] The total number of cattle driven to Ellsworth and Wichita, Kansas, in 1873 was
405,000,[29] but McCoy, in his *Historical Sketches of the Cattle Trade of
the West and Southwest*, gave 450,000 as the number delivered in
western Kansas that year.[30]

William M. Cox, livestock agent of the Kansas and Pacific, compiled
statistics on the cattle business in 1873. On July 20 his figures showed
the following totals:

	Head
Ellsworth	210,000
Wichita	75,000
Other Points	60,000
On the trail	55,000
Total	400,000

Later, he gave added receipts to be:

Ellsworth	60,000
Wichita	30,000
Other Points	10,000
Total	100,000
Grand Total	500,000

Commenting on these figures, the Kansas City *Journal* declared:

This is at least 100,000 more than the drive of 1872, and would probably
have been somewhat larger but for the fact that this market has been somewhat depressed during the summer by causes which deterred many from
driving late in the season, who would otherwise have brought their herds
through. But, as it is, the interest will be seen to be enormous. These cattle
may safely be averaged at $15. per head on arriving at Kansas soil, and at
that price it would take $7,500,000. to buy them. About 40,000 head have
been driven into Wyoming and Northern Colorado and about 20,000 to

[28] McCoy, *Historical Sketches,* pp. 248–249.
[29] Webb, *The Great Plains,* p. 223.
[30] Haley, "Survey of Texas Cattle Drives," p. 232, MS.; McCoy, *Historical
Sketches,* pp. 248–251.

Nebraska. About 50,000 will yet be driven into the Territories, and about 100,000 will be wintered in Kansas, leaving 290,000 head to be disposed of at the Kansas City market. Of these, from 20,000 to 30,000 head have already been marketed; 120,000 head will probably be taken by packers and converted into meats, and about 30,000 head will be tanked—that is, killed for their hides and tallow, because of the low price they command in market, leaving about 115,000 to go to butchers and feeders in other States than Kansas.[31]

About three-fifths of the cattle driven to Kansas that year, 1873, were stock animals—cows, heifers, yearlings, and steers less than four years of age—but there was little demand for them that season. Few buyers came from the northwestern territories,[32] and the requirements of the northern ranges had been filled by earlier shipments.[33] More-over, well-supplied buyers from the territories had changed their status and for a long time to come were to be sellers. Consequently, cattle-men were forced to hold their herds to fatten them for the fall market. But to accomplish this money had to be borrowed, and some of the cattlemen who were already in debt for their herds or who had not yet paid off their men upon arriving in Kansas were faced with more serious financial obligations. Still, the drovers preferred borrowing money to selling their cattle at the low prevailing prices. By the first of September Texas drovers in Kansas were in debt at least $1,500,000, and the greater part of this sum was due during the month of October.[34]

At this juncture the whole nation was precipitated into a financial panic, following the September 18, 1873, closing of the New York banking firm of Jay Cooke and Company.[35] Businesses all over the nation were paralyzed. Cattlemen who had borrowed money to be repaid in October were unable to meet their obligations, and the banks were not in a position to grant further extensions. No choice was left to the drover but to place his herd on the market and accept whatever price might be offered. But again a rainy season compounded troubles for the cattleman; the animals were unable to fatten on the coarse

---

[31] *Weekly Democratic Statesman,* October 16, 1873, III, 12. The above ac-count from the Kansas City *Journal* was republished in the *Statesman,* as were Cox's statistics.

[32] McCoy, *Historical Sketches,* p. 249.

[33] Webb, *The Great Plains,* p. 231.

[34] McCoy, *Historical Sketches,* p. 250.

[35] Webb, *The Great Plains,* p. 231.

soft grass. An estimated 90 per cent of them were unfit to be sold, and those marketed in the East brought little more than freight and other charges. The losses of all of the Texas drovers totaled 2 million dollars because of the panic. Scores of them became bankrupt, and few escaped heavy losses.

Thousands of stock cattle were sold at from one to one and a quarter cents a pound gross weight to be killed for their hides and tallow. Packers bought some of the best herds, while two-fifths of all cattle delivered in Kansas that year were wintered in the western portion of the state or driven into Colorado. Another 100,000 head were foraged in the northwestern states. Still others went to the Indians in the territories,[36] and many more were driven westward for grazing purposes. Not only did Colorado obtain a share, but Nevada, Wyoming, and New Mexico each received large numbers. And some cattlemen turned their herds toward the grasslands of the Indian Territory.[37]

The Panic of 1873 taught Texas cattlemen two lessons: they could no longer sell scrub stock to be ranged in the North, and from now on they must either deliver good beef or better cattle which could be easily fattened to increase their market value.

The drives of 1874 and 1875 amounted to only 166,000 and 151,000 head, respectively, indicating the effect of the disaster upon the Texas cattle business.[38] But the financial depression was not solely to blame for the decrease. The northern range was approaching a saturation point and needed no new stock, and the railroads, with more western mileage now, were taking cattle off the trails.

The effect of the panic was only temporary. By 1876 the cattle business was almost back to normal; the market was good,[39] and the cattle driven that year numbered 321,928.[40]

To complete the account of the Texas cattle business it is necessary to consider Texas packeries and rendering plants. In November 1870 the *Tri-Weekly Gazette* quoted the *Bulletin* of the coastal town of

[36] McCoy, *Historical Sketches,* pp. 250–252.

[37] James Cox, *Historical and Biographical Records of the Cattle Industry and the Cattlemen of Texas and Adjacent Territory,* pp. 97–98. Hereafter cited as Cox, *Cattle Industry of Texas.*

[38] Haley, "Survey of Texas Cattle Drives," p. 234, MS.; Cox, *Cattle Industry of Texas,* p. 87.

[39] Webb, *The Great Plains,* p. 232.

[40] Haley, "Survey of Texas Cattle Drives," p. 234, MS.; Cox, *Cattle Industry of Texas,* p. 87.

Indianola as reporting the existence of as many as ten beef packeries then in operation on Matagorda Bay and its tributaries. One of these plants, located at Tres Palacios, had rendered a hundred cattle a day throughout the summer of that year, and in the fall it handled the same number daily for packing purposes. Rockport and Fulton, Aransas Bay villages about three miles apart, had a total of six beef-packing establishments that slaughtered about 20,000 head of cattle in 1869 and shipped several thousand head alive, by boat, to New Orleans where prices were higher than they were locally.[41] One of the Fulton plants sold much of its output to the United States Navy in 1870.[42] Other packeries were in operation at Galveston,[43] Houston,[44] Anahuac, and Powder Horn during the early seventies.[45] These packing and rendering plants flourished before cattle prices rose as a result of greater demand in the North and thus drew the animals out of Texas. This increased market value finally forced the rendering plants out of business.[46]

In addition to cattle Texas had horses, ranking third among all states in 1870. Only Illinois and Ohio had more of these animals than the 622,000 estimated for the Lone Star State. Horses were cheaper in Texas than anywhere else in the nation except California. In the Gulf states the animals sold for almost three times the price paid for them in Texas, but part of the difference may be explained by the breed: the Texas horse was the mustang; the other Gulf states favored older breeds.

Texas counted 80,500 mules in 1870, ranking seventh among the states. But these mules brought the lowest prices of any in the country, probably because of their breed.[47] In 1874 the state comptroller reported that horses and mules in Texas numbered 871,278 and that they were valued at $21,187,030.

In 1870 Texas' hog population, estimated at 1 million, was tenth among the states. In 1872 Texas moved to ninth in this field, surpassing

[41] *Daily State Journal,* May 2, 1870, I, 96, quoting the Indianola *Bulletin.*
[42] *Tri-Weekly State Gazette,* November 21, 1870, III, 127.
[43] C. Appleton (ed.), *American Annual Cyclopaedia,* 1873, XIII, p. 742.
[44] Haley, "Survey of Texas Cattle Drives," p. 140, MS.
[45] *Ibid.,* pp. 140–141.
[46] *Ibid.,* p. 140.
[47] U. S. Department of Agriculture, *Report of the Secretary of Agriculture,* 1869, p. 47; McKay, "Texas under the Regime of E. J. Davis," p. 14, MS.

Pennsylvania. But these animals also brought low prices—the lowest in the nation—because they were of the razorback variety and because of the scarcity of markets in the state.

In 1870 Texas sheep numbered 1,272,000, and the herds continued to increase. Two years later, in 1872, the state ranking rose from eleventh to tenth. In 1874 the comptroller estimated that Texas had 1,632,971 sheep. Most were raised on the open range, and since markets were scarce and not easily accessible it is not surprising that these sheep too brought lower prices than those of any other state.[48]

AGRICULTURE

In the early seventies farming and cattle raising were the two most important Texas industries, and of all agricultural products corn and cotton ranked highest. During the previous decade, 1860–1870, Texas had risen from seventeenth to ninth in U. S. corn production, probably because the war had affected its crops less than those of other Southern states.[49] The average yield varied, with fair cultivation, from 25–30 bushels an acre in uplands to 50–60 bushels in river lands. Where irrigation was utilized, as in the Rio Grande Valley, corn yielded as much as 100 bushels an acre. But for the state as a whole corn cultivation was not particularly impressive.[50] In 1870 Texas produced 23,690,000 bushels, showing an average yield of 26.5 bushels for each of the 893,962 acres. With corn bringing $1.06 a bushel, the total crop valuation was $25,111,400. By 1874 a total increase of almost 8,000,000 bushels over the 1870 figures had been noted, but at the same time the price had dropped to 75 cents, making the value of the crop less.[51] Still, corn was the most profitable agricultural product produced during this period.[52]

The Negro labor problem gave the Texas cotton planter reason for anxiety, but in the years following the war the Lone Star State suffered less than did others in the South. In 1860 Texas produced 431,463 bales of cotton, ranking only behind Mississippi, Alabama, Louisiana, and Georgia. In 1870 Texas again ranked fifth, but the percentage indicated less of a loss than the others. Texas produced more than 75

[48] *Report of the Secretary of Agriculture,* 1871, p. 36.
[49] McKay, "Texas under the Regime of E. J. Davis," p. 6, MS.
[50] *Texas Almanac,* 1870, pp. 146–147.
[51] Homer S. Thrall, *A Pictorial History of Texas,* p. 731.
[52] McKay, "Texas under the Regime of E. J. Davis," p. 7, MS.

per cent of its 1860 yield; whereas for the others the figure was less than 50 per cent.[53]

In 1871 the Texas cotton crop was estimated at 293,450 bales, in 1872 343,450 bales, and in 1873 487,771 bales. By 1873 Texas had again equalled its 1860 production, but the rest of the cotton belt failed to do so until later.[54]

In cotton farming neither the white farmer nor the freedman could adjust himself well to the new situation. The planters had to do most of their own work; the Negroes, cherishing their new freedom, wandered from place to place, working only enough to keep from starving.[55] Farmers complained that the Negro held himself under no obligation to work, even when definite contracts had been effected. Thousands of acres of rich East Texas cotton land thus lay idle because labor could not be obtained. Although the production of cotton increased after 1870, this increase was due primarily to the larger acreage and increased labor by white owners.[56]

As a wheat-producing state Texas did not rank high. The 1870 yield amounted to 1,225,000 bushels, an average of 11.7 to the acre at a bushel value of $1.73.[57] Twenty-four other states enjoyed better yields. By 1874 Texas had increased its production more than 200,000 bushels to a total of 1,474,000 bushels, but the value had decreased to $1.35 a bushel, probably because of the effect of the panic of the previous year.

Oats constituted another important crop. In 1870 Texas produced 1,500,000 bushels, exceeding the wheat yield.[58] However, weather conditions in 1871 were evidently not as favorable for grains as in the previous season, for both wheat and oats production fell to less than half the 1870 amounts. Thereafter oats showed a steady gain until in 1874 the figure reached 1,118,000 bushels, but this was still less than the 1870 output.

[53] *Ninth Census of the United States, 1870,* III, 83–87.
[54] Matthew Brown Hammond, "Cotton Production in the South," in *The South in the Building of the Nation,* VI, 93; McKay, "Texas under the Regime of E. J. Davis," pp. 7–8, MS.
[55] *Texas Almanac,* 1871, p. 102.
[56] McKay, "Texas under the Regime of E. J. Davis," pp. 9–11, MS.
[57] *Report of the Secretary of Agriculture,* 1870, p. 34.
[58] Thrall, *Pictorial History of Texas,* p. 731.

During this same period the minor agricultural products included rye, barley, potatoes, tobacco, hay,[59] and sugar cane.[60]

Summarizing, it can be said that farming proved profitable in the early seventies. It has been suggested that one reason for this was that the Civil War had reduced the market value of land below the 1860 level,[61] but it is difficult to make an estimate of the average price of Texas land in 1870. A contemporaneous publication declared that plots suitable for homesteads, with sufficient wood and water and with good soil for farming, could be purchased at from $2 to $5 an acre anywhere in the state. Land convenient to railroads and markets was higher, the best unimproved tracts near the railroads selling at from $5 to $10 per acre. But improved land only five to ten miles away could be purchased for about the same figure,[62] and unimproved East Texas farm land near no railroad or town sold at from $1 to $5 per acre as late as 1873. Farm property in the northern part of the cotton belt, including Dallas, Collin, Fannin, Grayson, Hunt, and Lamar counties, was valued in 1872 at from $4 to $15 an acre. Much cheaper was the land in what was then known as West Texas; in Wilson, Karnes, Goliad, Kerr, Lampasas, Bosque, Wise, and adjacent counties thousands of acres could be bought at from 25 cents to $1 an acre.[63] In Central Texas, too, it could be purchased cheaply during the reconstruction period. C. J. Wilkerson of Denton County declared that in 1869 his father purchased 3,000 acres of Bell County land at sixty cents an acre.[64]

MINERAL RESOURCES

In 1870 mineral resources attracted scant interest, but of those known to exist the most important were iron, coal, copper, silver, lead, gold, bismuth, antimony, slate, and asphaltum.

Iron ore deposits were located in Burnet, Lampasas, Llano, Mason,

[59] *Ibid.* These statements were taken from the annual report published by the Agriculture Department in Washington.
[60] *Texas Almanac,* 1870, p. 149.
[61] McKay, "Texas under the Regime of E. J. Davis," p. 19, MS.
[62] *Ibid.,* p. 17; *Texas Almanac,* 1872, pp. 32, 77.
[63] *Texas Almanac,* 1871, p. 34; 1872, pp. 60, 63; 1873, p. 176.
[64] McKay, "Texas under the Regime of E. J. Davis," p. 20, MS.

McCulloch, San Saba, and other western counties. That found in Llano and Mason counties was better suited for steel manufacture than that of any of the other forty counties where it was found.[65] The only extensive iron works in the state was at Kellyville, four miles west of Jefferson in Marion County.[66]

Jack County possessed the most valuable coal deposit. The same vein ran through the counties of Young, Eastland, Palo Pinto, Brown, Comanche, Coleman, Callahan, Erath, and San Saba, and extended south to Bexar. This coal exhibited the same characteristics as that found in Missouri and other western states. Palo Pinto blacksmiths used bituminous coal found in their county.[67] Lignite was located in Webb, Atascosa, Frio, Bastrop, and other counties. It was soft, sulphurous, and ashy, but said to be of better quality than the German brown coal.[68] The lignite beds near Bastrop on Cedar Creek, west of the Colorado River, were measured and found to be five feet thick, in nearly horizontal layers.

In 1872 the regular coal measures of the state covered more than 6,000 square miles. There were also more than 10,000 square miles of lignite and other inferior coals which were then unavailable because of lack of development.[69]

Texas was believed to possess liberal copper deposits. A. R. Rossler, a former assistant state geologist, reported on the amount and quality:

Copper, covering as it does a large area of country, is almost inexhaustible, and will afford a vast fund of wealth for generations to come. A large portion of the counties of Archer, Wichita, Clay, Haskell, Territory of Bexar, counties of Pecos and Presidio—extending to the Rio Grande—is filled with immense hills of copper ore, some of which has been thoroughly tested and will yield on the average 55.44 per cent of metal; though some particular localities have produced specimens even as rich as 68 per cent, containing, besides, some silver, oxide of iron, etc.

[65] *Texas Almanac,* 1872, p. 126.
[66] *Ibid.,* p. 62.
[67] *Ibid.,* 1867, pp. 64–65.
[68] *Ibid.,* p. 128; Thrall, *Pictorial History of Texas,* p. 70. The account in Thrall is by A. R. Rossler, assistant state geologist in 1859, who at a later date made this report concerning the coal resources in Texas.
[69] *Texas Almanac,* 1872, p. 128.

. . . In 1870, after traversing the cretaceous and carboniferous series northward of Weatherford, Parker County, I was very agreeably surprised by a grand panorama of outcropping of this formation (copper ore). . . . At present, mining operations cannot be safely prosecuted, owing to the proximity of bands of prowling Indians.[70]

Lead and silver in limited amounts were found together in El Paso, Presidio, Bandera, and Llano counties. Gold, also in small quantities, was found in Llano, Mason, and a few other western counties.[71]

In the copper lands of Archer and Wichita counties bismuth was also mined, to sell for $5 a pound. Antimony existed in Llano and Mason counties; asphaltum in Hardin, Nacogdoches, Anderson, Bell, Travis, and Llano counties; gypsum, in what was then the largest known deposit in the world, in the northwestern portion of the state. The gypsum area included more than two hundred miles on the upper

[70] Thrall, *Pictorial History of Texas,* pp. 66–67.
[71] *Ibid.,* p. 67. The extent to which the minerals mentioned may be found today is enlightening, for the fields are not always where geologists of the early seventies believed, nor are they as profitable. There is some limited production of iron from the deposits of iron ores in the state but the principal deposits are found in Cherokee, Camp, Harrison, Anderson, Cass, Upshur, Henderson, Smith, Morris, Titus, and Rusk counties. The mining of bituminous coal is almost at a standstill, while lignite is obtained profitably by the strip-mining method in Milam County. Bituminous coal underlies a large area in north central and middle west Texas. Coal in the recent past was mined at Strawn in Palo Pinto County, Thurber in Erath County, and Bridgeport in Wise County. In Coleman and McCulloch counties are also deposits of bituminous coal. While in Maverick and Webb counties, a bituminous coal of low grade, called cannel coal, can be found. Lignite can also be mined over a wide belt that extends from Laredo to Texarkana, and deposits are to be found in Hopkins, Wood, Henderson, Bastrop, Bexar, Titus, Upshur, and Harrison. Copper is mined in an inappreciable amount in Culberson County. In the Trans-Pecos region, copper has been found in Presidio, Brewster, and Hudspeth counties and in the central portion of the state at Burnet and Llano counties. Deposits of copper lie in the Permian region of north central Texas, south and southwest of Wichita Falls and within Archer and the counties which center around it. Silver was mined at Shafter, Presidio County, but there is no mining of silver at present due to the low price of the ore, nor is there any production of gold. A belt of gypsum extends from Quanah, Hardeman County to Sweetwater, Nolan County; in both of the towns gypsum mills are in operation. Gypsum is also produced in Fisher, Hudspeth, Brooks, and Jim Hogg counties. *Texas Almanac,* 1958–1959, pp. 276–277.

149

Red River and its tributaries. This mineral had special value as a fertilizer.[72]

Nevertheless, mining was an infant industry in Texas during the administration of Governor E. J. Davis. Due to lack of capital and inadequate transportation facilities there was little incentive to extract and market the minerals.

[72] Thrall, *Pictorial History of Texas,* p. 70; *Texas Almanac,* 1872, p. 134.

7

MANUFACTURING, COMMERCE, AND TRANSPORTATION

MANUFACTURING AND INDUSTRY

BY 1867 cotton and woolen mills were to be found at Bastrop, New Braunfels, and Waco and three others were being constructed, two at Houston and one at Palestine. The Bastrop Manufacturing Company possessed 1,100 spindles and enough looms to produce from 800 to 1,000 yards of material daily, in addition to yarns. This company, the oldest of its kind in the state, was representative of the others then in existence.[1]

A conception of 1870 manufacturers may be acquired from a description of exhibits at the first state fair, held in Houston in May, 1870. The account was taken from a report prepared by fair directors. John H. Reagan was president.

The fair was attended by 25,000 to 30,000 people, 10,000 of them coming the second day alone; there were nine departments and nearly a thousand entries. Every one visiting the grounds expressed surprise and pleasure at the number and variety and quality of the articles exhibited, a large proportion of which were produced and manufactured in Texas. The cotton and woolen goods manufactured at New Braunfels and Houston compared favorably with goods of the same class from any part of the United States. Texas brooms and saddles were excellent. There were childen's carriages, buggies, rockaways, wagons, and a superbly built railway passenger car. A plow invented, patented, and manufactured out of Texas material by a Texas man won first honors. It came from Wise County on its own wheels, and on the journey of three hundred miles stopped on the way to break ground, thus paying its own expenses for travel. The best road wagon was

[1] *Texas Almanac*, 1867, p. 236.

151

made at Houston out of Texas material, and the iron work was manufactured at Texas foundries. Among other Texas inventions was a cotton-gin feeder, soon afterwards patented. A cotton press, produced at Houston, won the applause of all visitors. Of the six steam engines on the ground two were manufactured at Houston. There were exhibits of livestock, poultry, all kinds of kitchen products and many other things.[2]

Nor were these all of the Texas-manufactured products on display. Prizes were awarded for superior furniture, cabinet joiner's and turner's work, upholstery, clothing, boots, and shoes. Also in evidence were cigars made from Texas tobacco, cured meats, lard, and soap. Especially gratifying to Texans was the award won by a homemade buggy, which was judged by disinterested nonresidents[3] superior even to the celebrated "Concord" of New Hampshire.

But Texas was still in the handicraft stage. Large-scale manufacturing was absent; few of the scattered industries would even be considered in the factory class today. An 1870 list enumerated the more numerous of these scattered industries.

Flouring and grist mill products . . .	533
Sawed lumber	324
Blacksmithing	380
Carpentering and building	147
Saddlery and harness	115

Texas also possessed from ten to one hundred industries in each of the following fields: meat packing, wool carding and cloth dressing, and the production of boots and shoes, wheels for vehicles, metalware, furniture, tanned or curried leather, men's clothing, malt liquors, newspapers, bricks, guns, tobacco for cigars, saddlery hardware, bakery goods, watches and clocks, and agricultural implements. Most of these businesses employed from one to three persons.

Altogether, there were, in 1870, 2,399 manufacturing establishments employing 8,000 people who earned $1,787,835 annually. Investments in these businesses totaled $5,284,110; the annual value of all the products was $11,517,302.[4]

[2] Seth S. McKay, "Texas under the Regime of E. J. Davis," p. 29, MS.; *Texas Almanac,* 1872, p. 157.

[3] *Daily State Journal,* May 28, 1870, I, 103.

[4] U. S. Bureau of the Census, *Ninth Census of the United States, 1870,* III, 573; McKay, "Texas under the Regime of E. J. Davis," pp. 27–28, MS.; E. T. Miller, *A Financial History of Texas,* p. 158.

To encourage manufacturing the Twelfth Legislature passed a measure in November, 1871, exempting from taxes for five years the entire stock and property used in the making of cotton and woolen goods. The act also exempted all persons employed in the industry from the payment of any occupation tax for the same period.[5]

COMMERCE

Exports of merchandise from Galveston in 1870 amounted to $14,869,601. Eleven years later, in 1881, it had risen with some fluctuations to $26,685,248. Figures for all commerce handled through Galveston during the Davis administration were as follows:

Year	Imports	Exports
1870	$ 509,231	$14,869,601
1871	1,255,003	13,764,384
1872	1,741,000	12,211,774
1873	2,426,626	17,629,633[6]

Cotton shipping was the most important business of the city. Statistics for the years of the Davis administration show this picture:

Year	Receipts
1869	$133,466
1870	299,808
1871	204,718
1872	186,073
1873	333,502[7]

The 1872 cotton export decline was due to a shorter 1871 crop— some 60,000 bales less than that of the previous year.

About half of the cotton shipped from Galveston to other United States ports was eventually exported to foreign countries; of the total Texas cotton export about half went to Great Britain.

Other exports from Galveston deserve mention. In 1872 a total of thirty vessels departed from the port with 30 million feet of lumber worth $862,000. About half came from Texas and half from Louisi-

[5] H. P. N. Gammel, *Laws of Texas,* VII, 42.
[6] H. H. Bancroft, *History of the North Mexican States and Texas,* II, 567; 47th Congress, Second Session, *Executive Documents,* XVIII, lix–lx.
[7] C. Appleton (ed.), *American Annual Cyclopaedia,* 1873, XIII, 741.

ana. Wool exported averaged 4,100 bags a year for the period 1868–1872; during that same time exportation of hides averaged 351,000. Although most Texas cattle were driven to market in Kansas, 58,078 head were shipped from Galveston and Indianola in 1872.[8]

Notable imports were flour, malt, corn, oats, nails, potatoes, and sugar.[9]

Nine-tenths of the Texas foreign commerce went through Galveston. Steamers ran daily from Galveston to New Orleans, Indianola, and Corpus Christi. Weekly service linked Galveston with Havana, and semimonthly service connected the Texas port with Liverpool.[10]

Galveston was not, however, the only trading point. Another was landlocked El Paso, where imports received between July, 1870, and July, 1872, were valued at $847,279.52. A leading export there was wool; during this period 150,000 pounds were shipped out. At Corpus Christi, where foreign commerce averaged $2,000,000 during these years, the leading exports were wool, hides, skins, lead, bones, horns, and tallow, and the chief imports were lumber and assorted merchandise. Indianola also carried on a trade in livestock, lumber, and cattle products.[11]

In intrastate commerce Galveston, Jefferson, Clarksville, and San Antonio were important. Although isolated geographically, Galveston was well equipped for this trade: the Galveston, Houston, and Henderson Railroad connected the city with Houston, from which point the railroads diverged; also, a ten-mile-long canal connected Galveston Bay with the Brazos River.

Jefferson, linked with the Red River by Cypress Bayou and Caddo Lake, acted as the chief port and market for a northern section of the state, the section extending from the Red River to the frontier counties of the West.[12] It was long the most important trading center in North Texas. As a shipping point, in fact, it was second only to Galveston. Cotton, wheat, hides, and lumber were delivered to its wharves by

[8] *Texas Almanac,* 1873, p. 39; McKay, "Texas under the Regime of E. J. Davis," p. 31, MS.

[9] *Texas Almanac,* 1873, p. 40.

[10] Appleton, *American Annual Cyclopaedia,* 1873, XIII, 741.

[11] *Texas Almanac,* 1873, p. 43; McKay, "Texas under the Regime of E. J. Davis," pp. 32–33, MS. The chief markets of the trade of El Paso were Santa Fe, Chihuahua, and San Antonio. *Texas Almanac,* 1867, p. 103.

[12] Charles Shirley Potts, *Railroad Transportation in Texas,* p. 20.

wagon train. Then, loaded on small steamers, the goods were transported through the channel of the Big Cypress, across Caddo Lake and down the Red River to the Mississippi and New Orleans. Imports received at Jefferson were sent west to Dallas, Sherman, Fort Worth, and other frontier settlements. Expanding railroad facilities eventually resulted in Jefferson's decline in the early seventies.

Clarksville, also near the Red River, was a distribution point for that section of North Texas. The town received goods from New Orleans by way of the river. Steamboats deposited their cargoes at Rowland's Landing fifteen miles distant, and from there the goods were transported by wagon into town. But expanding rail facilities also doomed Clarksville as a commercial center, although at its height it boasted a trade area extending as far west as El Paso.

San Antonio served as a marketing point for a vast territory, largely unsettled, lying west of the Colorado River and south of Erath and Eastland counties. In this area were two important seaports, Corpus Christi and Indianola, and four minor ones, Port Lavaca, Matagorda, Texana, and Saluria. In the southern portion of the Rio Grande Valley, trade centers were Brownsville and Brazos Santiago.[13]

OVERLAND TRAVEL AND RIVER TRANSPORTATION

Before the arrival of the railroads overland trade was conducted by stagecoach or ox-drawn wagon. Highways were scarce— and rough, since road construction was limited mostly to clearing away brush and building bridges where streams could not be forded.[14] By 1870 stagecoach routes had fallen into a pattern: each had been laid out and surveyed by the "contractor" who owned the route, but the road was kept in repair by the counties through which it passed. Then, as the population increased, the counties began to open new roads which also became available for stagecoach use.

Stagecoach depots were located in all important towns along the routes, and fresh teams could be obtained there. With these periodic team changes a stage could average from five to eight miles an hour under good conditions, but bad weather often slowed it—and inconvenienced the passengers in other ways, for sometimes they were called upon to walk beside the vehicle and to prize mud from its wheels.[15]

The unpleasantness of stagecoach transportation on a rainy day may

[13] *Ibid.*, pp. 18–21.   [14] *Ibid.*, p. 13.   [15] *Ibid.*

be judged by this account describing a trip from Brenham to Austin in May, 1870.

> This may be good fun in fine weather, but after and during a rain, it's a pastime from which we pray: Good Lord, deliver us! We left Brenham on Tuesday night at nine o'clock, with a crowded stage, but a good team. The roads were rough and heavy, part of it being just opened through the woods. A most terrible thunder storm burst upon us; the rain came down in perfect torrents, the lights were put out from time to time, but "Joe" stood to his post like a man, and landed us safe in La Grange about nine o'clock A.M. After a pretty good breakfast, we started on the day's adventures. We found the river half-bank full, with quantities of drift wood. When about half across, the lashing on the block came partially undone, and made us very apprehensive that we would all go down the river together; but we finally got over safe, and took the mud at the rate of about three miles an hour, getting out and walking up hills. We reached Bastrop about nine o'clock at night, where we found the ferry-boat laid up for the night. We were told that as the water was high, the boat rickety, and the night dark, it was unsafe to cross; but the passengers wanted to proceed, having no desire of being handed over to the tender mercies of mine host for the night how much soever he and the ferryman might desire it. So after much bantering—the passengers protesting against the whole system of staging, hotel keeping, and ferrying, in all its ramifications—they proposed running the boat across light, leaving part of their number on the opposite bank to assist in landing the boat. This was finally acceded to, and we crossed over safely and went on our muddy way, reaching Austin nine hours behind time.[16]

Long journeys by stagecoach were not only uncomfortable; they were also expensive, for the usual fare was ten cents a mile. In addition to passengers the stages carried mail, and the slowness of delivery in wet weather must have proved a frequent source of irritation.[17]

One of the most important stage routes ran from San Antonio to El Paso and eventually to San Diego, California, passing through Fredericksburg, Fort Concho, Fort Stockton, Fort Davis, Fort Quitman, and Fort Bliss. The route covered 735 miles in Texas, and 150-mile branch line ran from San Antonio to Eagle Pass.

Between Fort Concho and El Paso the stages had to cross Indian in-

16 From a letter printed in the *Daily State Journal,* May 4, 1870, I, 82.
17 *Texas Almanac,* 1872, p. 57.

fested plains. Concerning this danger the 1870 *Texas Almanac* stated:

Entirely along this portion of the line the Comanches and Apaches, the most troublesome and bloodthirsty tribes of Indians, frequently commit severe depredations, not only to the mail line, but the government trains, and droves of cattle passing through the country. They frequently by their skill, if it may be called such, stampede every hoof of stock belonging to a mail station, and more frequently by the same means, manage to get possession of a whole cavayard of mules belonging to a government train, thus leaving the train and wagoners at a complete stand-still, their trains being loaded with stores for the different military posts along each line, and they in a wild Indian country without wood or water.

From Fort Davis to Presidio del Norte, about one hundred miles,[18] a weekly line ran. From Fort Concho another line ran to Fort Smith, Arkansas, where connection could be made with a stage that traveled to St. Louis. Fort Concho, being on the San Antonio-El Paso route, of course also offered a connection to California.[19]

Between Bremond and Waco the Sawyer mail lines traveled daily except Sunday. Stages also ran between Navasota and Hallville, where there was a connection with another Sawyer stage that went to Clarksville. The latter two sections provided triweekly service, as did a line from Waco to Clarksville. Another route, from Waco to Palestine, was covered once a week.

Stages ran triweekly from Columbus to La Grange, from Victoria to San Antonio, from Victoria to Austin, from Austin to San Antonio, and from Austin to Waco. No night travel was conducted on the Austin-to-Waco line, and the trip required from 6 A.M. to 4 P.M. of the following day. Another stage left Austin at 6 A.M. and arrived at San Antonio at 11 P.M. the same day. Before the construction of the railroads six-day schedules existed between Brenham and Austin, Austin and San Antonio, and Columbus and San Antonio.[20]

Ox-wagon transportation of freight was a thriving business in 1870.[21] Rates varied, but in 1867 the usual cost was about $1 for 100

[18] *Texas Almanac,* 1870, pp. 140–141.

[19] Potts, *Railroad Transportation in Texas,* p. 15.

[20] *Texas Almanac,* 1871, p. 188; McKay, "Texas under the Regime of E. J. Davis," pp. 37–38, MS.

[21] *Ninth Census of the United States, 1870,* I, 677; Potts, *Railroad Transportation in Texas,* p. 43.

pounds for each 100 miles.[22] Galveston, Houston, Jefferson, San Antonio, Port Lavaca, and Indianola each received a good share of the wagon trade.[23]

River transportation had always been limited because navigation was largely confined to short distances near the mouths of the streams.[24] The Red River, however, could be utilized as far up as Jefferson, and that port shipped annually between 75,000 and 100,000 bales of cotton to New Orleans.[25] In rainy seasons the Red River was also navigable above the "raft,"[26] an accumulation of driftwood near Fulton, Arkansas, that blocked the channel for many miles.

The Trinity River was long used for transportation as far up as Liberty, and the Brazos was regularly navigable to Richmond.[27] After an 1870 survey of the Trinity a report was issued declaring that the river could be made navigable over a distance of some six hundred miles at a cost of less than the price of ten miles of railroad.[28] This was a gross exaggeration, but it served to indicate that commercial centers near rivers had not, in 1870, lost sight of the river-trade profits despite the large fortunes made by railroads. Still, State Senator F. J. Parker was much too optimistic when he declared in 1867 that navigation was possible up the Rio Grande for a distance of 350 miles, and that several steamers were, in fact, so engaged.[29]

Victoria, on the Guadalupe, was accessible by flatboat, and after the mouth of the river had been deepened steamers were also able to make the trip from the Gulf. But with the San Antonio and Mexican Gulf Railroad passing through Victoria, linking it with markets at Port Lavaca and Indianola, there was small demand for river transportation.[30]

The lower sections of the Sabine and Neches rivers were navigable for ordinary steamboats, and during one-third of the year longer distances on both streams could be traversed.[31] Ordinarily, however, only

22 *Texas Almanac,* 1867, p. 224.
23 *Ibid.,* pp. 75, 77, 79–80, 120.
24 Potts, *Railroad Transportation in Texas,* p. 9.
25 *Texas Almanac,* 1867, p. 140.
26 *Ibid.,* 1870, p. 171.
27 Potts, *Railroad Transportation in Texas,* p. 10.
28 *Daily State Journal,* July 2, 1870, I, 133.
29 *Texas Almanac,* 1867, p. 88.
30 *Texas Almanac,* 1869, p. 89; McKay, "Texas under the Regime of E. J. Davis," pp. 39–40, MS.
31 *Texas Almanac,* 1867, p. 125.

flatboats could use the upper waters of the Neches and of the Angelina, which flowed into it.[32]

The Colorado was for a long time obstructed by a raft near its mouth. But about 1869 the stream carved a new course by-passing the obstruction, and the river then became navigable as far as La Grange.[33]

RAILROAD TRANSPORTATION

Railroad mileage prior to the Civil War was small indeed, and the roads were confined to a limited area in East Texas.[34] In 1861 the lines in operation totaled but 392 miles, and the bleak years that followed were hardly conducive to extensive construction. But despite the hardships, the total in 1870 had increased to 711 miles. Lines crept forward to new trade centers with growing vigor, and by 1873 mileage had increased to 1,578. By the close of the Davis administration, railroad construction had begun in earnest.[35]

First to begin a program of active construction following the war was the Houston and Texas Central.[36] By 1866 portions of the line were dilapidated; crossties, bridges, and superstructures generally were in a decayed state. The roadbed had deteriorated, and much machinery had worn out as a result of incessant employment during the war. Nevertheless, the company was able to get its entire floating debt funded in its bonds, which sold well in New York. With this money and other cash obtained through loans the company set about renewing equipment and recommenced the work of extension.[37] In August, 1870, the line received further help with the passage of the general railroad relief act, which saved a number of companies from being sold for debts owed to the permanent school fund. This provided considerable relief, for the railroad owed $450,000.[38]

By 1870 the Houston and Texas Central had purchased the Washington County Railroad, running from Brenham to Hempstead, and

[32] *Ibid.,* p. 74.

[33] *Ibid.,* 1869, p. 89; McKay, "Texas under the Regime of E. J. Davis," p. 40, MS.

[34] Potts, *Railroad Transportation in Texas,* map, p. 34.

[35] *Ibid.,* p. 43.

[36] *Ibid.,* p. 49.

[37] Houston *Union,* September 27, 1870, III, 22.

[38] Potts, *Railroad Transportation in Texas,* p. 90; Gammel, *Laws of Texas,* VI, 259–260.

had extended north from the old terminus at Millican to Calvert, 130 miles from Houston.[39] In 1871 the Hempstead-Brenham branch was brought into Austin. In 1872 another subsidiary line was opened, to Waco. The following year this branch, the Waco and Northwestern, was consolidated with the Houston and Texas Central, and for many years was operated as a part of it.[40] By 1873, this railroad had in operation 500 miles of track,[41] and the line, passing through Dallas and Sherman, had reached its final terminus at Denison.

The International Railroad was chartered in August, 1870, by the state Legislature, and the company was organized soon after. This line was to run from the northeast corner of the state, opposite Fulton, Arkansas, southwest through Jefferson, Palestine, Austin, and San Antonio to Laredo, where the road was to be continued to a Pacific terminus at Mazatlan, Mexico. From there a branch line would run to Mexico City. Another connection was planned, at the starting point opposite Fulton, with the Cairo and Fulton road.

Under its charter the company had a state-bond subsidy of $10,000 a mile and was required to build seventy-five miles annually. But the International was never able to collect these bonds, as has been explained. A land grant was substituted.

Construction of the International was begun at Hearne in 1871. In December, 1872, the line was opened to Longview, by way of Palestine. In September, 1873, the company was consolidated with the Houston and Great Northern Railroad and became the International and Great Northern.[42]

The Houston and Great Northern had been chartered in 1866 for the purpose of building a road from Houston to the Red River, where connection would be made with the Memphis and El Paso Railway at or near Clarksville. Construction was begun at Houston in 1870, and by 1872 trains were running over the route to Palestine, a distance of 151 miles. In 1870 the Houston and Great Northern purchased and became consolidated with the Houston Tap and Brazoria, a short road of fifty miles connecting Columbia on the Brazos with Houston. After the International had merged with the Houston and Great Northern,

[39] *Texas Almanac,* 1870, pp. 188–189.

[40] Potts, *Railroad Transportation in Texas,* p. 49.

[41] *Texas Almanac,* 1873, pp. 196–199; Charles Shirley Potts, "Railroad Transportation in Texas," *Texas Magazine,* II (May—October, 1910), 63.

[42] Potts, *Railroad Transportation in Texas,* pp. 54–55.

the new company (International and Great Northern) constructed a thirty-mile-long line from Hearne to Rockdale. This route was continued and reached Austin in 1876.[43]

The Texas and Pacific Railroad, created by a special act of the Legislature March 3, 1871,[44] came into being as the result of a consolidation of the old Southern Pacific, and the Southern Trans-Continental railways.[45] The Southern Trans-Continental, which had until 1870 borne the name of the Memphis, El Paso, and Pacific, was organized before the Civil War, being chartered in 1853 to provide service from the Mississippi River to the Pacific Ocean. The proposed construction was known as the "32 parallel" route although it did not follow that latitude exactly. As surveyed, it was to commence at Gaines' Landing on the Mississippi and extend westward by way of Camden, Arkansas, to the Red River, where it would follow along the north bank of the stream, via Fort Towson in the Choctaw nation, and cross the river at Preston in Grayson County. From there the road was to swing diagonally across Texas to El Paso, and from there traverse New Mexico, Arizona, and Southern California. It was to reach its terminus at San Diego.[46] But the convention held in 1867 to frame a new state constitution passed an ordinance, canceling the land reservation and charter previously granted to this company.[47]

Although a later ruling voided the convention ordinances that were not embodied in the Constitution, this action had a moral force that overwhelmed the credit of the Memphis, El Paso, and Pacific. To inspire new confidence the company was reincorporated in 1870 into an organization known as the Southern Trans-Continental Railroad Company.[48] Its route was much the same as that of the Memphis, El Paso, and Pacific, with the exceptions that from Fulton it followed the valley of the Red River on the south side instead of the north, and that construction began at Texarkana.

The Southern Pacific had been founded in 1856 to provide service from Vicksburg, on the Mississippi, to the Pacific Ocean, crossing North Texas and leaving the state at El Paso. By 1870 this company

---

[43] *Ibid.*, p. 55.
[44] Gammel, *Laws of Texas*, VII, 1623–1628.
[45] Potts, *Railroad Transportation in Texas,* p. 53.
[46] *Texas Almanac,* 1871, p. 179.
[47] Gammel, *Laws of Texas,* VI, 57.
[48] *Ibid.*, VI, 542–545.

had constructed its road from Shreveport, Louisiana, through Marshall to Longview, Texas.[49]

To speed railroad construction to the Pacific the Twelfth Legislature passed the previously-mentioned 1871 act, granting $6,000,000 in bonds to the Southern Trans-Continental and Southern Pacific companies, providing that both corporations sold out and consolidated with the new Texas and Pacific Railroad Company. In March, 1872, this change was effected.

The Texas and Pacific line was to be built from the eastern border of the state to the Pacific Ocean. Congress cooperated by promising twenty sections of land for every mile constructed in California and forty sections for every mile laid through Arizona and New Mexico. With a Pennsylvania Railroad official, Colonel Thomas A. Scott, leading the new corporation, construction immediately began. By 1873 the main line was ready for use between Longview and Dallas, 124 miles, and the Trans-Continental branch had been extended 56 miles to link Sherman and Brookston. By the same year another portion of the Trans-Continental line, known as the Jefferson branch, was completed between Marshall and Texarkana, 69 miles. By 1876 the main line had reached Fort Worth, and the Trans-Continental branch had been extended from Texarkana to Sherman.[50]

At the close of the Davis administration the Missouri, Kansas, and Texas Railroad was just entering the state. It had pushed through the Indian Territory to Denison, four miles south of the Red River. There it made connection with the Houston and Texas Central.[51]

Three years earlier, in 1870, the Twelfth Legislature had given the company, incorporated under Kansas laws, authority to construct a line across Texas from the Red River to the Rio Grande, with the proposed route going by way of Waco and Austin to Camargo on the Rio Grande. From there the line was to be extended to Mexico City.

Several minor railroads operated in the east and southeast sections of the state, but none of them had as much as one hundred miles of track. The Galveston, Houston, and Henderson extended only from Galveston to Houston, but for many years this was the exclusive link

[49] *Texas Almanac,* 1871, p. 182.
[50] Potts, *Railroad Transportation in Texas,* pp. 52–54; S. G. Reed, *A History of the Texas Railroads,* p. 362.
[51] *Texas Almanac,* 1873, p. 36.

COL. O. W. WHEELER'S HERD, EN ROUTE FOR KANSAS PACIFIC RAILWAY

PLATE 9. A cattle drive on the trail to Kansas. From the University of Texas
Archives.

PLATE 10. The Sam Houston Stage Coach preparing to leave 8th
Street and Congress Avenue in Austin for San Antonio in 1872. From
the Walter E. Long Collection.

between the two cities.[52] Similarly short was the 84-mile-long Galveston, Harrisburg, and San Antonio line.[53] In 1870 this company had been chartered and permitted to acquire the Buffalo Bayou, Brazos, and Colorado Railway and the Columbus Tap, two lines connecting Harrisburg and Columbus.[54] The terminus remained at Columbus until 1874, when construction was recommenced. By the following year the line reached Luling, 109 miles from Harrisburg.[55] About eight miles from Harrisburg a tap road to Houston made connection with the main line. Another connection, one with Galveston, was possible via the Galveston, Houston, and Henderson. This, however, entailed expense and delay in transferring freight, because the two lines had different gauges.[56]

A merger of the San Antonio and Mexican Gulf Railway and the Indianola road in May, 1871,[57] resulted in a new company: the Gulf, Western Texas, and Pacific, the purpose of which was to connect San Antonio with Port Lavaca. To further the work San Antonio citizens voted to purchase $100,000 in company stock. A branch line to Austin was planned, but in 1873 the length of the road in actual operation was only about forty miles, from Indianola to Victoria.[58]

The old Texas and New Orleans Railroad had completed a road from Houston to Orange in 1861, but it was abandoned after the Civil War.[59] After the company passed into receivership in 1870 a thirty-five mile stretch between Houston and West Liberty was rebuilt.[60] By the end of 1872 a company operating a railroad between Mobile and New Orleans had purchased the Texas and New Orleans, and this corporation became the Mobile, New Orleans, and Texas. It planned to connect Mobile and New Orleans with Houston.[61] Later, in 1876, another part of the old road between West Liberty and Orange was reopened.[62]

---

[52] *Ibid.*, p. 33.   [53] *Ibid.*, p. 34.
[54] Gammel, *Laws of Texas*, VI, 547–551.
[55] Potts, *Railroad Transportation in Texas*, p. 46.
[56] *Texas Almanac*, 1873, p. 34.
[57] Gammel, *Laws of Texas*, VI, 1663–1664.
[58] *Texas Almanac*, 1872, pp. 142–143; 1873, p. 35.
[59] Potts, *Railroad Transportation in Texas*, p. 38.
[60] *Texas Almanac*, 1871, p. 187.
[61] *Ibid.*, 1873, p. 35.
[62] Potts, *Railroad Transportation in Texas*, p. 38.

In northeast Texas, Jefferson residents backed the East Line and Red River Railroad Company in competition with the larger roads that were building into North Texas to the detriment of Jefferson trade.[63] This road was chartered in 1871 to be constructed from Jefferson to Sherman within four years of effecting permanent organization of the company.[64] Although construction had not begun at the beginning of 1873,[65] it was commenced soon afterward. By 1876 this line, a narrow-gauge, had been extended to Greenville, 124 miles away.[66]

The Dallas and Wichita received its charter in 1871 to build a road from Dallas to a point where the Wichita and Red rivers joined,[67] but by 1874 the line had been completed only between Dallas and Lewisville, a distance of about twenty miles.[68]

Railroad lines which years later would weave a web of steel across Texas thus had begun a vigorous expansion by the end of the carpetbag era. The size of the then-largest state was beginning to shrink.

[63] *Ibid.*, pp. 21, 63.
[64] Gammel, *Laws of Texas*, VI, 1188–1190.
[65] *Texas Almanac*, 1873, p. 38.
[66] Potts, *Railroad Transportation in Texas*, p. 63.
[67] Gammel, *Laws of Texas*, VII, 351–354.
[68] Potts, *Railroad Transportation in Texas*, p. 62.

8

THE FINANCIAL STORY

BETWEEN 1870 AND THE CLOSE of 1873 state expenditures were great and taxes were exceedingly high. A heavy debt had been accumulated. With the advent of the Radical Republicans the cost of state administration grew rapidly, for the Republicans not only increased the number of state employees; they also increased salaries and contingent expenses. In 1870, for instance, the governor, who had been receiving a yearly salary of $4,000 since 1866, was voted an increase of $1,000. Substantial raises were also given the secretary of state, the treasurer, the comptroller, the commissioner of the General Land Office, the chief clerks, and the district judges. These increases were unnecessary and placed an added strain on the taxpayers.

Expenditures were further increased by the Legislature, which met in numerous lengthy sessions and spent much time considering special measures, applying to individual corporations, a labor that might have been avoided by the passage of a general corporation act. The Legislature also encouraged needless spending by passing the printing act, the State Police law, and the mileage and per diem measure that provided generously for members.[1] The 1870 printing act provided liberal support for an official party newspaper for the state and for a partisan organ in each district.[2] The police act and the militia act combined resulted in drawing warrants authorizing payment of money from the treasury to the amount of $688,091 between 1871 and 1874

[1] E. T. Miller, *A Financial History of Texas,* pp. 160–161.
[2] H. P. N. Gammel, *Laws of Texas,* VI, 244–249.

165

—this was 15 per cent of all warrants drawn on the general revenue fund.[3]

Nor were the heavy expenditures confined to the legislative department. The cost of the judiciary more than doubled. Most of this expense stemmed from the reorganization of the courts after resumption of civil government, but there were other causes. For instance, fees paid to sheriffs and prosecuting attorneys were needlessly increased.

After 1871 large sums were diverted from the available school fund for frontier protection against Indian depredations; the total thus expended between 1871 and 1874 reached $524,963.[4] Meanwhile expenditures for asylums increased, probably commendably so, but there was evidence of jobbery in supply purchases and building repairs. On the other hand, penitentiary upkeep was not a problem during these years, for the state prison and the inmate labor as well were leased to a private operator, a policy begun in 1871 and continued for a little over a decade. The only state expense was incurred in providing transportation facilities for the convicts.[5]

Twelfth Legislature subsidies to the International, to Southern Pacific, and to Southern Trans-Continental railroads have been described, and they serve as examples of the extravagance of that session. Expenditures went beyond the means of the state and despite heavy taxation, bonds had to be sold to pay expenses. A large floating debt was thus accumulated. Conditions could have been much worse, however, had not Governor Davis been honest in the administration of the public finances.[6]

By February, 1871, the condition of the treasury had become exceedingly uncertain. An anti-Administration newspaper declared:

When E. J. Davis was *counted in* as Governor, we had a little money in the Treasury, and some little credit. One year of radical rule has changed this state of things, and left us without a dollar in the Treasury, and our credit so doubtful as to prevent the borrowing of simply a sum sufficient to

[3] Miller, *Financial History of Texas,* p. 162; Charles W. Ramsdell, *Reconstruction in Texas,* pp. 302, 312.

[4] *Senate Journal, 12th Legislature,* Adjourned Session, p. 206.

[5] Miller, *Financial History of Texas,* p. 162; "Report of Committee on Asylums," *House Journal, 14th Legislature,* p. 14; "Report of Committee on Public Buildings," *ibid.,* p. 161.

[6] Ramsdell, *Reconstruction in Texas,* p. 318; Miller, *Financial History of Texas,* p. 164.

pay the Legislature for plundering the people of their means, and squandering them amongst themselves.

The people have paid their taxes as willingly as could be expected, and with as little complaint as men usually do, who suffer the robber to rifle their pockets, at the muzzle of a loaded revolver. The Legislature is now ready to adjourn and go home, because there is no more money in the Treasury for it to plunder. . . . Nothing has been left undone to filch from the people their hard earned means and then squander them.[7]

On April 4, 1871, the fears of the Conservatives were confirmed. The state treasury was empty. Legislators could not obtain their per diem. State officials were forced to accept their salaries in comptroller's warrants. Payable on presentation to the treasurer, these warrants had to go then to the banks, displaying the treasurer's endorsement of acceptance. Even after that circuitous journey they could be realized only at a loss of from 10 to 12 per cent.[8] Within a week, by April 11, that discount schedule had increased to as much as 25 per cent. That same April 11 the legislative committee on appropriations estimated that $2,000,000 would be needed for the current fiscal year, which amounted to $2.50 for each man, woman, and child in the state.[9]

Taxation was the main money source, and the ad valorem tax on real and personal property was the most lucrative. Assessed by justices of the peace and collected by the sheriff,[10] these ad valorem taxes, state and local, became a heavy burden on the taxpayers. In 1871 the combined rates amounted to as much as $2.17 on each $100. But there were also state and county poll taxes, occupation taxes, and city taxes. Moreover, a levy of approximately $14,000,000 for railroad subsidies had to be provided for. An indication of the rate of tax increase may be had by comparing 1869, when all state and local taxes totaled only $1,129,577, to 1872, when assessed ad valorem, occupation, and local public-school taxes amounted to $4,584,275. Taking 10 per cent as a low average rate of interest on loanable capital, the state and county taxes of $2.17 would be equivalent to an income tax of 21 per cent. It is not surprising, then, that the indirect imposition of this rate through the property tax occasioned bitter dissatisfaction and con-

[7] *Flake's Daily Bulletin,* February 2, 1871, VI, 147.

[8] Frank Brown, "Annals of Travis County and the City of Austin," Ch. XXX, p. 37, MS.

[9] *Ibid.,* p. 38.

[10] Miller, *Financial History of Texas,* pp. 165–166.

demnation.[11] In protest, as mentioned, a state taxpayers' convention was held in Austin on September 22, 23, and 25, 1871, and though it seemed at the time to have accomplished little, it focused attention on the deplorably high levies and assisted in winning a Democratic victory at the polls that November.

Before 1870 corporations had been obliged to pay a property tax and an income tax. But in that year, 1870, the income tax ceased to be used, and a new system of collecting special corporation taxes was introduced: an annual tax of 2 per cent was levied on the gross receipts of railroad, insurance, and telegraph companies, in addition to the general property tax. The following year this was revised so that railroad and telegraph companies became subject to a 1 per cent tax on net receipts, life insurance companies to an annual occupation tax of $500, and fire and marine insurance firms to one of $250. A few days later still another alteration was made; a 1 per cent tax on gross receipts was substituted for the 1 per cent tax on net receipts. But this schedule was unfair to the railroads, which held a much larger amount of taxable property than did the telegraph companies. Consequently, the Legislature passed another bill a short time later excusing railroads from the property tax. The Governor vetoed it, declaring that since the counties were not allowed to tax railroad receipts, it was only just that the ad valorem tax should not be removed. The Legislature soon repealed the receipts tax, but the ad valorem property tax was left in force.

Another business tax levied during this period was the occupation tax, embracing an ever-expanding number of vocations after discontinuance of the income tax. Frequent changes were made in occupation taxes, those levied on the retail liquor business exhibiting especially radical fluctuations. Laws providing for these taxes were neither well framed nor well administered; penalties for nonpayment were light and checkups on collections were few.[12]

Beginning in 1871 adult male citizens also had to pay two poll taxes of $1 each,[13] one for the upkeep of the public schools and the other for the maintenance of roads and bridges. Prior to 1871 there had been an annual poll tax of $1 applying to all males over twenty-one years

[11] *Ibid.*, p. 167.
[12] Miller, *Financial History of Texas,* pp. 170–171.
[13] Gammel, *Laws of Texas,* VI, 945–946.

of age;[14] this same levy, in 1871, became the poll tax for schools and henceforth was to be paid by all men between the ages of twenty-one and sixty.[15] A person who failed to meet this obligation was not allowed to receive any state or county money due him until he paid the tax with interest.[16] The road and bridge poll tax was imposed at the discretion of the county court on every male citizen over twenty-one years of age, but any person could avoid its payment by working on roads or bridges at the rate of $1 per day.[17]

In addition to taxes the state raised money through the sale and hypothecation of bonds. During the years 1871–1874 receipts from bonds amounted to $1,406,650.60. The sum derived from taxation during the same period was $3,900,766.[18] Land sales also brought some money—but not much, because the state followed a policy of giving away the public domain to those who would live on it for three years and pay the land-office fees. School lands could not be given away to settlers or railroads, but the sale of them was small. In fact, during the Davis administration there was no provision for the disposal of school, university, and asylum lands;[19] the Constitution of 1869 prohibited the sale of certificates at the land office except to settlers of tracts not exceeding one hundred and sixty acres.[20]

A discussion of the Davis Administration finances would be incomplete without an examination of educational funds. The Constitution of 1869 had taken some important steps toward increasing an already-existent, though small, school fund by assigning to it all public-domain revenue, one-fourth of the annual receipts from taxation, and a poll tax of $1. The Constitution further stipulated that all endowments previously made to the fund should be confirmed and that the Legislature could raise such amounts in each school district as would be necessary to provide schoolhouses and to ensure the education of all eligible inhabitants.[21]

[14] Miller, *Financial History of Texas,* p. 171.
[15] Gammel, *Laws of Texas,* VI, 945.
[16] Miller, *Financial History of Texas,* p. 171.
[17] Gammel, *Laws of Texas,* VI, 946.
[18] Miller, *Financial History of Texas,* p. 172.
[19] *Ibid.,* p. 172.
[20] Gammel, *Laws of Texas,* VII, 395–427.
[21] *Ibid.*

Then an act passed on August 13, 1870, divided the general school funds into a permanent fund and an available fund.[22] Under provisions of the act the permanent fund consisted of all moneys standing to the credit of the "school fund" in the state treasury, all lands previously surveyed and set apart for establishing a primary school or academy, fines and forfeitures and land sales receipts that had already been set apart for school purposes, and all sums due the school fund from individuals and corporations. All this was to be consolidated and converted into United States bonds, and only the interest was to be applied to the support of public schools.

The available school fund was made up of one-fourth of the annual revenue derived from taxation, the annual poll tax of $1, and the interest accruing to the permanent fund. This was to be applied exclusively to they payment of teachers' salaries and to the expenses of the educational bureau.[23] The sum paid into the available fund during the years 1871–1874 amounted to $1,053,625.[24]

On April 22, 1871, the financial condition of the schools was further improved by the passage of an ad valorem property tax of one-fourth the amount of the direct ad valorem state tax on all the real and personal property owned in each school district. Money from this levy was to be used for construction of school buildings. The act itself carried out a provision of the Constitution of 1869 already mentioned.[25]

Two days later, on April 24, 1871, an act to organize and maintain a system of free public schools was passed. It gave the directors of each school district authority to levy a tax of not more than 1 per cent for the purpose of building schoolhouses and maintaining schools in their respective districts.[26] School finances were thus further increased, but the act evoked a storm of criticism from the taxpayers who met in Austin in September.[27] This law also stated that the available school fund should receive all of the interest accruing to the permanent school fund from the railroads or from any other source after March 30, 1870, one-fourth of the ad valorem and occupation taxes

[22] *Ibid.,* VI, 287–292.
[23] *Ibid.*
[24] Miller, *Financial History of Texas,* p. 173.
[25] Gammel, *Laws of Texas,* VI, 949.
[26] *Ibid.,* VI, 959–962.
[27] *Democratic Statesman,* September 23, 1871, I, 26.

assessed since that date, and such other taxes as had been provided by law for the support of public schools.[28]

During this period a question of particular significance for the permanent fund arose concerning the adjustment of the indebtedness of the railroads to the fund.[29] Since 1856 loans of $6,000 for every completed mile had been made from the permanent school fund to any railroad company that could prove construction of as much as twenty-five miles of track and completion of a graded section, of the same length, ready for rails and ties. To obtain the loan the railroad company was required to execute a bond for the amount of money received and to pay 8 per cent upon it annually.[30] After the war, however, the railroads were unable to meet their obligations, and as has been discussed, a general relief act was passed in August, 1870, permitting the companies to avoid being sold for debt by paying on November 1, 1870, six months' interest on the aggregate amount due—both principal and interest as it stood on May 1, 1870—and by paying an additional 1 per cent for the sinking fund. The companies were, of course, required to repeat these payments semiannually on May 1 and November 1 of each year.[31]

Of no importance during the Davis administration was the university fund. Laws were passed in 1870 and 1871 authorizing the sale of university lands to secure funds for building a university, but in both instances they were vetoed by Governor Davis. Soon after Coke became governor, however, a measure was passed—on April 8, 1874—providing for their sale.[32] Activity in behalf of an agricultural and mechanical college was more evident. As a result of a congressional act of 1862 and a supplementary act passed in 1866 the United State government gave Texas land scrip for 180,000 acres for the purpose of establishing such a college. Not until 1871 was the scrip placed on sale following the passage of a state law providing for the establishment of the college. It brought 87 cents an acre and a

[28] Gammel, *Laws of Texas,* VI, 959–962.
[29] This matter was discussed in detail in an earlier chapter and will only be mentioned here.
[30] Gammel, *Laws of Texas,* IV, 449; Charles Shirley Potts, *Railroad Transportation in Texas,* pp. 90–91.
[31] Gammel, *Laws of Texas,* VI, 259; Potts, *Railroad Transportation in Texas,* p. 91.
[32] Miller, *Financial History of Texas,* p. 175.

total of $156,600. The sum was invested in 7-per-cent frontier defense bonds of the state and in 10-per-cent bonds of Brazos County. Under the pretense that it was essential to purchase the lands required for the site of the college $12,000 was drawn from the fund, but the money was loaned, and the notes held by the comptroller were not paid. Nor was this all of the money lost, for $21,096 was spent on a worthless foundation for the main building.[33]

The public debt of the Davis Administration can be said to have begun in August, 1870, when $750,000 in 7-per-cent gold bonds, redeemable after twenty years and payable after forty years, were issued in order to maintain ranging companies on the frontier. The act initiating this also provided for a tax sufficient to pay the interest on the bonds and to provide a sinking fund of 2 per cent to pay the principal at maturity. The Governor was to direct the selling or hypothecating of the issues at the best price possible and to employ agents to sell them. The commission allowed to the agents was not to exceed 1 per cent.[34] When specifications went to the engraver Treasurer Honey and Comptroller Bledsoe refused to give their signatures for the bonds, declaring that the credit of the state would thus be placed in the hands of the engraver. Governor Davis, however, differed with them strongly, for he felt that the bonds had been correctly prepared and that there had been no error in specifications.[35] The absence of their signatures, as well as other faults, caused the New York *Herald* to comment:

An issue of $750,000 in Texas bonds will soon be on the market; and it will be well for our moneyed men to remember that said bonds are, in their origin, mere parenthetical, or inferential bonds, no act but a simple parenthesis or inference in an act, authorizing their issual; in their mode of preparation authenticated only by an engraved signature of the Governor, and destitute alike of the autograph of the State Treasurer or the certificate of registration of the State Comptroller; and, finally, in their prospect of ultimate redemption quite visionary, the people of Texas even now holding meetings in various parts of the State, and announcing beforehand to all whom it may concern that they will not pay this parenthetical issue of $750,000, ostensibly issued as bonds for frontier defense, but as the government at Washington has forbidden the raising of a State force on the border,

[33] *Ibid.*, pp. 175–176.
[34] Gammel, *Laws of Texas*, VI, 219–220.
[35] San Antonio *Daily Herald*, September 7, 1870, XIII, 214.

really meant to replenish the pockets of those robber reconstructionists who rule the State.[36]

This and similar publicity tended to undermine confidence in Texas credit; only 350 of the bonds were sold during this period. The transactions occurred in 1871 at an average price of 89.4. The gross amount obtained was $313,200, and after deducting commissions the sum stood at $312,000.[37] Of the 350 bonds sold, half were exchanged for cash held in the agricultural and mechanical college fund; the rest went to outside purchasers. Despite a noticeable lack of faith by the public, the interest on these bonds was met, and a sinking fund was established. By law this fund was to have been invested in interest bearing United States bonds,[38] but instead without benefit of statute it was used for the purpose of retiring the frontier defense bonds. By August 31, 1874, the amount of bonds thus redeemed was $53,000.

To alleviate the annual current-revenue deficiencies that began in fiscal 1870, bond sales were authorized. A $400,000 issue, in 10-per-cent bonds redeemable after two years and payable after five years, was authorized on May 2, 1871 to cover the deficiencies of 1871 and 1872. In December of 1871 another issue—of $2,000,000—was made, in 7-per-cent, twenty-year bonds. In neither instance was there any restriction as to selling price, and for the December issue there were no commission restrictions. Then, in 1873, the state faced the necessity of funding existing warrants. In consequence, $500,000 10-per-cent bonds were issued, redeemable after three years and payable after ten years.

Of the deficiency bonds, which had been issued under an act of May 2, 1871, 252 were sold during 1871 and 1872. At an average price of 93.5 they yielded $229,375.94, with the commissions already deducted. Of this, $156,433.47 was received in state warrants.[39] The deficiency bonds authorized under the act of December 2, 1871, however remained unsold—and only $89,800 of the 10-per-cent funding bonds had been issued to August 31, 1874. In addition to these bonds sold, 350 of the remaining frontier defense and 100 deficiency issues

---

[36] Austin *Daily Republican*, October 15, 1870, III, 116, quoting from the New York *Herald*.

[37] "Statement of the Comptroller," *House Journal, 16th Legislature*, First Session, p. 79; Miller, *Financial History of Texas*, p. 192.

[38] Gammel, *Laws of Texas*, VI, 220.

[39] *House Journal, 16th Legislature, First Session*, p. 79.

were hypothecated for $327,074.70 with Williams and Guion of New York.

By August 31, 1874, the funded debt of the state had been increased by a gross amount of $900,900. Of this, $57,100 was redeemed, leaving the net addition $843,800. In addition to this, there was a floating debt of $1,574,826.31, making a total debt contracted before the end of the Davis regime, of $2,418,626.31.[40] This did not, however, include the doubtfully valid debt of $809,311.67 due the school and university funds from railroads and other sources. The total of the recognized and doubtful debts thus was $3,227,937.98. Deducting a pre-reconstruction debt of $956,321.88 (a figure ascertained by the auditorial boards of 1868 and 1871), the university-fund debt with accrued interest, and the school fund debt, there remained $2,271,616.10, which was the reconstruction debt proper. The Davis administration was responsible for virtually all of it; obligations incurred before the end of Davis' term, on January 14, 1874, amounted to approximately $2,172,262.21.

Davis' debt policy is obviously subject to condemnation. Bonds were issued to meet revenue deficiencies created by extravagant spending. The funded debt bore as many as five different shapes and was issued under as many different laws. Had it been issued more uniformly it would have held a greater attraction for investors. Warrants were discounted as high as 50 per cent, and it was common to see men or boys hired by merchants wait in the treasurer's office from morning until night, day after day if necessary, for deposits of money to be made so that their warrants might be cashed.[41]

The most obvious characteristics, then, of the Davis financial system were its increases in expenditures, in taxation, and in the public debt. At that, however, although, it did not entirely escape dishonesty of state officials, Texas fared better than certain other Southern states, where theft was encouraged by carpetbag administrators.

[40] Miller, *Financial History of Texas,* p. 193.
[41] *Ibid.,* pp. 193–194.

SECTION III THE FRONTIER PROBLEM

THE NATIONAL AND STATE
INDIAN POLICIES

THE FEDERAL "PEACE POLICY"

THE INDIAN ADMINISTRATION of the federal government consisted of two programs, entirely distinct and apparently inconsistent. One regulated the treatment of potentially-hostile tribes like the Comanches, Kiowas, and Apaches. The other was concerned with the management of tribes that were less dangerous because of traditional friendship, numerical weakness, or location. The peaceful Indians, who were partially cared for by the United States government, are of scant importance to this study and will not be discussed. They did not menace the frontier. Emphasis will be placed instead on the savages who bolted reservations in the Indian Territory and on the still-at-large savages who swept down from the high plains; both groups had a common purpose, the spreading of death and destruction in the western portion of the state.

With respect to the hostile bands the federal government followed what was known as a "peace policy." Its purpose was to assemble the wandering tribes on reservations having clearly-defined boundaries. There civilian employees, working under agents, instructed them in agriculture and otherwise educated them as much as possible. Only when the Indians left their reservations to commit acts of murder, plunder, or theft did they come under the jurisdiction of the Army.

Theoretically the system might have been an excellent one, but in practicality it was not satisfactory. To make a cordon around the reservation a large army would have been required. This, of course, was not available, and the military protection offered to settlers living near the reservations was inadequate. Hostile tribes encountered little difficulty

177

in leaving the Indian Territory, descending into Texas, committing depredations, then returning to the safety of their reservations.[1] Moreover, Army officers were under orders not to allow their soldiers to enter reservations in pursuit, for as soon as the Indian returned to his government-provided home he fell wholly under the jurisdiction of the agents in charge. Troops located on reservations were stationed there only to assist the agents in preserving order.[2]

The Commissioner of Indian Affairs was Colonel E. S. Parker, himself a member of the Seneca tribe, an able administrator and a cultivated, honorable man.[3] Members of the Quaker sect were chosen as agents for the Indian Territory, consistent with the federal government "peace policy."[4] But many savages there refused to share this amity, for the Comanches, Kiowas, and Apaches residing in the Indian Territory were responsible for most of the depredations in Texas in the early seventies. These Indians maintained that they were free to roam at will in Texas, having been driven from their hunting grounds there by a superior force. They also declared they would never relinquish their claims to Texas soil and would never cease raiding there until an amicable settlement was reached. The Commissioner of Indian Affairs, anxious to end the depredations, recommended in 1870 that the federal government negotiate a reconciliation of differences.[5] But the mere suggestion of a treaty with any hostile Indians was repugnant to Texans. In the Brenham *Banner* one citizen, Dan McCary, commented:

The idea of making "treaties" with the Comanches is supremely absurd; just as well make treaties with rattlesnakes and Mexican tigers. Property will be stolen, men murdered, women ravished, and children carried into captivity on our frontier until the Indians are all killed off, or until they are all caught and caged like wild beasts in a show.[6]

[1] San Antonio *Daily Herald,* April 29, 1873, XVI, 100. This paper quoted a letter from General William T. Sherman to a friend.

[2] *Daily State Journal,* October 18, 1870, I, 223. This was a quotation from General Pope's orders to his men.

[3] *Ibid.,* January 6, 1871, I, 290, and October 4, 1870, I, 211. For Parker's initials, see Enoch Hoag to E. S. Parker, June 27, 1870, Letters Regarding Kiowa and Comanche Indians, 1870, MS.

[4] *Daily State Journal,* January 6, 1871, I, 290.

[5] *Annual Report of the Commissioner of Indian Affairs to the Secretary of the Interior for 1870–1871,* II, 719.

[6] *Daily State Journal,* December 22, 1870, I, 278, quoting from the Brenham *Banner.*

PLATE 11. Satanta, Kiowa chief, convicted perpetrator of the Salt Creek Massacre near Jacksboro in 1871. The Fort Worth *Star-Telegram,* Texas Collection.

PLATE 12. Big Tree, a Kiowa brave convicted, along with Satanta, for participating in the Salt Creek Massacre. The Fort Worth *Star-Telegram,* Texas Collection.

Apparently no formal peace treaty was made at this time.[7] It is true that early in 1870 the Kiowas promised to cease their depredations in Texas, but the declaration meant nothing to them. Their raiding parties continued as if no such word had been given.[8]

Secretary of Interior C. Delano was informed of these plundering expeditions, but he took no steps to halt them. Furthermore, after the savages returned to their reservations they were not punished, although invariably they would have murdered Texas residents. At Fort Sill, in the Indian Territory, Agent Laurie Tatum reported that the savages returned from raids and offered to sell captive women and children to the officers. He also said they brandished bloody scalps in the face of General B. H. Grierson and demanded presents, which were given them.[9]

In May, 1871, General W. T. Sherman visited Fort Sill and observed conditions with extreme displeasure. Amazed that the raiding Indians were allowed to remain unpunished, he wrote Adjutant General E. D. Townsend and offered a solution. The letter was dated May 24, 1871.

I advise the Indian Agent here be instructed to issue supplies only to Indians present, that when there is proof of murder and robbery the actual perpetrators be surrendered for trial and punishment. A few examples would have a salutary effect.

. . . By keeping the picket now at the mouth of the Cache creek and the other at Camp Radziminski active in the country south of Red River, these Comanches would find it more difficult to get out and still more so to get back on the Reservation with stolen stock. But the greatest advantage must result from refusing supplies to families whose adults are absent in Texas and in impowering the agents to surrender criminals. Now these Indians openly boast of their deeds of bravery in Texas and even show scalps taken in their raids.

[7] *Daily State Journal,* May 6, 1871, II, 86. A treaty between the United States and the Kiowa and Comanche Indians was made in October, 1867, in which a reservation was set apart for these Indians. Another treaty proclaimed in August, 1868, provided that the Apache tribe of Indians should become confederated and incorporated with the Comanches and Kiowas and accept the reservation in the Indian Territory as their permanent home. But the author found no evidence of any peace treaty being concluded in the early seventies.

[8] Tatum to Hoag, November 4, 1870. Letters Regarding Kiowa and Comanche Indians, 1870, MS.

[9] *Daily State Journal,* May 6, 1871, II, 86.

179

Though the Kiowas and Comanches have been located on this reservation for two years, I hear of none engaged in agriculture and Mr. Tatum told me to-day that not a single child of these two tribes was now at his school.

Their progress in civilization is a farce.[10]

Informed of Sherman's suggestion, Commissioner Parker immediately expressed his support of it to Interior Secretary Delano, whose department included the Indian Bureau. Delano himself also approved Sherman's plan. In June, 1871, he sent the following dispatch to Adjutant General Townsend:

. . . Your instructions to Superintendent Hoag to instruct Agent Tatum to issue supplies only to those Indians of the agency who are present on the reservation and withhold them from the families of those who are absent on raids, as requested by General Sherman, are eminently proper.

Inasmuch as the military authorities under the construction of your circular letter of July 12, 1869, to Superintendents and Agents of the Indian Department are unwilling to pursue and arrest criminal and predatory Indians within and upon the Indian Territory and to recover property taken by said Indians into said Territory, I suggest that you inform the War Department that hereafter, and until otherwise advised by your office, the military authorities may be permitted to enter the Indian Territory at all times in the pursuit and arrest of predatory and criminal Indians and for the purpose of recovering property and captives held by such Indians.[11]

Delano's suggestion, however, was unheeded by the Department of War. Reservation Indians continued to escape serious punishment for their crimes: at most, rations and annuity goods were forbidden those who held captives, and the Indians were not allowed to receive ransom for the return of their prisoners.[12]

The attitude of victimized Texas settlers toward the "peace policy" may well be imagined. Almost unprotected, they lived in constant dread of horrible death, an occurrence they had often witnessed; yet the savages who committed these atrocities seemed to be supported by the federal government. The insecurity and bewilderment of the uneasy settlers was evidenced in an appeal for protection sent to President Grant by Charles Howard, judge of the Thirteenth Judicial District and a Weatherford citizen.

[10] General W. T. Sherman to Adjutant General E. D. Townsend, May 24, 1871. Letters Regarding Kiowa and Comanche Indians, 1871, MS.

[11] C. Delano to E. S. Parker, June 20, 1871, *ibid.*

[12] *Annual Report of the Commissioner of Indian Affairs, 1872,* pp. 247–248.

. . . For a long time have this people (the frontier people of Texas) endured an almost uninterrupted war-fare bloody and savage at the hands of the several bands of Indians now falsely said to be upon the Ft. Sill Reservations. But sir those depredations have been growing from bad to worse until they are perfectly alarming to our people. I might give your Excellency scores of instances of recent date of murder, rape, and robbery which they have committed alone in the counties composing my Judicial District. It has been but a few days since the whole Lee family consisting of six persons were inhumanly butchered, three of them being females were ravished, murdered and most terribly mutilated. Then Mr. Dobs, Justice of Peace of Palo Pinto County was but last week murdered and scalped, his ears and nose were cut off. Mr. Peoples and Mr. Crawford of said county met the same fate. Wm. McCluskey was but yesterday shot down by those same bloody Quaker Pets upon his own threshold. I write to your Excellency, as to one who from your Exalted Position in our nation *can* if you *will* protect us from this inhuman butchery. . . .

. . . Your humble correspondent believes your Excellency to be endowed with at least a moderate amount of human feeling and a mind that cannot be trammeled by this one dread *Insane* Pseudo humanitarian Policy: called the "Quaker Indian Peace Policy." Am I mistaken?[13]

The peace policy, an obvious failure, again drew criticism from General Sherman in April, 1873, when he recommended that the Indian Bureau be placed under War Department control. Sherman asserted that the Indian problem could thus be dealt with much more efficiently. He observed:

From the organization of the government up to 1850, the Indians and Indian Bureau were under the war department, so that nearly all the civilization and Christianization of the Indians thus far accomplished occurred under army supervision. To-day, in case an Indian suffers a wrong, I believe he will be more likely to appeal to the commanding officers of the nearest military post than to his own agent; for in the one he sees with his eyes the evidence of a force to compel obedience, whereas in the other nothing of the kind. In like manner I believe the annuities to treaty Indians would reach the parties in interest quite as surely through army officers as through civilians. And when Indians have committed depredations—as is very common—and the annuities are chargeable with amount of damages, such stoppages could more safely be made by a commanding officer having soldiers at his back than by an agent afraid of his life—as too many of them are and have reason to be.

[13] Chas. Howard to President U. S. Grant, July 15, 1872. Letters Regarding Kiowa and Comanche Indians, 1872, MS.

Sherman also noted that not only were the Indians able to continue their depredations without punishment, but that under the protection of the Quaker Indian agents their plunder proved quite profitable.

. . . So that in fact, these reservations help them in their lucrative business, I am safe in saying that half the horses and mules now owned by the Kiowas, Comanches, Cheyennes, Arapahoes, Sioux, etc.—all treaty Indians, all at peace, with agencies and annuities—have been stolen from the United States or from citizens. I have myself seen, at the Kiowa and Comanche agency, and at several of the Sioux agencies, horses and mules branded "U.S." led up to be packed with the annuity goods, and I never heard of an agent demanding the restitution of one for that reason; and though murders are of so frequent occurrence, I do not hear of the murderers being surrendered, as is required by the treaties. . . . All I will venture to assert is, that the army has a much more difficult task now than if we were at actual war, and could anticipate depredations and follow the perpetrators to their very camps, as I did in the case of the Kiowas two years ago.[14]

Weak though the Quaker Indian policy was, it should not be presumed that Texans of the early seventies were without any military protection at all. To guard the northern and western frontiers soldiers were stationed at Fort Richardson in Jack County, Fort Griffin in Shackelford County, Fort Concho in Tom Green County, Fort McKavett in Menard County, and Fort Stockton in Pecos County. Chief threats to the outlying settlements north and west were the Kiowas and Comanches, who were mainly responsible for the construction of these fortifications. Along the southern border lay Fort Duncan in Maverick County, Fort Clark in Kinney County, and Forts Davis and Quitman in the Big Bend area. Personnel of these four forts were responsible for preventing the Kickapoos and other Indians residing in Mexico from conducting raiding parties into Texas.[15]

[14] San Antonio *Daily Herald,* April 29, 1873, XVI, 100. Sherman refers here to the part he played in the Jacksboro affair, which will be described in detail later.

[15] *Annual Report of the Commissioner of Indian Affairs, 1872,* p. 92; Carl Coke Rister, *The Southwestern Frontier,* pp. 44, 51–52, 61. The Commisioner of Indian Affairs in his report to the Secretary of the Interior for 1872 did not mention Fort Brown which was re-established on the lower Rio Grande in 1865. Neither did the report include Fort McIntosh, regarrisoned in the same region in 1867, nor Fort Bliss at El Paso which was reoccupied by soldiers in

Commanding these fortifications was General J. J. Reynolds, who had been the military executive in Texas when the state reentered the Union on March 30, 1870, and who was, of course, retained as commander of the Department of Texas, comprising Texas and Louisiana.[16] Although the number of soldiers was always inadequate, Reynolds handled the situation commendably. Early in 1872, however, he was relieved by General C. C. Augur.[17]

THE JACKSBORO TROUBLE

On May 18, 1871, at a point approximately seventeen miles southwest of Fort Richardson, a party of about 150 reservation Indians attacked and captured a ten-wagon train,[18] killing the wagon master and six teamsters. Several bodies were badly mutilated, and one man was chained to a wagon wheel and burned. Five men escaped; one of them, Thomas Brazeal, despite a painful foot injury, somehow dragged himself to Jacksboro and reported the affair.[19] The Indian band had been led by Satanta, Satank, and Big Tree of the Kiowa tribe.[20] But some Apaches and Cheyennes were said to be in the group, which had apparently set out to fight the Tonkawa Indians near Fort Griffin.[21]

General Sherman happened to be visiting Fort Richardson on a tour of inspection, and he immediately ordered all available men in companies A, D, E, and F of the Fourth Cavalry (commanded by Brevet

---

the same year (Rister, *The Southwestern Frontier*, pp. 64–65). These fortifications had been evacuated during the Civil War, and although re-established after it, were evidently not being used as late as 1872.

[16] Houston *Daily Union*, April 22, 1870, II, 38.

[17] *Daily State Journal*, February 4, 1872, III, 7. It is true that Reynolds was accused of showing undue favoritism in the awarding of contracts for transportation, but this was not proved.

[18] Laurie Tatum to Enoch Hoag, May 25, 1871, Letters Regarding Kiowa and Comanche Indians, 1871, MS.; James Cox, *Historical and Biographical Records of the Cattle Industry and the Cattlemen of Texas and Adjacent Territory*, p. 289. Hereafter cited as Cox, *Cattle Industry of Texas*.

[19] Tatum to Hoag, May 25, 1871, Letters Regarding Kiowa and Comanche Indians, 1871, MS.; *Annual Report of the Commissioner of Indian Affairs, 1872*, p. 502; Rister, *The Southwestern Frontier*, p. 128.

[20] Cox, *Cattle Industry of Texas*, p. 289.

[21] Tatum to Hoag, May 20, 1871, Letters Regarding Kiowa and Comanche Indians, 1871, MS.

Major General R. S. Mackenzie) to follow and punish the Indians.[22] But the savages escaped and vanished into the safety of the Indian Territory.

Two days later a delegation of citizens from Jack and Parker counties visited General Sherman to protest the lack of protection for settlements along the northern border. But Sherman was already aware of the problem, having observed results of Indian depredations during his journey from Fort McKavett to Fort Richardson. Inspector General Randolph B. Marcy, who had accompanied him, wrote in his journal on May 17:

> ... The remains of several ranches were observed, the occupants of which have either been killed or driven off to the more dense settlements by the Indians. Indeed, this rich and beautiful section does not contain as many white people to-day as it did when I visited it eighteen years ago, and, if the Indian marauders are not punished, the whole country seems to be in a fair way to become totally depopulated.[23]

Sherman needed no persuasion, then, to give the delegation his word to do all he could to effect reforms in the national military policy. Soon thereafter the General departed for Fort Sill, where he arrived May 23. General Marcy again provided a description of events, in a May 27 journal entry.

> This afternoon about four o'clock, several Kiowa chiefs, among them Satanta, Satank, Kicking Bird, and Lone Wolf, came to the agency to draw their rations. In a talk with agent Tatem, Satanta said he, with one hundred warriors, had made the recent attack upon the trains between Fort Richardson and Belknap; that they had killed seven teamsters and driven off forty-one mules. This he considered a meritorious exploit and said: "If any other Indian claimed the credit of it he would be a liar"; that he was the man who commanded. He pointed out Satank, Big Tree and another chief as having been with him in the action. The agent immediately reported the facts to General Sherman and requested him to arrest the Indians concerned; whereupon the General sent for them and Satanta acknowledged what he had stated to the agent, when the General informed him that he would place them in confinement and send them to Texas for trial by the civil authorities. Satanta, seeing that he was likely to get into trouble, replied that, although he was present at the fight, he did not kill anybody himself,

---

[22] Rister, *The Southwestern Frontier*, p. 128; J. W. Wilbarger, *Indian Depredations in Texas*, p. 554.

[23] Cox, *Cattle Industry of Texas*, p. 289.

neither did he blow his bugle. His young men wanted to have a little fight and to take a few white scalps, and he was prevailed upon to go with them merely to show them how to make war, but that he stood back during the engagement and merely gave directions. He added that some time ago the whites had killed three of his people and wounded more, so that this little affair made the accounts square, and that he was now ready to commence anew—cry quits. General Sherman told him it was a very cowardly thing for one hundred warriors to attack twelve poor teamsters who did not pretend to know how to fight. That if he desired to have a battle the soldiers were ready to meet them at any time. That he would send the three men to Texas for trial. Seeing no escape Satanta remarked that rather than be sent to Texas he preferred being shot on the spot . . .[24]

The chiefs were arrested. The rest of the Kiowas fled from the area, no doubt shocked that Agent Tatum allowed Sherman to arrest their leaders on the very reservation.[25] Northern border Texans were no less surprised, but their jubilation can be imagined. At last, they believed, hostile savages from the Indian Territory would be controlled. At this time the most popular man on the Texas frontier was, obviously General Sherman.[26]

A few days after the arrest of the Kiowa chieftains General Mackenzie arrived at Fort Sill, having followed their trail back to the reservation.[27] Sherman relinquished the prisoners to Mackenzie with orders to take them back to Jack County, where the crime had been committed. They were to be released to civil authorities at Jacksboro for trial. Mackenzie had the three chiefs bound and handcuffed and placed under guard in a wagon.

The journey had scarcely begun before Satank, wrapped in a blanket, began boasting loudly to his two comrades that he was a brave warrior and a great chief, and complaining that he was too old to be thus mistreated. About a mile from the post he pointed, with his shackled hands, to a tree near a ford and said, "I shall never go beyond that tree." He then began singing a mournful death song:

Oh Sun, you remain forever, but we Kaitensko must die.
Oh Earth, you remain forever, but we Kaitensko must die.

[24] *Ibid.*, p. 290–291.
[25] *Tri-Weekly State Gazette,* June 21, 1871, IV, 61.
[26] *Daily State Journal,* June 13, 1871, II, 118.
[27] Rister, *The Southwestern Frontier,* p. 132; *Daily State Journal,* June 21, 1871, IV, 61.

Unobserved by his guards, he had gnawed the flesh from one of his wrists. This allowed him room to squeeze his hand out of the shackle. He threw a blanket off his shoulders, seized a knife he had hidden under it, and attacked one of the two guards riding with them. Both soldiers leaped from the wagon, leaving their weapons behind in their haste. Satank grabbed a rifle and aimed it at the guards, but before he could fire he was killed by a mounted trooper riding nearby.

The other two chiefs, Satanta and Big Tree, were safely delivered to Jacksboro, where they were brought to trial in district court on July 5, 1871. The case was sensational, for in addition to the ghastliness of the crime this was the first time reservation Indians had been surrendered to civil authorities for trial. The defendants were represented by Thomas Ball and J. A. Woolfork of Weatherford; prosecuting attorney was S. W. T. Lanham, who later became governor of Texas.[28] During the trial Satanta spoke in his own behalf and exhibited all the sagacity and cunning credited to him. Denying none of the charges, he dwelt on his tribal influence and the revenge that the Kiowas would surely reap if he were executed.

Both chiefs, tried separately, were given death sentences.[29] But when the Superintendent of Indian Affairs, Enoch Hoag, learned the outcome he begged President Grant to intervene, declaring that if the two were executed an Indian war would no doubt follow.[30] This and other pressure brought a Federal request to Governor Davis that he commute the sentences to life imprisonment, and he did this.[31] The two Indians were taken to Huntsville under guard and placed in the state penitentiary.[32]

Kiowas on the reservation were told that the fate of their chiefs depended on future behavior of the tribe, but their conduct did not improve noticeably though the frequency of their frontier raids decreased. The Kiowa agent, a Quaker of unquestioned ability, declared

[28] Rister, *The Southwestern Frontier,* pp. 132–133; Wilbarger, *Indian Depredations in Texas,* pp. 562–563, 567–568; Cox, *Cattle Industry of Texas,* p. 291.

[29] *Daily State Journal,* July 18, 1871, II, 146.

[30] Rister, *The Southwestern Frontier,* pp. 137–138.

[31] Ed. R. Smith to E. J. Davis, October 7, 1873, Letters Regarding Kiowa and Comanche Indians, 1873, MS.

[32] Rister, *The Southwestern Frontier,* p. 138.

that the tribe remained uncontrollable and that nothing short of military authority with punishment by troops would subject them.[33]

At this juncture all Southwest tribes apparently began preparing for war. Seriously concerned, President Grant summoned leaders of the Cheyenne, Arapahoe, Comanche, Kiowa, and Apache tribes to Washington to talk peace. The Kiowas, at first reluctant, consented to go only after receiving a promise that they would be allowed to confer with Satanta and Big Tree somewhere along the route. St. Louis was selected, and Satanta and Big Tree were taken there from Huntsville in July, 1872, under heavy guard. Lone Wolf and other Kiowa braves conferred with them.

At St. Louis Satanta and Big Tree were delivered to the Special Commissioner of Indian Affairs, H. E. Alford. With the two chiefs went a letter from Governor Davis to Secretary of the Interior Delano in which Davis set down two conditions he deemed essential to the future of Texas: surrender of all arms and horses by all Fort Sill Indians and daily muster of all savages on the reservation. But the Governor did not assent to the release of the two Indians on any terms,[34] and they were returned to Huntsville.

In the Washington conferences, however, the Commissioner of Indian Affairs ignored Davis' stipulations and promised the Kiowa representatives that Satanta and Big Tree would be released about April 1, 1873, if the tribe would discontinue its attacks on the settlements.[35] This was a presumptuous move, because the Governor of Texas and not the President of the United States had authority over the two Indians. Furthermore, at about the same time, the Texas legislature voted overwhelmingly to ask Governor Davis not to grant any request for the liberation of the two chiefs.

When General Sherman learned of the federal offer to release them he wrote Secretary Delano:

. . . I hope when Satanta is released and when he is actually killed at the head of a raiding party off the reservation (as certain as next year comes),

[33] *Annual Report of the Commissioner of Indian Affairs, 1872,* pp. 136–137.

[34] Henry E. Alford to E. P. Smith, September 20, 1873, Letters Regarding Kiowa and Comanche Indians, 1873, MS.

[35] Rister, *The Southwestern Frontier,* p. 140.

you will simply decree that the Kiowas are outlawed, their property confiscated, and their most valuable reservation restored to the public domain.

. . . I believe that Satanta has done fifty murders. Indeed, my idea is that the Indian by nature can't help it. He should no more be tempted by a horse or a convenient scalp than a child should with candy.[36]

Nevertheless, on March 22, 1873, Secretary Delano dispatched a letter to Governor Davis[37] declaring that since the federal government had promised the Kiowas their chiefs' freedom provided tribal conduct was good, President Grant would be glad to see Satanta and Big Tree pardoned on April 15.[38] Kiowa conduct, the Secretary added, warranted the release. Davis did not agree to liberate them on that date, but later he consented to discuss their proposed freedom at an autumn council in the Indian Territory. This convened at Fort Sill on October 4. Present besides Governor Davis were E. P. Smith, who had become commissioner of Indian affairs in 1873; Enoch Hoag, Indian superintendent; all Indian agents; and chiefs of the Kiowas, Comanches, Wichitas, Caddoes, and plains Apaches. Two days later, on October 6, Governor Davis agreed to release the two Kiowas if the council would accept certain conditions:

. . . I will now tell you my terms for releasing Satanta and Big Tree. Listen. The Kiowas and Comanches to go on that part of the cultivated land in the neighborhood of Fort Sill the location to be so that they may adopt the habits of the whites and cultivate the land and raise cattle like the Cherokees and give up the use of their horses and arms. This movement to commence at once and in the meantime to prevent misunderstanding they will have white men for agents who will remain in their camps and see them all daily so they cannot go on raids. They will draw their rations for three days at a time each man answering for their own rations. If absent it will be taken for granted he is raiding into Texas. Further that the Comanches who have been raiding recently in Texas will be given up and those who remain at peace shall put themselves under the direction of the United States troops and aid in arresting the others—who will be turned over to the authorities of Texas and tried by law. All identified horses to be returned. Satanta and Big Tree to be held until General Davidson at Fort Sill is satisfied all is carried out. After release Satanta and Big Tree must

---

[36] Rister, *The Southwestern Frontier*, pp. 140–141. W. T. Sherman to Delano, April 23, 1873. MS., Semi-official Letters of W. T. Sherman, 1872–1878, MS.

[37] San Antonio *Daily Herald*, April 19, 1873, XVI, 92.

[38] *Ibid.*, April 3, 1873, XVI, 78.

understand that they are at any time liable to be rearrested and punished for their old crimes if they break these conditions that they are not pardoned for I still hold the right to rearrest them. I have consulted with General Davidson and know if you really desire peace you must carry out these terms.[39]

The October 6 meeting disappointed the Kiowas, who expected their chiefs to be released at once. Commissioner Smith told Governor Davis the next day that since the Indians had fulfilled the requirements of the Secretary of the Interior, they felt they were being treated unjustly in not having Satanta and Big Tree returned to them. Furthermore, they could not understand why it was not possible for the President of the United States himself to order the release. Commissioner Smith added:

. . . I have reason to fear that the Kiowas will join the Comanches on the war-path almost immediately, giving as their reason that they have lost faith in the government, then if we are obliged to fight them, it will necessarily be done with the misgiving that the Indians themselves are not altogether in fault.

Smith urged Governor Davis to release Satanta and Big Tree immediately. He promised that if Davis would do this the government would compel the Indians to comply with the Governor's release conditions.[40] Davis accepted these terms, and at a council held the next morning, October 8, the Kiowas were informed that their chiefs would be liberated.[41]

Many Texans disapproved of Davis' action.[42] The *Weekly Demo-*

[39] Record of Indian Council at Fort Sill, October 8, 1873, Report signed by General W. T. Sherman, Letters Regarding Kiowa and Comanche Indians, 1873, MS.

[40] E. P. Smith to E. J. Davis, October 7, 1873, Letters Regarding Kiowa and Comanche Indians, 1873, MS.

[41] E. P. Smith to C. Delano, October 8, 1873, Letters Regarding Kiowa and Comanche Indians, 1873, MS.

[42] San Antonio *Daily Herald,* April 16, 1873. Certain persons had predicted the liberation of Satanta and Big Tree by Governor Davis as soon as it became known that President Grant desired to give them their freedom. The following poem taken from this issue of the newspaper illustrates the reaction of not only the anonymous author but of many other Texans to Grant's desire:

> *By Order of the President*
> Turn loose Satanta and Big Tree!
> How can they ever vex us?
> If they are set at liberty

cratic Statesman accused Davis of working a trade with Grant to obtain federal patronage for Texas.[43] Certain U. S. Army officers were equally unhappy about the decision, and General Sherman was so disgusted that he wrote the Governor:

I believe in making a tour of your frontier with a small escort, I ran the risk of my life; and I said what I now say to you, that I will not again voluntarily assume that risk in the interest of your frontier,[44] that I believe Satanta and Big Tree will have their revenge if they have not already had it, and that if they are to have scalps, that yours is the first that should be taken.[45]

Sherman was evidently correct in his prediction. The Commissioner of Indian Affairs declared in his report for 1874 there was little doubt that the Kiowas had disregarded their covenant of the preceding year and had joined the Comanches, who were definitely known to be raiding into Texas. The Commissioner expressed a belief that it would be impossible to halt these depredations without vigorous operations by federal military forces.[46] Such operations, however, were not to be instituted until after the carpetbag era had come to a close.

> Away down South in Texas.
> They'll never take so far a stroll
> To dare to face me on my throne,
> In my imperial capitol,
> Where everything is now my own. . . .
> What do *I* care for murders there?
> They'll never be as many fold
> As you can hear yet, everywhere
> Of Grant's blood-thirsty army told—
> I'm used to extremes, and can smile
> If homesteads burn and persons bleed,
> I want a horse to trot a mile,
> And who can bring me such a steed?
> Turn loose Satanta and Big Tree!
> To send me presents. Yet, do not tell
> That, in return for liberty,
> I hope they'll chastise Texans well.

[43] *Weekly Democratic Statesman,* October 16, 1873, III, 12.

[44] Sherman was speaking here of the inspection tour he made through Texas in 1871 at the time of the Kiowa raid near Jacksboro.

[45] Rister, *The Southwestern Frontier,* p. 142. W. T. Sherman to Davis, February 16, 1874, Semi-official Letters of W. T. Sherman, 1872–1878, MS.

[46] *Annual Report of the Commissioner of Indian Affairs, 1874,* pp. 9–10.

THE FRONTIER FORCES AND THE MINUTE MEN

State Indian policy was put into effect by frontier forces and Minute Men. The first of these was provided for in an act passed by the Twelfth Legislature on June 13, 1870, authorizing the Governor to raise and muster into state service twenty companies of Rangers[47] to be used in protecting the northern and western frontiers from Indian depredations. Each company was to consist of a captain, a lieutenant, a medical officer, three sergeants, four corporals, fifty privates, a bugler, and a farrier. Membership was to be composed of citizens residing in frontier counties; they were to be recruited for one-year periods. This force was made subject to the orders of the governor, who was empowered to disband it when it was no longer needed.[48] Another measure passed on August 12, 1870, provided for the maintenance of these ranging companies, stipulating that $750,000 in state bonds were to be issued and sold, with the entire proceeds going to the force.[49]

By the close of 1870 fourteen Ranger companies had been organized. With the exception of one company that had been mustered out of service in November, 1870, they were stationed in frontier areas where savages from the Indian Territory or Indians from Mexico raided most frequently.[50] One company was stationed in each of the following counties: Erath, Kerr, Wise, Starr, Zapata, Mason, Lampasas, Gillespie, El Paso, Kimble, and Coleman;[51] and two companies were ordered to Uvalde County. The ranging forces, however, proved too expensive for the state to maintain, and the bonds issued for frontier defense could not be sold or hypothecated except at very low figures; their value was lessened by criticism from individuals who did not approve of their issuance. Consequently, the thirteen companies were consolidated into seven, but even these could not be financed. By June 15, 1871, they had all been mustered out of service.[52]

[47] Not to be confused with the Texas Rangers of historical fame. See footnote 81 in Chapter I.

[48] Gammel, *Laws of Texas*, VI, 179–182.

[49] *Ibid.*, VI, 34–36.

[50] *Report of the Adjutant General of Texas for 1870*, p. 7. Captain Franklin Jones' Company A was mustered out of the service on November 11, 1870.

[51] *Adjutant General's Report to Honorable E. B. Pickett, President of the Constitutional Convention*, p. 2. This source gives the frontier forces organized under the law of June 13, 1870.

[52] *Report of the Adjutant General of Texas for 1872*, p. 7.

Protection provided by ranging companies was not adequate anyway. Their numbers were not sufficient to enable them to patrol the vast stretches of the Texas frontier with a great degree of effectiveness. The length of time of their united service, however, was not sufficient to give them a fair test. None of the units served longer than nine months; the first company was mustered into the service on August 21, 1870, and all of them had been withdrawn by June 15, 1871. Moreover, companies were consolidated or mustered out during that period so that by the time of their final disbandment only three of the original fourteen companies remained in active service.[53]

During their brief existence ranging companies were able to recover 130 head of cattle evidently stolen by Mexican thieves and to recapture 94 horses and mules taken by Indians. In various encounters with savages 21 Indians were killed; the Rangers lost three dead and five wounded.[54]

Cost of maintaining these companies was $458,996.51. (Of this sum, however, $5,826.03 was lost through the alleged dishonesties of Adjutant General Davidson and State Treasurer Honey.) Thus the entire expenditure averaged $2.90 a day for each man employed.[55] This should not, of course, be confused with actual salaries, which ranged from $100 a month for captains to $50 for privates.[56] Such modest pay did not compensate for the dangers of the work.

To visualize the risks involved a twentieth-century reader might study some of the old Ranger reports. One was submitted on December 9, 1870, by H. J. Richarz, captain of Company E, stationed at Fort Inge in Uvalde County. He reported to the Adjutant General an Indian engagement in which eight savages were killed and fifteen wounded. At the same time three Rangers met their death—the only fatalities during the period the law was in operation—and one of them was the Captain's son. Captain Richarz's account stated:

Since my last report we have had hard and bloody work here. I will endeavor to make this as short as possible. At daybreak, on the fifth of December, I started on a scout with fourteen men and three citizens who had

[53] *Adjutant General's Report to Honorable E. B. Pickett, President of the Constitutional Convention,* p. 2; *Report of the Adjutant General of Texas for 1870,* p. 7.

[54] *Adjutant General's Report to Honorable E. B. Pickett, President of the Constitutional Convention,* p. 4.

[55] *Ibid.,* p. 3.   [56] *Report of the Adjutant General of Texas for 1873,* p. 4.

volunteered to scout the country between the Nueces and the Rio Grande, in order to intercept that band of Indians who stole the horses a hundred miles from here near Fort Ewel. That same day I met messengers from Fort Duncan, who brought the news that about three hundred Comanches and Kiowas, and about two hundred Kickapoos and Lipans, divided in parties from fifty to one hundred warriors, all armed with rifles, Spencer rifles, and pistols, besides their customary arms, were sweeping this part in every direction. Before I left, I had ordered my lieutenant to keep the force held in readiness to mount on half an hour's notice. This party had just come in from a fifteen days' scout to the Devil's River Mountains.

Twenty-five miles from the Rio Grande, I met a messenger and some United States officers, who informed me that the scouting party of my company I had mentioned in my last report under command of Dr. Woodbridge, our medical officer, who had volunteered, and Corporal Eckhart, consisting of fourteen men (one man having been left behind, his horse being lame) on an open prairie, twelve miles from the Rio Grande, had overtaken that band of Comanches who had killed David Adams and two Mexicans near the Pendencia, had gallantly charged them, and had stood their ground against seventy well armed savages, and had defeated them, killing eight warriors and wounding about fifteen. I ascertained at the same time that this band of Indians, after they were beaten, had retreated towards the Rio Grande, and that Dr. Woodbridge's party had buried one of my Rangers, Lorenze Biediger, who fell in the commencement of the battle, and were camping near the battle ground to rest their own worn out horses. So I turned my command toward the lower Chaparoso creek; not finding the trail of the Indians there, I made for the Nueces.

During the night of the eighth of December, my guide, whom I had sent towards the Eagle Pass road to meet a spy, returning to my camp, informed me that another band of Indians had appeared near my post at Fort Inge, and in overwhelming numbers, had attacked two of my Rangers at the Blanco, sixteen miles east of Fort Inge, and had killed them. Their names are Walter Richarz (my son) and Joseph Riff.

Another band, the Kickapoos, had been seen near Uvalde, raiding in the direction of the Frio River. I broke up in the night; arrived before daybreak at the post, and found, to my satisfaction that Lieutenant Wanz had started with the reserve force in hot pursuit of the murderers of my son and Joseph Riff. Before daybreak the same night, that party who returned with me had started in a northerly direction to fall in the trail of the Lieutenant, or eventually to intercept the savages on their way to the Canadian river or Indian reserve. With the last three men I had intended to start at daybreak the same night towards the Rio Grande, to assist Dr. Woodbridge's party, as I was informed that Old Castro, the chief of the Lipans, had avowed at Piedras Negras that he would revenge his red brethren for the loss inflicted by Dr. Woodbridge's party upon their allies. But I met the Doctor coming back into the post, who had no loss other than the man above mentioned, and carrying the shield of one of the Comanche chiefs killed in the action, as a trophy. The report, as above stated, is correct in substance. Dr. Woodbridge reports that he can not praise enough the bravery and fighting qualities of my men. Without a moment's hesitation this little band had charged seventy well armed savages (three of my men were absent on a reconnoitering scout when the fight commenced). The savages had formed two battle lines on a rising ground, and had soon outflanked my small band. The Indians fought like demons at first, and when an Indian tumbled from his horse dead or wounded, his place was instantly filled with warriors from out the second line.

Mr. Woodbridge, stunned by a blow upon his forehead by an Indian, fell off his horse, but several of my braves though fighting themselves as against overwhelming numbers came to his rescue, and in a second the Doctor had recovered himself so as to join in the work again. His horse was wounded and lost. The Indians meanwhile seeing that they had to deal with a new sort of combatant gave up the contest and fell back, as did my men; they rallied about three hundred yards from the battle ground. I have to mention that when the action was in progress, the three men who were on the reconnoitering tour, drawn by the heavy firing, joined in the attack on the left flank, killing a chief of the Indians. I hope that this lesson given to the savages by that heroic little band of Rangers will do some good; and I am pretty sure that I shall be able to report another success in a few days.

At the same time, referring to my last report, I would like to have some reinforcements; at any rate to be authorized to fill up my company to the number as organized at first. My men and horses have not had any rest worth speaking of since their arrival here. The grass is getting worse every day, and as the tribes protected by the Mexicans have a secure base of operation of two hundred and fifty miles long, watching my movements under the eyes of the United States garrison, having distinctly and formally notified me that they had determined to drive me from the place, and sweep the country to Bexar county, it is not reasonable to be expected that I can always successfully operate in every direction against a half a thousand well armed savages with thirty-eight privates, not to mention that I am not able to have two strong scouts out in different directions at the same time. Though we will not count numbers, if we fight, I may lose too many men without having the satisfaction to destroy the enemy. If it was not for this cursed international law, I know very well what to do to clean out these bloody savages on the other side of the Rio Grande.[57]

[57] *Daily State Journal,* December 4, 1870, I, 271.

PLATE 13. Satank, Kiowa leader in the Salt Creek Massacre, later killed near Fort Sill attempting to escape from his captors. The Fort Worth *Star-Telegram,* Texas Collection.

PLATE 14. A Plains Indian on the reservation at Fort Sill during the early 1870's. The Fort Worth *Star-Telegram*, Texas Collection.

Another report was submitted by Lieutenant A. C. Hill of Company F (commanded by Captain D. P. Baker) describing an Indian battle in North Texas in February, 1871:

I have the honor to report to you a fight with nine of our men and forty Indians well armed with Henry rifles, Needle guns, six shooters, bows and arrows. One of our men severely wounded. Two Indians killed, dead on the ground and quite a number of wounded. One horse slightly wounded.

On the morning of the 7th inst. Sergeant Cobb who is commanding at Perryman Station received word that Indians had gone east to the Settlements down Clear Creek. He started immediately and followed the trail about 30 miles and came in sight of the Indians on the high prairie near the corners of Wise, Cook, Denton, and Montague counties. The Indians were well armed and half their number were mounted on good horses. So soon as the Indians discovered our men they retreated to a draw of high grass, just over the first rise, with infantry concealed and cavalry formed on right and left. As our brave boys dashed up the Indians rose and attempted to surround them. The chief was instantly killed and clung to his horse until his horse dashed through the lines and kicked him loose just in the rear of our men. This gave them check for a few moments. Little Billy Sorrells, son of Mr. F. M. Sorrells, was wounded on the hip with a six-shooter ball. The chief had two six-shooters. Billy was wounded in the first charge but fought bravely to the end. They got the chief's horse with his very fine silver bridle, worth forty dollars, his extra fine bow and quiver, and his richly adorned cap with plumes; and was about to lift his scalp when the enemy dashed up to rescue the body of their chief, which brought them again in close combat. Gus Hasroot being a little to one side, an Indian dashed up to him to spear him. The boys all thought Gus was gone up, but he made a lucky shot that dropped the Indian dead before him, but a few steps off. A. J. Sowel, while contending and exchanging several shots with one, was satisfied he had got him badly hurt, judging from the staggering retreat he made.

Sergeant Cobb withdrew his men in good order to a better position, not taking time to secure the so much desired scalp. The sergeant came out bloody all over, but could not give a satisfactory account of it. The Indians powwowed and yelled mournfully over the remains of their chief and warriors that were killed and wounded.

The sergeant took Billy to the nearest house and secured a good physician to attend him until our surgeon could go up, and left two of our men with him.

. . . All the citizens say with one accord, and proudly too, they never saw Rangers like these, to contend with such great odds. Allow me to give you the names of the entire squad to hold in remembrance: Sgt. E. H.

195

Cobb, Wm. Caruthers, George Howel, D. W. Edwards, J. R. Ewers, A. J. Sowel, A. J. Wilhoit, Darkin Cleveland, Wm. R. Sorrells, Gus Hasroot. The Indians waved their battle flag defiantly with their death mask on it, to all Texans. The chief in his clownish movements tried to daunt our brave Boys, but they have not forgotten their brutal work so recently committed on the Families in that vicinity. They were like the Boys who remembered the Alamo. . . . Every moon makes the number less of both man and horse, in this unfortunate part of our noble lone Star State.[58]

A report signed on January 23, 1871, by Captain James Swisher of Company P, stationed at Camp Colorado in Coleman County, told of an encounter on the western frontier.

I have to report that on the night of the 5th inst., a runner from Mr. Sam Gohlson's ranche on Jim Ned creek, in Coleman county, informed me that a party of Indians had captured twenty-five horses from Mr. Gohlson the night before.

With a detail of ten men and ten days subsistence, I at once proceeded to the ranche of Mr. Gohlson, who joined me with eight of his men and a four-mule wagon loaded with forage and subsistence, when we immediately started in pursuit.

On the first day we followed the trail twenty miles, passing three horses dropped by the Indians, and camped on Jim Ned creek.

On the second day we traveled in a northwest direction; saw two beeves killed by the Indians, and passed two of their camps and stopped for the night on the head of Elm creek.

On the third day we followed the trail in the same direction, passed two more horses dropped by the Indians and camped on "Rock creek" a tributary of the Brazos.

On the fourth day, we passed through "Rocky Pass," crossed the Overland Mail Route near "Church Mountain" and camped five miles beyond.

On the fifth day, being still some distance in the rear of the Indians, I concluded to pack the wagon mules and make a four days' scout before giving up the chase. Early that morning, and before the mules were packed I started on the trail with three men, directing the others to follow as soon as possible, and had not gone more than a half mile before we discovered several Indians chasing cattle and others herding horses. After sending one man back to hasten on the remainder of the party, chase was immediately given, and we had a running fight for ten miles, when on reaching Cedar Mountain they abandoned their horses and entered a cave. The cave is

---

[58] *Adjutant General's Report to Honorable E. B. Pickett, President of the Constitutional Convention*, p. 3; *Daily State Journal*, February 25, 1871, II, 26; Letters of the Frontier Forces, 1871, MSS.

about twenty miles west of Church Mountain on the waters of the Clear Fork of the Brazos. Here the remainder of the party came up, but the cave being so deep and hollowed out below it was impossible to get at the Indians without sacrificing too many of my men. We surrounded the cave, however, and a scattering fire was kept up until dark. The night being very dark, it was impossible to guard the cave, and the men having had nothing to eat or drink since morning, we drew off to get water. We returned to the cave the next morning, and found on the trail twelve or fifteen blankets, one shield, one Indian saddle and bridle, tent cloth, shot pouch, some children's clothing, etc. At the cave we found the body of an Indian, a blanket covered with blood and several shots through it, and a hat recognized as the one worn by J. A. Dofflemeyer, when he was killed by the Indians on Mule Water Creek last September. I am satisfied that there were several other Indians killed, who were carried off or buried in the cedar brake. We captured thirty-eight horses, but ten of them were lost on the route back during a severe snow storm. The captured horses were left with Mr. Gohlson, at Camp Colorado subject to your orders. We had but one man wounded in the fight.[59]

Despite their frequent heroism the Rangers did thankless work. Initially the federal government furnished the men rations and forage, but it soon discontinued the practice, and Texas had difficulty in providing either.[60] Nor could the men be sure of receiving their salaries. In July, 1871, thirty-six former members of Company N, at that time all private citizens residing at San Elizario in El Paso County, wrote Governor Davis that they had not received one cent of pay, even though they had been employed for more than nine months—the entire time the ranging companies were in existence.[61] Moreover, U. S. Army officers along the frontier were not always considerate in their treatment of the Rangers. General Reynolds, commander of the Department of Texas, apparently was concerned for the welfare of the state, but some of his subordinates were less cooperative, and in particular they felt that the Ranger forces were a reflection on their own work. When one Ranger captain reported to the commander at Fort Bliss he was told that the only orders were to keep away from the fort. In other instances state troops allegedly were required to carry

[59] *Daily State Journal,* February 2, 1871, II, 6.
[60] *Report of the Adjutant General of Texas for 1870,* p. 63.
[61] Signed letter by thirty-six citizens of San Elizario to E. J. Davis, July 15, 1871, Letters of the Frontier Forces, 1871, MS.

mail for the Army and to hunt deserters instead of scouting for savages, which was their only legitimate duty.[62]

After the ranging companies were mustered out in 1871 Texas was for several months without any form of state protection. But on November 25, 1871, the second session of the Twelfth Legislature passed an act providing for twenty-four companies of Minute Men, who would be enlisted for one year, to continue the protection of the border settlements. This service was limited from the start, however, for the act stipulated that the time of employment in the field should not exceed ten days a month.

Each company was to consist of one lieutenant elected by the members, two sergeants, two corporals and fifteen men. The units were to be stationed in each of the following counties: Montague, Cooke, Wise, Jack, Parker, Palo Pinto, Erath, Comanche, Brown, San Saba, Hamilton, Lampasas, Burnet, Llano, Mason, Gillespie, Blanco, Kerr, Kendall, Bandera, Uvalde, Maverick, and Webb. Company recruits were required to be citizens of the county in which the unit was located, or of the adjoining county, and they had to provide their own horses. Salary was to be two dollars a day while in actual service; this money was to come out of the cash received by the governor from the hypothecation of frontier defense bonds.[63] But before the governor could use any of it for the Minute Men he was required to pay off the Ranger companies.

Organization of the new force proceeded slowly. At the end of May, 1872, only seven companies were active. By the end of that October, however, all twenty-four units had been mustered into service. The actual expense for their maintenance from the time of organization to the close of 1872 amounted to $21,692.00. Estimated total expense, assuming that each company served a complete year, was set at $107,492.75. Cost of financing the Minute Men was only one-fourth that for the ranging companies—and Adjutant General Frank L. Britton declared them to be more effective.[64]

Their activities closely resembled those of the Rangers, and so did the reports that were submitted to the Adjutant General. Lieutenant James Ingram, commander of Company A in Blanco County, stated in February, 1872, that large bodies of Indians were plaguing his dis-

[62] *Daily State Journal,* December 16, 1870, I, 273.
[63] Gammel, *Laws of Texas,* VII, 36–37.
[64] *Report of the Adjutant General of Texas for 1872,* pp. 7–8.

Minute Companies in Operation under the Law of November 25, 1871*

Co.	Station County	Commander	No. Men	Organized
A	Blanco	James Ingram	19	Jan. 4, 1872
B	Wise	G. W. Stevens	19	Mar. 2, 1872
C	Kendall	C. A. Patton	19	Feb. 4, 1872
D	Comanche	J. A. Wright	19	Mar. 25, 1872
E	Kerr	H. Schwethelm	19	Apr. 6, 1872
F	Gillespie	B. F. Casey	19	Apr. 18, 1872
G	Brown	G. H. Adams	19	June 5, 1872
I	Cooke	J. M. Waide	19	Apr. 24, 1872
K	Bandera	R. Ballantyne	19	July 2, 1872
L	Coleman	J. M. Elkins	19	Volunteer without pay
M	Lampasas	G. E. Haynie	19	Aug. 10, 1872
N	San Saba	W. H. Ledbetter	19	Aug. 13, 1872
O	Burnet	Jno. Alexander	19	Aug. 19, 1872
P	Parker	J. C. Gilleland	19	Aug. 19, 1872
Q	Llano	F. C. Stewart	19	Aug. 21, 1872
R	Mason	D. Herster	19	Aug. 26, 1872
S	Jack	N. Atkinson	19	Aug. 23, 1872
T	Palo Pinto	D. H. McClure	19	Aug. 22, 1872
U	Montague	J. J. Willingham	19	Apr. 20, 1872
V	Medina	George Haley	19	Sept. 6, 1872
W	Webb	J. D. Martinez	19	Oct. 2, 1872
X	Maverick	M. Barrs	19	Oct. 8, 1872
Y	Uvalde	D. A. Bates	19	Oct. 12, 1872
Z	Erath	C. M. O'Neal	19	Oct. 12, 1872

456

* Information from the *Adjutant General's Report to Honorable E. B. Pickett, President of The Constitutional Convention*, pp. 4–5.

trict and that one band had captured a white woman. Despite vigorous pursuit, he said, he had still not been able to round up the savages. Then in August he reported that the Indians were still numerous in Blanco County and that his men had only recently engaged them in battle. But the encounter had been disappointing, as his men had been forced to withdraw. Nevertheless, they had killed two Indians and wounded several others. Three of Ingram's men were wounded.

Lieutenant G. W. Stevens, leader of Company B in Wise County, reported on April 13, 1872, that he had captured thirteen horses from the Indians. About four months later, on August 11, he wrote of a fight between nine of his men and one hundred savages in which all of his horses were lost and one of his rangers was killed. Despite these odds the Texans had been able to dispatch the chief and twenty Indians. In August, 1872, a letter from Company F, in Gillespie County, declared that one man had taken two stolen horses from the Indians. About the same time Lieutenant J. M. Waide, commanding Company I in Cooke County, reported that his men had recaptured fifty animals from the savages. Thus the Minute Men recovered sixty-five horses and killed twenty-three Indians during 1872. Of their own men, only one was killed and three were wounded.[65]

The Thirteenth Legislature passed a bill on June 2, 1873, amending the first section of the act that created the Minute Men. Originally this section had declared that twenty-four companies should be mustered into service for one year. By the amendment the governor was given authority to muster for a twelve-months term a company in any frontier county where Indian raids were being conducted. The state was thus no longer obliged to maintain a definite number of companies, and the governor was given more freedom in handling the problem of frontier protection. Furthermore, the amendment specified no counties in which Minute Men were to be placed; they were to be located where most needed. Otherwise the original measure remained unchanged.[66]

Following passage of this act the number of companies was increased from twenty-four to twenty-eight. Companies were removed from Burnet, Medina, Webb, Maverick, and Bandera; newly organized units were stationed in Kinney, Menard, Callahan, and Gillespie.[67] Then, on November 1, 1873, Governor Davis issued an order for the organization of seven ranging companies to serve for four months, to afford the troubled frontier further protection. Four of these com-

---

[65] *Adjutant General's Report to Honorable E. B. Pickett, President of the Constitutional Convention*, pp. 4–5.

[66] Gammel, *Laws of Texas*, VII, 631.

[67] *Adjutant General's Report to Honorable E. B. Pickett, President of the Constitutional Convention*, p. 6; *Report of the Adjutant General of Texas for 1873*, p. 4.

Ranging Companies called out by
Governor Davis on November 1, 1873*

Station	Co. Commander	Lt.	Sgt.	Cpl.	Pvt.	Total	Organized
Wise	G. W. Stevens	2	4	8	60	75	Nov. 26, 1873
Jack	S. W. Eastin	2	4	8	60	75	Dec. 3, 1873
Palo Pinto	W. C. McAdams	2	4	8	60	75	Dec. 13, 1873
Parker Erath	W. L. Hunter	2	4	8	60	75	Dec. 24, 1873
Comanche	M. R. Green	2	4	4	64	75	Jan. 17, 1874
Montague	G. W. Campbell	2	4	8	60	75	Dec. 13, 1873
Young Brown	A. C. Tackett	—	2	4	34	41	Jan. 6, 1874
McCulloch San Saba	J. G. Connell	2	4	8	60	75	Jan. 6, 1874
	8	14	30	56	458	566	

* Information from the *Adjutant General's Report to Honorable E. B. Pickett, President of The Constitutional Convention*, p. 8.

panies had been mustered into the service by the close of 1873,[68] which virtually marked the end of the Davis administration.

The following year, 1874, the Minute Men recovered one hundred seventeen horses, killed four Indians, and suffered no losses of their own.[69] The only record of the ranging companies mustered into the service by Governor Davis was contained in a report made by the Adjutant General. The statement declared that some men belonging to a ranging company under Captain W. C. McAdams in Palo Pinto County had encountered a band of Indians in that section and recaptured some horses stolen by them.[70]

During the Fourteenth Legislature members of both the ranging companies and the Minute organizations, unpaid during Davis' term, received the money due them for past services. A deficiency appropriation act passed on May 4, 1874,[71] provided the sum of $121,476.56 to meet these obligations.[72]

[68] *Report of the Adjutant General of Texas for 1873*, p. 4.
[69] *Adjutant General's Report to Honorable E. B. Pickett, President of the Constitutional Convention*, pp. 6–7.
[70] *Ibid.*, p. 8.
[71] Gammel, *Laws of Texas*, VIII, 233.
[72] *Adjutant General's Report to Honorable E. B. Pickett, President of the Constitutional Convention*, p. 8.

It is obvious, then, that during the Davis administration the state did relatively little to protect the frontier. The ranging force provided for in the act of 1870 was so poorly supported that it had to be disbanded after only a few months. The Minute Men, created to fill the vacancy, proved to be inadequate, because they could serve only ten days out of the month. Ranging companies created by order of Governor Davis in November, 1873, also accomplished little. Having mustered them into service for only a four-month period, Davis still could give them nothing more than a promise of compensation, which was little incentive to strenuous action. But the primary reason for the failure of these organizations was the vast frontier extending hundreds upon hundreds of miles. It made the problem of protection far too great for any of these small groups to cope with successfully.

During the next administration the frontier protection act of 1870 and the laws creating the Minute Men were repealed. But the same measure that removed these acts also created a Ranger force of a more permanent character.[73]

THE REMOVAL OF THE KICKAPOOS

The purpose of the fortifications along the Rio Grande, as mentioned, was to protect the southern part of the state from depredations of the Kickapoo Indians. These savages resided on the Mexican side of the Rio Grande near the town of Santa Rosa, but their frequent raids into Texas constantly menaced lives and property along the border.[74] It was obviously essential that they be either controlled or removed to a United States reservation. In May, 1870, the Twelfth Legislature passed a joint resolution asking Congress to stop Mexican harboring of these Indians, declaring that during the past five years the Kickapoos and Lipans had been guilty of conducting depredations.[75] (Evidence proves, however, that the raiding parties were largely Kickapoo, and in July, 1870, the commander of Fort Duncan declared that there were at that date no Lipans in Mexico.)[76]

Some 500 warriors were in the Kickapoo tribe, which mingled freely with the Mexican people although not enjoying legal rights

---

[73] Gammel, *Laws of Texas,* VIII, 86–89.
[74] *Daily State Journal,* May 11, 1870, I, 88.
[75] Gammel, *Laws of Texas,* VI, 415–416.
[76] *Annual Report of the Commissioner of Indian Affairs, 1871,* p. 792.

accorded citizens of that country. They were, however, allowed to keep all stock captured from other Indian tribes, and this was a privilege that proved frustrating to some Anglo-Texans. Frequently residents of Southwest Texas visited Mexico to recover stock stolen by these Indians, but in Mexico at that time the word of a savage carried more weight than the oath of a United States citizen. The Kickapoos' counterbrand, when enforced by the mere assertion that the stock had been captured from another Indian tribe, was sufficient proof of rightful ownership, and the victimized Texan had no alternative but to return to his own country.

Like the Indians who raided the northern and western frontiers of the state, the marauding Kickapoos left in Texas a trail stained with blood. This gruesome fact was noted by Speaker Ira H. Evans when he addressed the Twelfth Legislature House of Representatives during discussion of the joint resolution asking help from Congress.

For the capture and detention of half a dozen of her citizens, England went to war with Abyssinia at an expense of many millions of dollars and the cost of many lives; but for the murder of one hundred of her citizens, the United States has not even raised her voice in protest to the government which has so long harbored and abetted the murderers, while claiming to be a friendly power.[77]

In July, 1870, Major Z. R. Bliss, commander of Fort Duncan, suggested that a closer surveillance be kept on Kickapoo activities by employing as scouts some Seminole Negroes residing near Santa Rosa.[78] General Reynolds gave Bliss permission to hire as many as twenty, and Bliss immediately entered into negotiations. With John Kibbitt, chief of the tribe, he arranged for the scouts to receive adequate compensation and to be given farm land on Elm Creek, five

[77] *Daily State Journal,* May 11, 1870, I, 88.

[78] This group of Seminole Negroes had belonged to chief Wild Cat's band and had left the United States reservation many years before the Civil War. Kibbitt and Gopher John, another Seminole Negro chief, had settled on the Santa Rosa Mexican reservation with Wild Cat. During the Civil War, all of the Seminole Indians in Mexico returned to the United States reservation in Arkansas. Gopher John, the principal chief of the Seminole Negroes, and Kibbitt, remained in Mexico through the war, fearing to return to the United States on account of slavery. Gopher John had moved from Santa Rosa to a point about 200 miles southwest of the town. Another band of Seminole Negroes lived near Matamoras. *Annual Report of the Commissioner of Indian Affairs,* 1871, pp 792–793.

miles from Fort Duncan but still on the military reservation. These Seminole Negroes proved to know nothing about the Texas countryside, nor were they cognizant of where the Kickapoos crossed the river river on their forays. Nevertheless, they understood Kickapoo habits thoroughly and made excellent scouts. For the same purpose Bliss also employed members of the peaceful Tonkawa tribe.

Kibbitt, an intelligent and reliable man, attempted to persuade the Kickapoo chief to agree to a conference with Major Bliss about the future actions of the Kickapoos. But Kibbitt informed the Major early in July, 1870, that the chief had refused, declaring that he would never visit Fort Duncan. He said the Mexicans had told him he would be killed if he ever appeared there. Kibbitt provided another bit of intelligence: all of the stock the Kickapoos owned had been stolen from Texas, and they feared that if they came to Fort Duncan they would lose their horses and cattle and be punished for their thefts. Kibbitt held the opinion that neither promises nor treaties would induce the Kickapoos to come to the fort.[79]

Congress passed an act on July 15, 1870, and another on March 3, 1871, providing for the removal from the Border to the Indian Territory of the Kickapoos and other roving Indian bands.[80] But the Kickapoos refused to move, and General Reynolds, who had just returned from official visits to Fort Clark and Fort Duncan, said he knew the reason: the Indians had been retained in Mexico by bribes from corrupt Mexican officials, he declared. Reynolds also commented on Kickapoo depredations:

. . . The marauders with their stolen stock have been time and again traced to the Rio Grande, and I am reliably informed that parties in pursuit can often see, from the north side of the river, their stock in possession of other parties, collected in convenient droves on the south side for sale or distribution to the interior of Mexico.

The gradual but heavy loss of property is very discouraging to the people; they are becoming restless, not to say desperate, and seeing the apparent determination of Mexican officials to retain the Kickapoo Indians in Mexico, as a cloak for the evil deeds of the Mexican people,[81] they talk now

[79] *Ibid.*   [80] *Ibid., 1873,* p. 17.

[81] He is evidently referring here to the work of Mexican cattle bandits as well as to the bribe-giving Mexican officials. These bandits are also said to have carried on thieving expeditions extensively. *Tri-Weekly State Gazette,* February 19, 1872, IV, 185.

quite freely of organizing themselves into armed bands and crossing into Mexico to recover their stolen property.

... The ranchmen live from ten to thirty miles apart, and incursions from the south side of the Rio Grande in small parties cannot be prevented by a reasonable force in Texas, unaided by any force, civil or military, from the Mexican side.

It is believed that these depredations can be effectually and permanently stopped by pursuing marauding bands into Mexico with troops accompanied by owners of the stock and records of the brands.[82]

During his visit to South Texas, General Reynolds persuaded the Kickapoos at least to hold a council on the subject of removal to an Indian reservation in the United States. The tribe seemed inclined to make the change but, as mentioned, postponed a decision because of the gifts of arms, ammunition, and money received from certain Mexicans—and because of past profits made from selling stolen stock to these same Mexicans.[83] So they continued to maraud.

Most Kickapoo depredations in Texas occurred north and northwest of Eagle Pass. The tribe probably also ranged into the lower Rio Grande Valley, since there was no United States cavalry post located on the river south of Fort Duncan, which was near Eagle Pass. But it was not the Kickapoos alone who caused anxiety in the minds of settlers of extreme southern Texas. They were also harried by mounted Mexican cattle thieves. Fully 260 miles of border country south of Eagle Pass was left virtually unprotected against horsemen, for although U.S. infantry companies were stationed at intervals of every hundred miles or so, foot soldiers were not able to cope with mounted enemies. Regarding these Mexican thieving expeditions a Texas newspaper declared:

... The stock west of the Nueces is being driven over the Rio Grande by every available pass. At one crossing in Hidalgo County five thousand head of beeves have been driven since last June by armed bands, who collect and drive the stolen cattle for the merchants and traders in Mexico, who receive the stolen property and are the allies and sleeping partners of the thieves.

It is also charged that General Cortina, commanding the Mexican forces on the Rio Grande, protects and shelters this organized robbery, so that no

[82] J. J. Reynolds to E. D. Townsend, July 28, 1871, Executive Letters of Governor E. J. Davis, 1871, MS.
[83] *Daily State Journal*, July 2, 1871, II, 135.

redress can be obtained from Mexican law. Unless something effectual is done the settlers complain that the stock interest between the Rio Grande and Nueces rivers will be ruined. The thieves ride in companies, well mounted and strongly armed. They defy the resistance of the scattered ranchmen, and in broad daylight harry the country and drive off their plunder into Mexico.[84]

Early in February, 1872, Texas Congressman J. C. Conner introduced a resolution in the U.S. House of Representatives regarding the Indian and Mexican depredations in South Texas, with the purpose of focusing the attention of the United States on these ravages and thus arousing sentiment for their suppression. Conner reported that the Mexican bandits had raided so extensively and so successfully that Texas cattle, all bearing their original bands, were selling in the Mexican states of Tamaulipas, Nuevo Leon, and Coahuila at much lower prices than in any section of the Lone Star State. He declared that even as far in the interior as Monterrey and Saltillo these stolen cattle were sold at the same low prices. Since the thieves had not incurred any expenses in buying or raising the cattle they could, of course, dispose of them cheaply and still realize comfortable profits.[85]

As a result of Conner's work Congress passed a joint resolution on May 7, 1872, providing for the appointment of commissioners to inquire into the Texas depredations. Named to the group were three men—Thomas P. Robb, Richard H. Savage, and Thomas O. Osborn[86] —but by October their appropriation had been exhausted. On December 16 President Grant transmitted to Congress their report,[87] but it was incomplete because lack of funds had halted the investigation. Still, it brought results. U.S. forts along the Rio Grande were reinforced, and this enabled General R. S. McKenzie to deliver a sharp blow against the Kickapoos early in 1873. But the encounter effected no permanent change in the situation.[88] On January 11, 1873, the com-

[84] *Ibid.,* September 26, 1871, II, 206.

[85] *Tri-Weekly State Gazette,* February 19, 1872, IV, 185.

[86] Forty-third Congress, First Session, *Executive Document No. 257* (Serial No. 1615), p. 32.

[87] James D. Richardson, *Messages and Papers of the Presidents, 1789–1897,* VII, 207.

[88] Forty-third Congress, First Session, *Executive Document No. 257* (Serial No. 1615), pp. 31–32.

missioners were sent back to Texas, having received a supplemental appropriation.

They arrived at Brownsville February 6 and remained there about three weeks. Then they visited sites of all outrages, following the Rio Grande from the Gulf inland. At Brownsville, Ringgold Barracks, Corpus Christi, Santa Gertrudis, San Diego, Laredo, El Sauz, Eagle Pass, Brackettville, Fort Clark, Uvalde, and, finally, San Antonio the commissioners met in session, obtaining proofs of Border raids and general testimony concerning operations of the nomadic Indians on the northern and northwestern frontiers. The commissioners took 736 depositions, which combined with those taken the year before totaled 1,000. In addition, 423 grievance petitions claiming $48,496,234.25 damages were gathered from settlers in southern and southwestern Texas; of this figure the losses resulting exclusively from raids of Indians residing in Mexico amounted to $721,492.60. From cattlemen in western and northwestern Texas came another 354 petitions claiming $44,572,415.43 losses from raids by Kiowas, Comanches, and Apaches.[89]

Concurrently with the commissioners' second session Secretary of War William G. Belknap and General Philip H. Sheridan also visited the Border area, inspecting the frontier over a stretch of several hundred miles. They also saw at first hand evidences of the depredations committed by the Indian and Mexican raiders.[90]

In June, 1873, the commissioners completed their final report. They asserted that the Border situation had remained unchanged from the previous year, and they suggested the following solution to the problem:

. . . The serious state of affairs heretofore reported can only be concluded by the removal of the marauding Kickapoos to their proper reservation, the performance of plain duty by the Mexican river authorities and an equitable adjustment of these claims. . . .

The raids of Mexican marauders cannot be entirely stopped by the United States forces, however watchful, and it is presumed that the operations of the Texan regiment of volunteers, recently authorized by the legislature of Texas, will not bring about the desired result, which can only be brought about by a resolute determination on the part of the national government of the republic of Mexico to put down in a most summary manner, these

[89] *Ibid.,* pp. 1–3.
[90] San Antonio *Daily Herald,* April 29, 1873, XVI, 100.

irregular bands of banditti who for many years past have impoverished Western Texas and wantonly shed the blood of her citizens.

. . . It is for the government of the United States to open this region to improvement by giving to those who live under the shadow of its flag on the distant Rio Grande that effectual protection which they deserve to life and property, a protection due citizens and residents whose members have been depleted by the arrow of the Indian and the knife and the pistol of the Mexican assassin.[91]

This report was not presented to Congress unitil May 26, 1874,[92] which was after the close of the Davis administration, but the preliminary report submitted in December, 1872, became an important factor in the removal of the Kickapoo, and the commission thus earned a niche in this study of the carpetbag era.

In April, 1873, state officials at Austin were informed that General T. J. Williams and H. M. Atkinson had been appointed members of a commission to oversee removal of the Kickapoo Indians from Santa Rosa, Mexico, to the Indian Territory. Williams carried letters written by the Mexican minister at Washington to the governors of Coahuila and Nuevo Leon, soliciting their help in effecting the removal. The Secretary of War ordered General Augur, commanding the Department of Texas, to assist the commission as appropriate, and Secretary of State Hamilton Fish gave similar instructions to all U.S. consular officials in Mexico. The Secretary of the Interior delegated authority to the commission to outfit the Indians for the trip, and Governor Davis instructed peace officers to provide any assistance needed in transporting the Kickapoos across Texas.[93] Finally, after a series of councils and removal of certain barriers thrown up by disreputable Mexicans, the commission succeeded in moving three or four hundred Kickapoos. By the end of 1873 the tribe had been established in the Indian Territory.[94]

Indian raids along the Rio Grande did not end with the removal of the Kickapoos. The commission extended the promise of a safe transit and a home in the Indian Territory to the other wandering

[91] Forty-third Congress, First Session, *Executive Document No. 257* (Serial No. 1615), pp. 31–32.

[92] Richardson, *Messages and Papers of the Presidents,* VII, 266.

[93] *Daily State Gazette,* April 23, 1873, VI, 96.

[94] *Annual Report of the Commissioner of Indian Affairs, 1873,* p. 17.

tribes in Mexico who belonged to the United States. There is no evidence, however, that they accepted the invitation. These tribes included fragmentary bands of Seminoles, Comanches, and perhaps others. Mescalero Apaches and Mexican thieves of cattle remained a problem in that area as well.[95]

In his annual message to Congress on December 7, 1874, President Grant discussed the Border situation:

. . . Marauding on the frontiers between Mexico and Texas still takes place, despite the vigilance of the civil and military authorities in that quarter. The difficulty in checking such trespasses along the course of a river of such length as the Rio Grande, and so often fordable, is obvious. It is hoped that the efforts of this Government will be seconded by those of Mexico to the effectual suppression of these acts of wrong.[96]

Additional protection was to be provided for Texas Border settlements two years later by a congressional act of July 24, 1876, that increased the cavalry force.[97]

[95] *Daily State Gazette,* April 23, 1873, VI, 96.
[96] Richardson, *Messages and Papers of the Presidents,* VII, 290.
[97] *Ibid.,* p. 418.

10

INDIAN DEPREDATIONS

INTRODUCTION

THE NORTHERN AND WESTERN FRONTIERS, as mentioned, were devastated during E. J. Davis' term by raids of savage Comanches, Kiowas, and Apaches,[1] and the Border suffered serious damage from raids of marauding Kickapoos, Mescalero Apaches, and Mexican bandits.[2]

On the northern and western frontiers depredations were not limited to reservation Indians, although most raids were conducted by these savages. The Qua-ha-das, or Staked Plains Indians, contributed a share of the trouble. Although a branch of the Comanche tribe, the Qua-ha-das had never been confined to the reservation,[3] and they resided for a time on the headwaters of the Red River, approximately one hundred fifty miles southwest of Fort Sill. Their predatory character was indicated by Fort Sill Indian Agent Laurie Tatum, who said he had been informed that by December, 1870, the Qua-ha-das had already stolen all the horses and mules they wanted from Texas and were planning to kill all the white men and steal all the women and children until they drove back the settlements two or three days' journey farther east. The Indians asserted they were thus only regaining property stolen from them by Texans.[4]

---

[1] *Annual Report of the Commissioner of Indian Affairs to the Secretary of the Interior, 1872,* p. 42.

[2] Forty-third Congress, First Session, *Executive Document No. 257* (Serial No. 1615), pp. 14–27; *Daily State Journal,* April 20, 1871, II, 72.

[3] *Annual Report of the Commissioner of Indian Affairs, 1872,* pp. 93–94.

[4] Laurie Tatum to Enoch Hoag, December 15, 1870, and Tatum to Hoag, October 27, 1870, Letters Regarding Kiowa and Comanche Indians, 1870, MS.

PLATE 15. Austin citizens watch deeds of derring-do on Congress Avenue in the early 1870's. From the University of Texas Archives.

PLATE 16. An Austin street during the Reconstruction period: East 6th Street in 1866. From the University of Texas Archives.

DEPREDATIONS OF THE COMANCHES, KIOWAS, AND APACHES

Specific incidents, better than any other kind of description, afforded a conception of the dangers braved by Texas frontier settlers during the era of the carpetbaggers. One occurred in Mason County in July, 1870. At that time a German family named Buckmeyer was residing in Loyal Valley. The parents were still mourning the loss of a son, stolen by savages several months earlier, when the Indians, probably Kiowa or Comanche, paid a second visit, in the afternoon of July 18. Buckmeyer and his eldest son were away from the house at the time.

A band of eight Indians suddenly appeared, sending Mrs. Buckmeyer and her children fleeing inside. Frantically they barricaded the door, but the savages fired Spencer rifles into the window, then threw large stones into the opening they had made. Discovering that there was no man in the house, the Indians dismounted and tried to force their way in. Anticipating this, Mrs. Buckmeyer grabbed a double-barreled shotgun, and when one savage tried to crawl through the window she pulled the trigger, showering him with a load of buckshot. A few minutes later another savage appeared at the window and she fired again.

Two casualties were enough for the Indians, who fled, whooping and yelling. Mrs. Buckmeyer later found that before their departure they had broken into an adjoining room and had destroyed bedding, clothing, harnesses, and other articles kept there, leaving the household almost bare of necessities. They had also stolen all the horses.[5] Still, by her brave, quick action Mrs. Buckmeyer had saved herself and the children from certain capture and possible death.

During that same month—July, 1870—between fifty and a hundred Kiowas from the reservation descended on a small settlement about seventeen miles west of Montague, killed a man named Koozer and captured his wife and five children, murdered two other men, and seized a sixth child, named Kilgore. The savages also stole a number

---

[5] *Daily State Journal*, July 29, 1870, I, 55. This paper published a letter from Otto Donop, a prominent citizen of Mason County to Honorable Fritz Tegner dated July 20, 1870. It is from this account that the above incident is taken.

of horses and killed several head of cattle.[6] Reporting this raid to the Superintendent of Indian Affairs, Agent Laurie Tatum asked if the Interior Department would sustain him in paying a reward for the prisoners, if their release could not otherwise be obtained. Tatum declared that the immediate families did not possess enough money for ransom, but he stated that the captives could be found easily: they were on the very reservation, in the Kiowa camp.[7] Apparently the federal government paid the ransom; accounts of the period state that members of the Koozer family were released for a price of $600 each.[8]

During the same summer of 1870 a geologist, A. R. Rossler,[9] set off with an escort provided by the Sixth Cavalry at Fort Richardson to explore the copper region of northwest Texas. With his escort far in advance Rossler and a small party entered the Wichita country. Suddenly the group was attacked by Indians, and only Rossler escaped with his life. The escort galloped back, and the soldiers accompanied him to Fort Griffin.[10]

A Texas newspaper of August 24, 1870, describes conditions on the western frontier at this time.

The counties of Llano, Mason, and Gillespie swarm with savages. The farmers are shot down in their fields, and their stock stolen before their eyes and in open day. Not for twenty years back have the Indians been so bold, well armed and numerous as now. At Llano, the frontier is breaking up in consequence of these incessant and ferocious raids.[11]

[6] A similar attack occurred in Montague County a few months later on December 2, 1870. A house located about twelve miles southeast of the town of Montague was forcibly entered at night by the Indians, who killed and scalped one woman and murdered three children. Another woman, a Mrs. Keener, was mortally wounded. A small boy, who received only a slight wound, escaped and gave the information of the attack. The Indians evidently did not discover three other children who remained in the house unhurt. It is obvious that the women were without male protection, for there is no mention whatever of any such aid being given them.
George H. Smith to Enoch Hoag, December 13, 1870, Letters Regarding Kiowa and Comanche Indians, 1870, MS.
[7] Laurie Tatum to Enoch Hoag, July 29, 1870, *ibid.*
[8] Austin *Daily Republican*, September 27, 1870, III, 100.
[9] Homer S. Thrall, *A Pictorial History of Texas*, p. 66. This source gives Rossler's initials.
[10] Galveston *Weekly Civilian*, June 23, 1870, XXIII, 7.
[11] *Daily State Journal*, August 24, 1870, I, 176.

A letter from San Saba, however, disagreed with part of the preceding observation.

... The Indians are not worse than usual. Only one man killed, two children captured, and about seventy-five head of horses driven away during the past "light moon" in this vicinity.[12]

A dispatch from Lampasas County, dated August 15, 1870, pictured conditions there.

... During the last moon our entire county, and as far as reports can be credited, other surrounding counties, have been infested by large bodies of hostile Indians, evidently on the war path. They have been seen in different portions of this county, in large bodies, by different responsible citizens. They made a raid near our town, and drove off quite a number of fine horses belonging to our citizens.

... About ten days since, Capt. P. H. Healy, a citizen of this place, and a man universally respected and esteemed by all who knew him, was most foully and brutally murdered and scalped by the red fiends of hell. He was coming into town in a wagon drawn by a yoke of steers, and when about ten miles west of this place, he was set upon by the Indians, and having only a single six-shooter, was evidently soon overpowered and murdered. His body was found a few days afterwards most horribly mutilated, and was brought into town and buried....

... I learn also that a large party of Indians passed near the town of Belton, Bell county, on the Nolan, and carried off some fifty head of horses. They also carried off a large number of horses from the Gabriel in Burnet county, and doubtless are at this date prowling about in this county.

The truth is, if something is not done soon for the relief of the frontier it will have to be abandoned.[13]

Another raid occurring in this section at Cedar Mills, Burnet County, early in December, 1870, is illustrative of the depredations committed in that vicinity. The following open letter to the Austin *Daily Republican* thus described this Indian visit:

Within the last few days the Indians have been infesting our settlements to a fearful extent, and the people everywhere seem to be in a fever of excitement over the depredations committed by these savage fiends.

The report is that, after doing a great deal of mischief in Brown county, they come down into Blanco, and that while resting at noon on the 6th inst., a party of men ran upon them and scattered them. Owing to Indian cunning

[12] Galveston *Weekly Civilian*, June 23, 1870, XXIII, 7.
[13] *Daily State Journal*, August 20, 1870, I, 173.

the whites were unable to follow them to any great distance; for as soon as they were discovered, they plunged into the dense cedar brakes where it is almost a matter of impossibility to follow them on horseback. They soon emerged into the beautiful valley along the west bank of the Colorado, in the neighborhood of Mr. Fowler's and there displayed their skill in deeds of barbarity and cruelty. They gathered horses in the Fowler Valley, herding them by the side of the field. Several hands were at work in the fields near by. Two of the savages left the balance to gather horses, and proceeded across the field where the hands were working. Immediately on their appearance two of the hands ran off and made their escape, leaving two Negro girls to whatever fate the Indians might decree. One of them ran some five or six hundred yards but was finally overtaken and killed—the other, only ten years old, was made a prisoner and carried off.

The savages were seen several times during the same day, gathering and herding horses along the west bank of the Colorado. How many horses they collected is not known, but it is supposed that the number is very considerable.

On the morning of the 7th inst., as Mr. Sam Holland was riding from Mormon Mills to the town of Burnet he was suddenly surprised and attacked by the same party of Indians that had committed depredations west of Colorado. Being upon an excellent horse he could outrun all but two. He was fired at several times during the chase. He returned the fire five times, but without being conscious of inflicting any injury upon the savages. After being chased for some distance, he met an old Negro man going to mill in a two-horse wagon. Mr. Holland called to him and told him to prepare to fight, but the old fellow, so terrified at the Indians and the noise made by them, wheeled his horses around, and went at double quick toward town. Mr. Holland saw that it was useless to contend against so many Indians— for they were trying all the time to surround him—and to make the best of a bad bargain, concluded to make his way into a thicket. The Negro thought it was not good policy to ride in a wagon driven by the Indians, and so he took to a thicket also; leaving the Indians in full command of the wagon and team.

Just a few minutes before the Indians chased Mr. Holland, they killed the Negro that they captured in the field of Mr. Fowler, but she was not found until some time the next day.

As soon as the report was circulated that the Indians were in the county, a party of men from the town of Burnet and vicinity immediately made pursuit, but to very little purpose; for, pursuing their usual plan, the savages left the country with what horses they had and recrossed the river higher up. Reliable information has since been received to the effect that in their exit from this county, they murdered a gentleman by the name of

214

Whitlock and his entire family; at the same time burning his house and all furniture.[14]

Among the many depositions gathered by the U. S. commission investigating depredations on the Texas frontier was one made by a 13-year-old boy, Clinton L. Smith of Dripping Springs, in Kendall County. Two years earlier, in 1870, he had been engaged in herding his father's stock when a mounted group of twelve Apaches and two Mexicans suddenly appeared, seized him and his younger brother Jefferson, and carried them away. Their father, Henry L. Smith, heard their screams and ran toward the spot, but he arrived too late. He could only stand and watch the terrified children being borne away.

The two boys were taken northwestward, across the Brazos River. At a Comanche camp Clinton Smith was traded to a Comanche chief, Mah-way, for four hourses, some beads, powder, and lead, but the Comanche refused to take Clinton's brother because he was too young. The Apaches later carried him off to Mexico.

Clinton's new captors were continually on the march. They wanted to cross the Staked Plains to avoid meeting United States troops, but an existing drouth prevented this. They kept a little to the south of the plains, hunting buffalo as they traveled. Clinton and other young captives were kept busy packing buffalo meat, washing robes, and herding horses. They were whipped terribly, yet if they cried they risked death; some were actually killed for that reason.

Clinton was eventually exchanged at Fort Sill for an Indian squaw, and he was sent home. He did not see his brother again until May, 1873, when Jefferson was returned to Dripping Springs, released through the efforts of William Schuchardt, United States commercial agent at Piedras Negras, who bought him from the Lipan Indians for $250.

Jefferson Smith also appeared before the commission but was not examined; he was to young to understand the oath and his mind had been affected by ill treatment. His body bore the marks of severe beatings and perhaps other injuries as well: at one point in their captivity he and his brother had been put astride a wild buffalo and turned loose, and both were thrown immediately.[15]

[14] Austin *Daily Republican,* December 14, 1870, III, 165.
[15] Forty-third Congress, First Session, *Executive Document No. 257* (Serial No. 1615), pp. 26–27.

Another graphic account of capture was related by Martina Diaz, who made a deposition before the commission. On December 2, 1871, she and her husband were traveling from Laredo to San Antonio in a wagon train when, at a point about fifty miles from Laredo, thirty Comanches attacked. The savages delivered an overpowering fire, killing a woman named Guadalupe Rodriguez, then they plundered the wagons. Martina Diaz and a boy, Ceferino Trevino, were captured, and for the ensuing three months, at the mercy of their captors, they traveled through rugged, desolate country, until the Comanches at last brought them to the tribal camp in the Sierra Nevada mountains. All this time Martina Diaz, now a slave, belonged to a chief named Youngcost who outraged her. She endured his cruelty until the following year, when he died. Sometime shortly after her capture the Comanches fought a United States cavalry unit. She observed that her captors were apparently victorious, for they returned with arms, provisions, a white man's scalp, and a pair of saddlebags. She later testified that her own life was threatened on this occasion, perhaps because she betrayed emotion.

Martina Diaz had been a captive for several months when a party of some two hundred Mescaleros visited the camp. She observed that they held many women and children captives. She was able to learn something from them concerning their captors' operations and the activities of the Mexican Apaches, but she obtained this at the risk of her life. The Indians killed captives seeking such information; they allowed prisoners to speak only about current happenings of the camp, and they limited conversation to the Comanche tongue.

Early in December, 1872, the Comanche band camped near Fort Sill to exchange some white boys and to negotiate other business with the agent. For several days the Indians remained there, and Martina Diaz was almost insane with desire to escape. She could even see the fort in the distance.

About a week after arrival she overheard a conversation between two squaws, who plainly indicated their contempt for Anglo-Americans and for the reservation policy. One said to the other:

Didn't these damned fools, Americans, give us fine things for the few Texas rats we delivered to them? But never mind; our brothers are now getting some more Texan boys and horses, with which we will get our warriors and women back again from them, and then we will rise and leave their reservation, and will show these foolish white men how much the

Comanche can be coaxed to live in peace with them and eat bacon and salt stuff on their reservations.

That same evening Martina Diaz learned that the Comanches had concluded their negotiations. Fearing that they would leave the area at once, she determined to escape that night, despite forbidding weather. To avoid creating suspicion among her captors she abused the Anglo-American prisoners before the two squaws whose conversation she had overheard. Finally the Indian women retired for the night, but Martina Diaz, now in her tent, waited. By midnight she felt certain that everyone was asleep. She crawled under the side of her shelter, stumbled out into a cold, rainy night, and ran. When she at last reached the agent's home at Fort Sill her feet were cut and bleeding. Fearful all the while of being killed by a sentry, she walked up to the house and knocked. Receiving no answer, she called out in English, asking for the door to be opened. Finally she was convinced that her entreaty had not been heard, so she passed the rest of the night sleeping in a nearby alley. There she was found the next morning. After solicitous treatment by the women of the post she was returned to her home in San Antonio.[16]

Late in the spring of 1872 news came out of Fort Sill that all Indian warriors of the Comanche and Kiowa tribes had left the reservation to raid into Texas and that Qua-ha-das, Apaches, and Cheyennes might soon follow.[17] Then, on September 1, 1872, Agent Laurie Tatum reported the outcome:

During the fall and winter of last year, and the early part of the present season, the Indians of this agency except the Qua-ha-da band of Comanches came regularly for their rations and repeatedly gave assurance of amity and peace during this year, but no sooner had their horses recuperated from the winter's exhaustion than the Kiowa Indians determined to go on the war path during the summer, and I have cause to believe that a few of the Apaches and a large number of the Comanches have joined them in their raids. The frontier settlers of Texas have been extreme sufferers from their numerous thefts and atrocities, taking in some instances all of the stock of a new settler. They have taken one young woman and two children captives and murdered in Texas twenty-one persons that I have heard of.

[16] Forty-third Congress, First Session, *Executive Document No. 257* (Serial No. 1615), pp. 25–26.
[17] *Daily State Journal,* June 1, 1872, III, 109.

From the 8th of last fifth-month to the 18th of eighth-month, I have withheld rations from the Kiowa Indians on account of their atrocities. At the latter date, they brought in two of the captives, Susanna and Milly F. Lee,[18] who with their brother John were taken by them on the ninth of the sixth month, 1872. They promised to bring in their brother in two weeks. Until then, I do not intend to issue to them again unless so instructed . . .[19]

Commissioner of Indian Affairs E. P. Smith provided additional information in his annual report of 1872, declaring that during the past two years the Kiowas had murdered no fewer than 100 innocent persons and had stolen as many as 1,000 horses and mules.[20] Agent Tatum, reporting at the same time, stated that Kiowas, Comanches, and Apaches owned among them at least 16,500 horses and mules taken from Texas.[21]

DEPREDATIONS OF THE INDIANS FROM MEXICO AND THE MEXICAN BORDER THIEVES

Border depredations of the Kickapoos and the Mexican stock thieves have been mentioned, but again certain selected incidents can serve to give a more vivid picture of these raids and those by Mescalero Apaches.

One deposition came to the U.S. commissioners from James O. Luby, who had resided on the Border for eleven years and was aware of many Indian raids. He stated that on August 10, 1870, he observed eight mounted Kickapoos near Fort Ewell, Texas, driving a herd of stolen horses toward Mexico. All of the Indians were intoxicated; they had just robbed a ranch and had obtained liquor, among other booty. Luby also declared that a few months later, on December 3, a party of forty-two Kickapoos attacked Nogalitas ranch in Encinal County, besieging it for two hours, then hit the Charco Largo and Quirogas ranches. The next day Luby was among the men who pursued these savages, and he found many dead farm animals, their bodies riddled with arrows, along the road between Charco Largo and Quirogas ranches. At Quirogas Luby saw a Mexican woman the Kickapoos had

---

18 The Lee children had been captured near Fort Griffin. G. W. Schofield to J. A. Augur, August 19, 1872, Letters Regarding Kiowa and Comanche Indians, 1872, MS.

19 *Annual Report of the Commissioner of Indian Affairs, 1872,* pp. 247–248.

20 *Ibid.,* pp. 136–137.

21 *Ibid.,* p. 41.

murdered, and he was told that a man had also been killed nearby. On their raid the Indians had stolen Luby's own saddle horse. Although he was positive the animal had been taken to Mexico, his efforts to obtain it proved unsuccessful.

Luby concluded his deposition with a description of three Kickapoo raids near San Diego, Texas, in 1872. The Indians appeared during the dark of the moon, as was their custom, and after plundering for three or four days returned to Mexico with their loot.[22]

Another deposition describing Kickapoo marauding was provided by Albert Turpe, Maverick County district court clerk, who had actually visited the tribe's center of operations at Santa Rosa, Mexico, numerous times. There he had observed the disreputable dealings the Kickapoo and Pottawatomie Indians carried on with certain Mexican traders in a market place at a Mexican mission called Nacimiento, twenty-five miles northwest of Santa Rosa. One merchant, Jesus Galan, extended credit to the Kickapoos provided that they repaid with stolen Texas stock, at three dollars a head for horses and mules.

Albert Turpe stated that his brother Richard had formerly lived near Santa Rosa, and thus had closely observed activities of the Indians. One of them, a Kickapoo named John Taylor, often led a band of Indian braves into Texas. Upon his return he invariably boasted of the number of killings and on one occasion brandished the scalp of a woman. Richard Turpe estimated that it had been acquired only two or three weeks earlier.

In his deposition Albert Turpe also described an 1870 Indian fight in which the Kickapoos overwhelmed a combination of Mescaleros and Lipans, forcing them to retreat to Monclova Vieja, some eighteen miles above Piedras Negras. Turpe was in Mexico at the time and observed the beaten Indians. At their camp he found several captives. Most of them were Mexicans, but one was a white girl about nine or ten years old. He spoke to the child in both English and German, and though she seemed to understand, she did not answer. Possibly previous discipline by her captors had taught her discretion. Turpe attempted to take her with him across the Rio Grande into Texas, but the Indians guessed his intention and drove him away with a shower of arrows. Plunging into a nearby stream, he made his escape. Later,

[22] Forty-third Congress, First Session, *Executive Document No. 257* (Serial No. 1615), p. 15.

Turpe offered $200 in specie to any Mexican who would bring the child to Texas, but she was soon spirited away by her captors and vanished, possibly forever.[23]

Although this South Texas frontier was virtually without federal and state protection, the settlers themselves offered courageous resistance to the marauders when they had time to organize. A letter written on December 28, 1872, by C. A. Beeman of Oakville, in Live Oak County, described one instance.

. . . The first alarm was given about noon on yesterday, that Mr. Andrew Eullons had been chased by a party of Indians some eight miles west of this town. Little time was lost in mounting and equipping a party of fifteen, who found the trail and followed it some distance that evening but night was coming on—very dark and misting rain—they were forced to call a halt and encamp for the night. At daylight this morning they were again on the trail, which the moist condition of the soil permitted them to follow without difficulty, and about 9 o'clock, A.M., they came upon the Indians at "Turkey Creek," where they had stopped to prepare breakfast. Making a genuine Texas charge, they took the Indians entirely by surprise, and succeeded in killing the entire party, five in number. . . .

The fight occurred about forty miles west of this place.[24]

Not all citizens were so eager for retaliation, however, because some of them actually profited by the raids. The federal commissioners included this comment in their report:

. . . With regret the commissioners report that at the town of Laredo, the feeling was so strong in connection with the debasing circle of Mexican local influence, illicit trade, and hostility to Americans that, although the drum had been beaten on one occasion to rally the inhabitants of that town generally to repel an attack of the Kickapoos, and the bodies of men murdered by them, often been brought into the town, but few resident witnesses could be found who could state what tribes of Indians depredated upon them. As the town of New Laredo, Mexico, opposite, is often visited by Kickapoos who trade there, this uncertainty has but one explanation—a strong sympathy with the corrupt local influences on the Mexican side.[25]

[23] Forty-third Congress, First Session, *Executive Document No. 257* (Serial No. 1615), pp. 22–23.

[24] *Tri-Weekly State Gazette,* January 6, 1873, VI, 11.

[25] Forty-third Congress, First Session, *Executive Document No. 257* (Serial No. 1615), p. 14.

Among Kickapoo notorieties was horse thieving. Levi English, a Rio Grande Valley stockman, told the commissioners about an 1871 raid in which eighty of these Indians participated. The savages killed and wounded several persons and stole three hundred horses. The animals were, of course, taken to Mexico; there Texas stockmen bought some of them from the Kickapoos and brought them back across the Rio Grande.

English also furnished information concerning activities of the Mexican border thieves. He recalled that in 1870 he and a group of his ranch hands were attacked by a band of savages and Mexicans disguised as Indians who stole his camping equipment and thirteen horses. Determined to recover the animals, he and a group of his friends followed the marauders and overtook them on the banks of the Rio Grande. The thieves, mounted on English's horses, put up a furious fire and compelled the Texans to retreat, but in the brief encounter English and a companion killed one of the bandits, who proved to be a well-known Mexican.

Again in 1872 English joined forces with other stockmen to pursue these marauders, and once he was accompanied by thirty State Police commanded by the celebrated Captain L. H. McNelly. On that occasion they followed the trail of about one thousand stolen cattle, but they were forced to halt at the Rio Grande; the cattle had already been taken into Mexico.[26]

Many Mexican bandits exhibited a cruelty worthy of the Indians they often accompanied. One especially horrible incident occurred at Howard's Well, in what was to become Crockett County, on April 20, 1872, when several teamsters were burned to death by Indians and a group of more than twenty Mexicans.[27]

Mexican authorities did practically nothing to hinder these thieving excursions. In fact, one man, Edward N. Gray of San Diego, Texas, stated in his deposition that Mexican officials admitted to him that they could not stop the marauding. Gray also declared that when stolen stock entered Mexico it was often confiscated by Mexican army officers. Some of his own horses and mules stolen by Mexican bandits were later used by Lieutenant Colonel Juan Flores of the Mexican army to mount some of his men.[28]

Further evidence of the depredations of the Mexican border thieves

[26] *Ibid.,* pp. 10–11.   [27] *Ibid.,* p. 14.   [28] *Ibid.,* p. 16.

was brought forward by Beauford P. Vivion in his deposition before the United States frontier commission. Vivion, like English, a stock-raiser of the Rio Grande section, declared that early in June, 1871, he was informed by a friend, Alcalde Trompo Garcia, of Piotes, Mexico, that the Texan's stolen cattle, as well as those of this brother, had been confiscated by a Mexican named Silas Gonzales with the aid of certain others of his nationality. Garcia further explained to Vivion that the cattle, after being brought into Mexico, had been driven to Amole, a place located about twenty miles from Piotes and evidently in the vicinity of Piedras Negras. His informant offered to go with Vivion to show him the property, but the stock-raiser being alone, feared that he would be killed should he make the attempt and declined. A few days later, Alcalde Garcia called at Vivion's home in Eagle Pass and told the Texan that about 1,500 cattle stolen from Texas were located at a ranch near Santa Rosa, belonging to Nasario Luna, a Mexican. The alcalde again offered to take Vivion to Luna's ranch in order that the American stock-raiser might locate his cattle. But since he was positive that Luna was both a desperate character and a murderer, Vivion refused to try to regain his property from the bandit.

In August, 1871, Vivion was returning from a trip to Monterrey, Mexico, when he encountered a large herd of cattle, a number of which bore Texas brands. He asked the Mexican drover where he obtained the animals and was told that they had been bought from Nasario Luna. Vivion explained to him that the stock had been stolen, but to this the drover replied: "You can take the cattle if you choose." However, Vivion did not make such an attempt, as he was alone, while the drover was accompanied by eight companions.[29]

In 1871 a description of Mescalero Apache depredations was compiled by M. E. Kelly, customs collector at Presidio del Norte, and forwarded to Senator A. J. Fountain, chairman of the Committee on Indian Affairs of the Twelfth Legislature. These Mescaleros raided into Texas along the upper Rio Grande, keeping settlers there in constant fear for their lives. Kelly stated that the savages ranged from Mexico to the Guadalupe mountains in El Paso County and that the tribe, consisting of some three hundred persons, often made temporary peace with certain Mexican towns in order to trade off stolen stock. During 1870 and up to April, 1871, Kelly reported, these Indians had killed

[29] *Ibid.*, p. 9.

at least twenty-two Texas settlers, wounded eleven, and captured three. During this period they had stolen 117 horses and 233 cattle with a total value of more than $12,000 and had taken wagons, goods, and other personal property worth $5,700.[30]

Life and property along the Texas frontier during E. J. Davis' carpetbag administration were thus in constant danger, and many settlements were devastated. Only the more densely populated eastern and southeastern sections of the state were immune to these constant depredations.

[30] *Daily State Journal,* April 20, 1871, II, 72.

SECTION IV THE SOCIAL SCENE UNDER THE CARPETBAGGERS

Nov

DAILY LIFE IN TEXAS

LIVING CONDITIONS AND CUSTOMS

THE SOCIAL PICTURE in Texas tended to vary with the topography and climate of its extensive area. Residents of the eastern and southeastern portions suffered from the Civil War to a greater extent than did those of any other section, since they were more interested in raising cotton. Negro slaves had been widely used in this region, and it is not surprising that planters encountered difficulty in adjusting to free labor.

People who lived nearer the center of the state were not so materially affected, for there cotton farming had not acquired the importance it had attained in the older eastern section. Frontier settlers in the north, west, and southwest were virtually undisturbed, economically, by the outcome of the war but of course faced a greater challenge to economic development in the constant Indian depredations.

The breakup of the plantation system after the war, the increased immigration in the early seventies, and the homestead act passed by the Twelfth Legislature all tended to increase the number of small farmers. The following description of these agriculturists, however, applies particularly to those who resided in the eastern and northeastern portions of the state.

The small farm of the early seventies usually possessed a limited number of livestock: ten or fifteen cows, a yoke or two of oxen, perhaps twenty sheep, a horse or two, a dozen razorback hogs, and a number of chickens, ducks, geese, and turkeys. Usually each family had a garden and an orchard producing vegetables and fruits for home consumption. Several cattle would be killed every year, the meat cured,

227

and the skins taken to the nearest tannery. Most clothes were home-made, and the housewife spent much time spinning and weaving wool, cotton, and flax. Dyes used for the clothing were obtained from walnut hulls, oak bark, indigo, and cochineal. The wife also knitted socks, stockings, and mittens for her family and made carpets, candles, soap, and mattresses.[1] Her husband built furniture, broke his field with a turn plow, cultivated row crops with a "double-shovel" or with a "bull-tongue" and a "sweep." At that time cotton and corn were planted by hand.

Land was enclosed by a "stake and rider,"[2] a rail fence to protect it from stock. Rock fences were also used, as were, in East Texas, rose and *bois-d'arc* hedges. Barbed wire, invented in 1873, would later supplant other types of fencing.[3]

Game was abundant, and a farmer, especially in the wooded areas, had little difficulty obtaining all the wild meat he desired: deer, geese, turkeys, prairie chickens, ducks, quail, and squirrels. For refrigeration he used a spring or a well. Branch water was usually considered pure enough for drinking purposes.[4]

The typical town of this period was small and usually built along one wide street, which in wet weather presented a serious obstacle to travel of any kind. In county seats, stores clustered around the courthouse square. In small towns were found two or three general stores, a drugstore or two, and several saloons.

General stores offered a limited variety of groceries, a few dry goods, and an insignificant amount of hardware and furniture.[5] The grocery area might display home-cured meats, eggs, sugar, homemade

[1] W. O. Hebison, *Early Days in Texas and Rains County*, pp. 8–9. Hebison declared that dripping lye soap was made by almost every farm woman. The ash hopper, a homemade utensil, was generally used in making soap. The ashes were soaked to the dripping stage, and then the drip was collected and placed with boiling lye and grease scraps. The grease scraps were at once eaten up by the lye, leaving the newly made soap. Scraps of hog meat were generally used for soap grease, but if this could not be obtained, it was said that the flesh from a fat opossum made an acceptable substitute.

[2] Seth S. McKay, "Texas under the Regime of E. J. Davis," pp. 63–70, MS.

[3] Walter Prescott Webb, *The Great Plains*, pp. 281–300.

[4] McKay, "Texas under the Regime of E. J. Davis," pp. 63–70, MS.; Hebison, *Early Days in Texas*, pp. 8–9.

[5] Statement of Mrs. Eliza Rosewood to the author, March 27, 1938.

228

syrup, butter, cheese, coffee, lemon and soda crackers, dried herring, codfish, and dried fruits—prunes, apples, and currants. In the larger towns canned fruits and preserves were also available.[6] The dry goods area contained denim goods, calico, gingham, and hats. Before Christmas such delicacies as peppermint stick candy might be displayed to tempt the children, but toys were few and not well made. Only the basic necessities in hardware and furniture were kept.

A small-town drugstore carried a variety of patent medicines, most with glowing advertisements on their dusty exteriors guaranteeing to cure a long line of man's infirmities. For Negroes the druggist himself frequently served as a doctor.[7] But even persons able to afford a professional physician received inferior care compared to their twentieth-century descendants. A local doctor in the early seventies did not concern himself with the germ theory, nor did he operate for appendicitis or do any abdominal work. He emphasized the use of quinine and calomel and believed that milk was harmful to the sick. He sometimes doubled as a dentist.[8]

Down the street from the doctor's austere office might have been a hotel, and in the small town of the early seventies this was scarcely ornate. The bill of fare was limited, and the cooking was not likely to impress a gourmet. Found on the table were skillet-made cornbread, home-cured meat, eggs, coffee, and milk. Water for the meal was drawn from a well or a cistern. A transient could usually expect sleeping companions: another member of his own sex (for there were not enough beds to give guests the luxury of a private one) and numerous bedbugs. These insects were often so plentiful and so hearty that "they would almost lift a man up and carry him off."[9]

Always present in any small town was a saloon, which was invariably a gathering place for a certain male segment of the population. The hot politics, strong liquor, and ready pistol found there were not conducive to the maintenance of friendships, and gunfights occasionally disturbed the customers.

In the vicinity of Fort Griffin buffalo drives were being conducted,

[6] Houston *Union,* November 15, 1870, III, 60.

[7] Statement of Mrs. Eliza Rosewood.

[8] *Ibid.*; San Angelo *Standard Times,* May 3, 1934, Sec. IV, p. 4, Vol. 51, No. 1.

[9] Statement of Mrs. Eliza Rosewood.

and the prosperous hunters descended thirstily on a town called the "Flat."[10] One of their favorite saloons at the "Flat," the "Beehive," bore near its front entrance a sign that proclaimed:

> In this hive we are all alive,
> Good whiskey makes us funny,
> And if you are dry
> Step in and try
> The flavor of our honey.[11]

In West Texas saloons, dance-hall girls enlivened festivities, and at the "Flat" the most famous of these creatures was red-haired Lottie Deno, "the poker Queen," who was said to be the equal of the most proficient gamblers in the West.

During the buffalo drives the "Flat" reached its uproarious zenith. Although some staid citizens resided there, the place was jammed with gamblers, desperadoes, horse thieves, cattle rustlers and women who suited the tastes of such rascals. For a time the place was entirely without law enforcement, for civilian disturbances were of no concern to the soldiers at Fort Griffin. Eventually the sober citizens of the town formed a vigilante organization which controlled the lawlessness. Thereafter the town thrived on a higher plane; the good citizens, ignoring the dens of iniquity, were proud of the hotel, the several stores carrying excellent merchandise, and a school building, which on Sundays served as a church.[12]

Throughout the early seventies buffalo hunting remained a lucrative sport for West Texans. Countless herds still roamed the plains,[13] and hunters could often kill from twenty-five to forty head a day. One of the most proficient shots was Wylie Poe of Fort McKavett, credited with killing as many as ninety in one stand. These hunters frequently worked in bands of about twelve, while another dozen men followed in wagons to do the skinning and to save whatever meat was needed. Thousands of hides were brought to Fort Concho[14] and to the "Flat" each year.[15] Thus massacring the buffalo was wasteful, but it helped

[10] Sallie Reynolds Matthews, *Interwoven*, pp. 119–121.
[11] *Ibid.*, p. 53.
[12] *Ibid.*, pp. 119–121.
[13] San Angelo *Standard Times*, May 3, 1834, Sec. IV, p. 16, Vol. 51, No. 1.
[14] *Ibid.*
[15] Matthews, *Interwoven*, p. 118.

solve the Indian problem: with the disappearance of the animal went the chief means by which the Indian could obtain food while on a raiding expedition.

The most profitable and permanent business of this western area, however, was not buffalo hunting but cattle ranching. And its central figure, the cowboy, through his songs, stories, speech, and gunfighting, has become the subject of an extensive literature.[16]

Each cowboy employed by a ranch had to provide his own saddle, bridle, spurs, and bedding. Called a "hot roll," bedding consisted of a few quilts and blankets rolled in canvas to protect them from rain. Management furnished the horses, usually from eight to ten for each man. With fifteen men employed the ranch provided as many as 150 horses.

Spring and fall roundups were held each year, but the one in the spring was more important, for then the calves were branded. Work was done in roundup districts, each of which included several ranges. All the ranches in the district participated. Before each roundup the stockmen met to choose a superintendent for the event and to select a meeting place for each outfit. At a central point within the district the outfits, accompanied by chuck wagons and cooks, would gather. Eventually as many as three hundred men might appear at the site, and their horses numbered between two and three thousand. Now the superintendent, or roundup boss, named his lieutenants, gave them details of cowboys, and ordered them to cover designated sections of the range. From four to six days usually were required to work a range; the men left camp in squads, but then separated and in a fanlike man-

---

[16] J. Marvin Hunter, *The Trail Drivers of Texas,* pp. 332–334. Mr. Hunter says this concerning the apt phraseology of the cowboy:

I think I may claim these few samples of cowboy lingo are characterized by simplicity, strength, and directness and it may be added accuracy. Of a tall man he does not like, the cowboy says: "He's just as long as a snake, and he drags the ground when he walks." Although a cow is one of the most stupid of animals, when a cowboy says that a man has good cow sense he means to pay him a high compliment. An "eye baller" is a person who pokes himself into other people's business; going courting is: "goin gallin," "sittin the bag" or "sittin her"; "cutting a rusty" means doing your best; moving fast is "faggin," "leffin here," "sailing away," or "going like the heel flies are after him." . . . When a fellow makes a night of it, he is said to have "stayed out with the dry cattle." When a delicate situation arises, there is said to be "hair in the butter." The water on the plains is sometimes so muddy that the cowboy says "he has to chew it before he can swallow it." When there is room for doubt about his knowledge, he is said to know as much about it as a "hog does about a side saddle." A man who is good at roping is said to "sling the catgut well."

231

ner scoured the country. They brought the cattle to a circle near the roundup camp, and by noon of the first day as many as two or three thousand head might be gathered. At this juncture the superintendent designated men to hold the herd.

Next the cattle were separated into individual herds. The owner of the range on which the work was being done made the first "cut." Cowboys, on cutting horses, worked out of the herd all his branded cows and calves that followed them and left them in a separate herd. Then the next man took his cut. New calves were branded during cutting or later by the owner.

Day after day this work was repeated until the first range had been combed. Then the men moved to the next range, but when they left, the range owner remained behind with his herd or made provisions for it to be held on his property by some of his help. He also saw to it that any cattle belonging to him and found on other ranges during the roundup should be cut out and returned to him. From the first of the cutting there were of course as many separate herds as there were owners.[17]

Like branding, cattle drives occurred in the spring, for then there was plenty of grass and no cold weather to fear. During the first few days of the drive the cattle were pushed to longer distances to trail-break them, but thereafter the distance covered each day averaged from twelve to fifteen miles. Riding ahead of the herd to lead it were "pointers," the most experienced men. Behind them followed flank riders, then swing horsemen, and finally, drag men. These cowboys worked in pairs, across the herd from each other, and the foreman circled the herd from time to time.

The worst menace to cattle drivers was the stampede. Anything might cause it: a flash of lightning, a burst of thunder, any unusual sound. Once the cattle stampeded they lost all reason and would even run blindly over the edge of a cliff or into a ravine. The headlong flight could be ended only by forcing the animals to run in a circle; then they milled round and round until calm returned. But it was far better to prevent a stampede than it was to try to halt one, and for this reason the cowmen sang to their herd after the animals had been bedded down at night.[18]

[17] Webb, *The Great Plains*, pp. 255–258.
[18] *Ibid.*, pp. 264–268; Charles A. Siringo, *Riata and Spurs*, p. 26.

As mentioned, Abilene, Kansas, was the chief market for drovers in the early seventies, and the town was well fixed to provide entertainment sufficiently boisterous for the amusement of men who had spent weeks on the trail. Saloons, dance hall girls, and gambling tables provided outlets for emotions and for money. Gunplay was not unusual, and the news of another killing aroused little excitement. Here the earnings of many a cowboy were exhausted after only a few days in the town.[19]

Although this was Kansas, it was also typical of social life on the Texas frontier, which centered around the man rather than the woman. For obvious reasons women were scarce in the area, but men were thrown together in cattle roundups, in drives, in buffalo hunting, and in patrolling against marauding Indians. The comparatively few women who resided in the area led isolated lives far distant from the nearest neighbor. No doubt many wives who ventured West had no idea that the Indians were still a menace or that the country remained a wilderness, but when they learned the truth most of them made admirable attempts to adapt to the hazardous situation.[20]

On the more sedate side, Texas in 1870 had 843 churches with a total membership of 199,100 people.[21] Most church members were Methodist and Baptists, with the Methodists in a majority by a few thousand.

A typical rural church was constructed of logs, but if one had not been built a log schoolhouse or a private residence was sometimes used. Usually a circuit rider was employed as pastor, but occasionally a local resident, such as a schoolmaster, doubled as a minister.

In late summer, after most crops had been harvested, revival meetings were held, usually beneath a brush arbor near the church. It has been said that when a strong man "got religion" at one of these meetings his shouting could be heard all over the countryside and that several men were needed to hold him down. Revival meetings were important events in the early seventies and were well attended, men sitting on one side and women on the other. The congregation often sat through sermons from an hour and a half to two hours long, and during that time the split log or plank benches must have become quite

[19] Siringo, *Riata and Spurs*, p. 223.
[20] San Angelo *Standard Times*, May 3, 1834, Sec. III, p. 13, Vol. 51, No. 1.
[21] U. S. Bureau of the Census, *Ninth Census of the United States, 1870*, I, 506.

233

uncomfortable. Sleep was out of the question, because most benches had no backs. The preacher, however, suffered, too. He was not paid well—certainly not in proportion to the length of his sermons—and often received compensation only in the form of food and clothing.[22]

Other niceties appeared, somewhat paradoxically, in the rough-hewn Texas of the early seventies. Temperance and women's suffrage movements had been launched by that time, and a prominent temperance leader, the Reverend James Young, had organized an order known as the "Friends of Temperance." By the spring of 1870 he had formed about thirty local councils, but they were not widely influential;[23] the Lone Star State was not really ready for the movement.

Neither was it ready for the suffragists. The first campaign for women's rights in Texas was launched by Dr. Mary J. Walker, who lectured throughout the more peaceful areas of the state in April, 1870. Among the towns she visited were Columbus, Richmond, and Brenham, but none of them received her enthusiastically.[24] Richmond proved to be most inhospitable of all; there she was met at the railway depot and pelted with eggs, some of which obviously had no other use.[25]

More sophisticated amusement than this was available to residents of larger cities, where horse racing, baseball, theatricals, dancing, and railroad excursions were popular. Horse races were held in Houston each spring, and betting was lively. In April, 1870, the Blooded Stock Association of Texas, which held its races in Houston, even provided a brass band to create additional enthusiasm.[26]

[22] Hebison, *Early Days in Texas,* pp. 19–20.

[23] Houston *Daily Union,* March 15, 1870, I, 5. In this same issue of the paper but in a different account, it is stated that Young had organized a society of seventy-two members taken from the children of Houston, which was called the "Band of Hope." The members of this organization pledged themselves to neither drink liquor, use tobacco, nor swear.

[24] Houston *Daily Union,* April 20, 1870, II, 36.

[25] *Ibid. The Daily Union* reported the incident as follows:
We learn from Dr. Mary Walker that a few rowdies, forgetful of the slight claim they may have to manhood, pelted her with unsavory eggs at the depot in Richmond, Texas, yesterday. Where was the boasted chivalry of whom the democratic press love to prate, when this shameless—vile outrage was permitted upon a defenseless woman whose sole offense was in asking that which every American regardless of sex, color, or previous condition, has a right to demand and enjoy—free speech? Can such creatures have mothers and sisters?

[26] *Ibid.,* April 2, 1870, II, 21.

Another possibility for betting lay in baseball games. Many towns fielded their own clubs; the "Merry Nines" of Calvert, the "Pioneers" of Houston, and the "Island City" team of Galveston were among the leaders. Games were often played in the morning, beginning at a little after nine.

Popular in the cities were theatrical performances. In 1870 Galveston had several theaters whose boards boasted some of the best talent to be found. Accordingly, prices were high. In the newest theater the regular cost of admission was $2.50 for any seat in the house.[27]

Also popular—in rural as well as urban areas—was dancing, especially the "Quadrille," "Virginia Reel," "Shooting the Buffalo."[28] When a rural family decided to have a dance one or two young men were dispatched on horseback to inform the desired guests.[29] All-night dances were not unusual, and a single fiddle produced the music. Sometimes a Negro fiddler would be hired to play.[30]

After completion of the Houston and Texas Central to Austin, railroad excursions became a popular form of recreation. A gala celebration held when the service was inaugurated started the fad. The Houston *Daily Telegraph* gives the following account of that first excursion to Austin.

Twelve passenger and two baggage cars left Houston, of which six were well filled with delegates from Houston and Galveston. The engine drawing the first train was just from the shop and its smokestack proving defective, affected its capacity for speed considerably. Added to this, the boxes of one car became so hot as to make it necessary to switch it off and leave it. At most of the depots along the route, delegations were in waiting, so that by the time the trains left McDade, the party was estimated at about six hundred . . .

All along the upper portion of the road from McDade, small parties congregated to see the cars pass. The gray-headed grandfather, and the infant in its mother's arms were alike there, many of them hearing the whistle for the first time. Cattle hurried off in alarm, and the scarce broken mustang did his best to unseat his rider, all however, to no purpose . . .

[27] McKay, "Texas under the Regime of E. J. Davis," p. 66, MS.; *Flake's Daily Bulletin,* January 30 and February 1, 1870, V, 186 and 187.

[28] McKay, "Texas under the Regime of E. J. Davis," p. 76, MS.

[29] *Ibid.,* pp. 75–76. McKay quotes two letters to him; one from C. J. Wilkerson of Denton, Texas, dated April 2, 1919; and the other from W. B. Bell of Honey Grove, Texas, written on March 30, 1919.

[30] Oral statement of D. D. Fowler of Georgetown, Texas, June 6, 1934.

Inside the cars the time seems to pass pleasantly amid conversation, laugh and song, "the flow of champagne and the feat of the lunch-box." Looking for the officers of the road, however, one generally finds them on the platform noting the construction of the road.

About half past six the cars reached the depot, amid wild cheering and the salvos of artillery. Had they arrived at the appointed time, they would have met a grand reception, as all the civic companies, the cadets, and the military were out to welcome them.

At a comparatively early hour the assembly began to gather at the capitol and by half past ten the floors of both the Representative Hall and Senate Chamber were fairly covered with gallantry and beauty whirling in the mazes of the dance, or promenading in an endless chain.[31]

Five other diversions entertained rural residents: singing, Sunday school picnics, log rollings, house raisings, and quilting parties.

Singings were usually held on Sunday evenings at the church or schoolhouse, or at the home of one of the residents. All members of the community were invited; only sacred songs were sung. Similarly religious in nature was the Sunday school picnic, an all-day event that took place at some attractive spot along a river bank or beneath the shelter of a grove of trees. Attendance was not restricted to Sunday school members, for many of them brought friends from outside the class.

Practical as well as diverting was the event called log rolling. When a resident of a timbered region wanted to clear a portion of his land he asked his male neighbors over to assist him. Smaller trees were cut and removed easily, but large logs had to be rolled with "pry poles," used as levers. The term "log rolling" thus developed. Similarly practical was house raising, for to a recently married man or a new settler the construction of a home loomed as a formidable task. But most Texans in the early seventies cooperated—this was a necessity—so a man's neighbors assembled and helped him build his house. Straight-bodied trees were felled; from them logs were cut to the desired length, hauled by oxen to the building site, lifted into place, and notched down. After the walls were thus constructed the log of a large pine or grained oak tree was cut into boards to cover the house. The puncheon floor required timber that would split straight. With that done an adz was used to smooth the surface of the boards, which were laid on sills and fitted as snugly as possible.

[31] Houston *Daily Telegraph,* January 3, 1872, **XXIX,** 59.

For women of the community quilting parties were both practical and pleasurable. Gathering on invitation at the home of a neighbor, they assisted her with the year's quilting. This was done willingly, for after the work had been completed the hostess usually treated her guests to a party or a dance.[32]

Another event, one with universal appeal, was the state fair. The first one was held at Houston in May, 1870, sponsored by the Agricultural, Mechanical and Blood Stock Association of Texas. More than forty thousand people attended during the six days of the fair; Texas farm products, livestock, and manufactured goods were exhibited. A lasting cultural contribution of this event was the organization of the Texas Historical Society on May 23, 1870. Officers of the Society were all prominent Texans, the first president being Ashbel Smith.[33]

URBAN DEVELOPMENT

Residing in Texas in 1870 were 818,175 people; of the thirty-four states then in the Union the Lone Star State ranked nineteenth in population. Population density that year averaged 3.1 persons to each square mile, the least of any Southern state. Only 2.15% of all United States population was claimed by Texas.

That same 1870 census yielded the following statistics:

Population	1860	1870	Gain in Percentage
White	420,819	564,700	34.17
Negro	182,921	253,475	38.57
Total	603,730	818,175	35.52

During the 1860–1870 period Negro population for the nation as a whole increased 9.21 per cent. Texas' sizable increase in this cate-

[32] McKay, "Texas under the Regime of E. J. Davis," pp. 72–76, MS.; Hebison, *Early Days in Texas*, p. 25.

[33] Houston *Daily Union*, May 24, 1870, II, 61. A few of the other important figures who were officers in the Texas Historical Society at the time of its organization were: J. H. Reagan, F. R. Lubbock, E. M. Pease, J. H. Bell, Guy M. Bryan, H. R. Runnels, E. J. Davis, J. D. Giddings, O. M. Roberts, J. W. Throckmorton, and H. S. Thrall.

gory moved it from tenth to ninth ranking in numbers of Negroes.[34]

Of the people residing in the state in 1870, nine-tenths (756,168 persons, were natives of Texas or of another state in the Union. Of this figure 51 per cent had been born in the state. Foreign-born residents totaled 62,411, with Germans the most numerous—23,976. Mexicans, a close second, numbered 23,520. Other nationalities, in order, were Irish, French, English, Austrian, Bohemian, Scotch, and Swiss, but they were much less numerous. Natives of Canada, Poland, Norway, and Sweden were also present, but in numbers less than five hundred.[35]

In 1870 the chief city of Texas, in population and commercial importance, was Galveston. Located on the eastern end of a long island, at the mouth of Galveston Bay, it possessed three miles of wharf frontage. Its 1870 population was 13,898, but it was growing rapidly and by 1880 was to have 22,248 inhabitants.[36] The Galveston of 1873 was a well-planned city with wide streets lined with flower gardens. Further enhancing its beauty were six public squares, an esplanade two miles long, and two parks, one of eighty and the other of twenty-five acres. Nine miles of street railway were in operation. Contributing to the skyline were thirteen hotels, three markethouses, an opera house, two theaters, three concert halls, and many other buildings.

Important factories included two iron foundries, six machine shops, a gas works for lighting the city, and a beef preserving company. In the field of finance, there were two national banks with an aggregate capital of $800,000, a savings bank with $175,000 capital, two banking and insurance companies, four insurance companies proper, and twenty-three joint stock companies possessing an aggregate capital of $12,211,000.[37] Educational institutions were also numerous, though all of them were private schools: Galveston Medical College, Catholic College, Convent for Females, German Lutheran School, and many others.[38]

Although Galveston was a bustling city, it was vulnerable to certain

[34] *Ninth Census of the United States, 1870,* I, preface; McKay, "Texas under the Regime of E. J. Davis," p. 59, MS.

[35] *Ninth Census of the United States, 1870,* I, Table 6; McKay, "Texas under the Regime of E. J. Davis," p. 61, MS.

[36] Texas Department of Insurance Statistics and History, *The Resources, Soil, and Climate of Texas,* p. 111. Hereafter cited as *Resources, Soil, and Climate.*

[37] C. Appleton (ed.), *American Annual Cyclopaedia,* 1873, XIII, 742.

[38] *Texas Almanac,* 1871, p. 112.

recurring perils. One was yellow fever, which broke out in the autumn of 1870, terrifying the populace and sending two thousand persons in flight out of the city.[39] The dreaded disease struck again in 1873.[40]

The second largest Texas city was San Antonio, with an 1870 population of approximately twelve thousand. Inhabitants of Mexican ancestry were in the minority but of course influenced the character of the city. While it possessed Texas' most important military post, San Antonio was also proud of its several educational institutions. One was a free public school with more than two hundred pupils. Stone bridges arched across the San Antonio and San Pedro rivers, which furnished water that irrigated nearby crops.[41]

The third largest Texas city was Houston; its 1870 population was approximately nine thousand.[42] The city, located on the west bank of Buffalo Bayou at the head of tidewater navigation there, lay within fifty miles of the Gulf of Mexico. Even in the early seventies, before the ship channel connecting it with the sea had been constructed, Houston was an important commercial center, the terminus for several railroad lines.[43] By 1871 Houston possessed two cotton and woolen mills, six brickyards, three packing plants, three foundries, and three machine shops. Within the city were manufactured steam engines, railroad cars, wagons, carriages, buggies, furniture, cigars, soap, and many other items. In the Houston vicinity at least twelve sawmills were profitably employed in cutting pine and cypress on Buffalo and San Jacinto bayous,[44] and even as early as 1867 Houston possessed a few mercantile establishments carrying on an annual trade of almost a million dollars each.

The most important town in the northeastern part of the state was Jefferson, situated at the head of navigation on Cypress Bayou and, as mentioned, acting as supply point for a large trade territory. In 1870 Jefferson had four thousand inhabitants,[45] but the town was growing

[39] Houston *Daily Union,* October 2, 1870, II, 27.
[40] Frank Brown, "Annals of Travis County and the City of Austin," Ch. XXXII, p. 39, MS.
[41] *Texas Almanac,* 1871, p. 94.
[42] *Ninth Census of the United States, 1870,* I, Table 3.
[43] *Resources, Soil, and Climate,* p. 136.
[44] *Texas Almanac,* 1871, pp. 163–164.
[45] *Ninth Census of the United States, 1870,* I, Table 3; McKay, "Texas under the Regime of E. J. Davis," p. 61, MS.

tremendously. In one year sixty brick stores were built, and business was so heavy that many of them stayed open all night. Among industries in 1873 were a large packing plant, an ice factory, a cotton compress, and a brewery.[46] Gas lights illuminated the city. But Jefferson's glory was brief; with the spreading of the railroads into the interior and the development of Marshall as a rail center the town declined. A few years after the close of the Davis administration it ceased to be of any importance.[47]

In 1870 Austin counted 5,680 residents.[48] The town, built on a series of hills, looked down on the Colorado River, which lay in the distance. Standing on a hill at the head of Congress Avenue was the capitol, considered a commodious and well-arranged building at the time. At the foot of Congress Avenue a pontoon bridge was constructed across the Colorado in the winter of 1871.[49]

In 1871 Austin had eight churches and twice as many schools. Three or four schools taught Negroes exclusively; in them white Northerners and freedmen acted as instructors. The following year, 1872, was especially prosperous for Austin, for in the November election the city won permanent possession of the capitol, and the western branch of the Houston and Texas Central Railroad had been completed to Austin—late in December, 1871.[50]

Dallas, Fort Worth, Waco, and El Paso were all small towns. Of the four Waco was largest. Illustrative of the state's rural predominance was the Washington County population, which surpassed other Texas counties by several thousand. Yet no large town was located there.[51]

EDUCATION

By passage of the school laws of 1870 and 1871, the Radical Republican Twelfth Legislature created a public school system.

[46] McKay, "Texas under the Regime of E. J. Davis," p. 67, MS. Here McKay quotes a letter from Mrs. Zach Lamar written to him from Pittsburg, Texas, on March 8, 1919. The *Texas Almanac,* 1871, p. 135, declared that in 1871 Jefferson had a population of 12,000.

[47] McKay, "Texas under the Regime of E. J. Davis," pp. 67–68, MS.

[48] Brown, "Annals of Travis County," Ch. XXX, p. 32, MS.

[49] *Ibid.,* p. 26.

[50] Brown, "Annals of Travis County," Ch. XXX, p. 76, MS.

[51] *Ninth Census of the United States, 1870,* I, Table 3; *Texas Almanac,* 1871, p. 103; McKay, "Texas under the Regime of E. J. Davis," p. 61, MS.

The most important of these laws, the act of 1871, provided for the appointment by the Governor of a state superintendent, who was to share authority in school affairs with a state board of education consisting of himself, the Governor, and the legislature. The superintendent was to appoint thirty-five district supervisors, who were to enforce the regulations adopted by the state board of education. Each of these supervisors was in turn to appoint five citizens in every district to act as a district board of directors. The public thus had no control over the management of the school system, but the people were required to pay taxes and to send their children to school.[52]

Following the passage of the act of 1871 Governor Davis appointed Colonel Jacob C. De Gress the first state superintendent of public instruction. De Gress, a Union Army veteran, had come to Texas in June, 1865, when he had been appointed provost marshal and assistant commissioner of the Freedman's Bureau for the eastern district of Texas.[53]

De Gress had no practical school experience, and he was certainly no teacher. He set about organizing and managing the school system in a militaristic manner, showing little consideration for the desires or financial ability of the citizens of the state.

De Gress served until February, 1874,[54] despised most of the time by the Democrats. When that party won a majority in the Legislature following the election of 1872 investigation of his conduct in office was ordered. A joint committee report late in the spring of 1873 declared:

. . . Your committee respectfully submit that the Superintendent, being by virtue of the present school law, vested with almost despotic power, and requiring with the disposition of an inquisitor, the submission of every official act of his subordinates to his own critical inspection, should be held to a strict responsibility for every piece of impropriety which may have come to his knowledge, and which he had not sought to correct.[55]

Despite this disapproval, De Gress continued to serve until February, 1874, a month after the Davis administration had ended. Evi-

[52] H. P. N. Gammel, *Laws of Texas,* VI, 959–962; Frederick Eby, *The Development of Education in Texas,* pp. 160–161, 542.

[53] Frank Brown, "Annals of Travis County," Ch. XXX, p. 39, MS.

[54] Eby, *Development of Education in Texas,* p. 161.

[55] *House Journal, 13th Legislature,* p. 798.

dently the grudge against him had been dissipated by the passage of a new public school act on May 23, 1873, which vested in the people the power once held by the state superintendent.[56] De Gress eventually gained considerable popularity, for though he was a Republican he was elected mayor of the Democratic city of Austin in 1878 and served three consecutive terms, with increasing majorities.[57]

In September, 1871, the scholastic population—including all persons of school age—stood at 229,568. In December of that same year 1,324 schools were in operation and 63,504 pupils attended them. During the following year enrollment increased to 129,542, which amounted to 56 per cent of the scholastic population. But during 1873–1874 attendance dropped to 102,689, only 38 per cent of a scholastic population of 269,451, despite the passage of the public school act of May 23, 1873. Although the law provided for compulsory attendance, the measure was not well enforced.

Schools were divided into first, second, and third classes. Curriculum of third-class schools (primary grades) consisted of spelling, reading, penmanship, geography, and primary arithmetic. In second-class schools (elementary grades) spelling, reading, penmanship, higher geography, mental and practical arithmetic, elementary English grammar, and United States history were taught. In first-class schools (advanced) the course included spelling, reading, penmanship, mental and higher arithmetic, English grammar, English composition, modern history, physical geography, Constitution of the United States, and other courses that the pupils might be competent to pursue. Teaching of Spanish, French, or German was permitted, but not for more than two hours a day. All girls were required to take needlework.[58]

Stiff taxes levied by the Radicals evoked much opposition to the school system; this dissatisfaction became obvious at the previously-described taxpayers' convention. Many people also objected to the system because the superintendent and board exercised extraordinary powers, leaving citizens of the state with no voice in the operation of the schools that their children were compelled to attend. Nor did a majority approve of the compulsory attendance provision of the school act of 1871. They felt that this was a direct violation of the rights

[56] Gammel, *Laws of Texas*, VII, 536–547.
[57] Brown, "Annals of Travis County," Ch. XXX–XXXI, p. 39, MS.
[58] Eby, *Development of Education in Texas*, pp. 161–162; Gammel, *Laws of Texas*, VII, 536–547.

of the parents, that the law-prescribed age of six was too young to send a child to school, and that the maximum age of eighteen was too old. Moreover, the school acts provided for the education of the Negro, a matter displeasing to many who feared that schools would soon be "integrated," to use a twentieth-century term. Further dissatisfaction arose over the extravagance of Superintendent De Gress and the State Board: disbursements far surpassed available funds. For 1872–1873 the available fund was $478,820.34, but the sum disbursed totaled $1,144,535.55.[59]

Even at that, not every teacher received his salary. During the spring of 1873, in fact, Harris County teachers petitioned the Legislature to pay them for past services, declaring that since their salaries had been withheld they had been reduced to privation.[60]

The Radicals thus blundered obviously in the operation of their school system, yet it should not be forgotten that through them the doors of the free school were first opened in Texas. The system actually was rather efficient, but its centralization, especially the arbitrary powers of the superintendent and board, scarcely suited individualistic Texans. The bad features of the system, however, were removed in 1873, when the powers of the state superintendent and the board were displaced. Paradoxically, Texans paid scant attention to this 1873 law, even though complete control of the system was placed in their hands. State residents soon returned to the practice of relying on private schools, as they had done before the Civil War.[61]

During the early seventies a number of private colleges came into existence through the efforts of certain Protestant churches. In 1873 Methodists founded Southwestern University at Georgetown, merging the older schools of Rutersville College, Wesleyan College, McKenzie College, and Soule University; Presbyterians built Austin College, established at Huntsville but later moved to Sherman, and Trinity University, opened at Tehuacana, then moved to Waxahachie and, years

[59] Eby, *Development of Education in Texas,* pp. 162–166.
[60] San Antonio *Daily Herald,* April 29, 1873, XVI, 100.
[61] Eby, *Development of Education in Texas,* pp. 167–168. The features of the Radical school law were many years later reincorporated into the system. Upon this subject, Eby declares: ". . . It is worthy of note, however, that although the system was repudiated by the returning Democratic party of that time, and all of its efficient features eliminated, yet during the past two decades a number of these same features have again been incorporated into the school system by the authority of the people of Texas . . ."

243

later, to San Antonio;[62] Disciples of Christ established Add-Ran College at Thorp Springs, then moved it to Waco and finally to Fort Worth, where it is now Texas Christian University.[63] The first Negro college in Texas, Wiley University, was founded at Marshall in 1873 by the Freedmen's Aid Society of the Methodist church. It remained the only Negro school of any importance in Texas for a number of years.[64]

Also in operation were privately-owned academies, which usually admitted both boys and girls. Providing an idea of the instruction offered is a description of one conducted at Gilmer by Professor Morgan H. Looney. The school, which was in session ten months of the year, averaged in enrollment about two hundred students. It offered work in English, composition, higher mathematics, ancient languages, and other studies. Students were required to adhere to strict rules, and they were supervised at all times. Political and religious arguments were not tolerated, and boys and girls were not allowed to talk to each other except when school work required it. This last rule was occasionally suspended, and a boy was sometimes allowed to call on a girl on Saturday night, provided he did not stay later than nine o'clock.

The close of each school day was marked by a general spelling lesson. At the end of the school session examinations lasting three days were held, and outsiders were invited to watch. The number of visitors attending these examinations was sometimes estimated at between six and eight hundred.[65]

[62] H. H. Bancroft, *History of the North Mexican States and Texas*, XVI, 546; J. J. Lane, *History of Education in Texas*, p. 83.
[63] Lane, *History of Education in Texas*, p. 100.
[64] *Ibid.*, p. 76.
[65] Dudley G. Wooten, *A Comprehensive History of Texas*, II, 466.

12

PROBLEMS OF LAW ENFORCEMENT

CRIME

ON THE DARKER SIDE of the social picture were the many crimes committed in Texas during the carpetbag era. The unsatisfactory efforts of the State Police and of the poorly maintained frontier forces to control this outlawry have been fully discussed, but it should be noted that the evil condition preceded them. From January, 1869, to March 20, 1870, at least 590 murders were committed in Texas—an average of more than one murder a day during the fifteen-month period.[1] Shortly before General J. J. Reynolds relinquished command of the Fifth Military District in the spring of 1870 he commented on the situation.

For the suppression of bands of desperadoes which have infested almost every part of the State and the arrest of parties indicted for murder, it has been necessary to furnish military aid to the civil officers.

These parties have usually met with armed resistance, and in the encounters which ensued several persons have been killed. With very few exceptions, indictments for murder have been found against these persons, and in every case they invited their fate by refusing arrest and in resisting by force of arms the lawfully constituted authorities of this State and of the United States.[2]

Many offenses were committed by freedmen. The transition from slavery to citizenship seemed to be more than the Negro, whose ex-

[1] Report of the Secretary of State, James P. Newcomb, to the State Senate, June 18, 1870, in *Daily State Journal,* June 19, 1870, I, 122.
[2] Forty-Second Congress, Second Session, *Report of the Joint Select Committee to Inquire into the Condition of Affairs in the Late Insurrectionary States Made to the Two Houses of Congress* (Serial No. 1529), p. 19.

perience was certainly limited, could easily make. Lacking proper leadership he sometimes turned to crime, a tendency that was discussed by Bancroft:

. . . As a result of this abrupt change from slavery to political equality with the whites, not only was a conflict between the two races inaugurated, but the debased Negroes, no longer debarred the use of spirituous liquor, under its influence incessantly, engaged in frays among themselves, which generally terminated in bloodshed. The number of murders committed during this period was unparalleled in any epoch of Texas history . . . and what was worse, the judiciary was inadequate to punish . . .[3]

Former slaveholders, who were in many instances true friends of the Negroes, were not allowed to aid in the readjustment. Sole responsibility was given instead to the Freedmen's Bureau, a branch of the United States Army to advise and protect the ex-slaves. Generally, however, the main contribution of the Bureau consisted of arousing within the Negro a distrust for his former master and persuading the ex-slave to join the Union League, an organization that solicited votes for the Radical Republicans.[4] Through the Union League the freedman was taught that only the Union-Republican party would guarantee to protect his rights as a free man.[5]

The Freedmen's Bureau was abolished in 1872, and the Negroes could no longer depend on that organization for their subsistence.[6] In order to survive, many therefore were compelled to work as tenant farmers for the whites, and this brought on another abuse: by threats of ejection some white landlords forced their Negro laborers to refrain from voting or participating in any other political activity.[7] Tenant farming did, however, have its benefits. With the Negro

[3] H. H. Bancroft, *History of the North Mexican States and Texas,* XVI, 511. Bancroft declared that Hepworth Dixon in his book *White Conquest,* p. 331, which was written in 1875, stated that "We learn on good authority that there were 3,000 murders in Texas last year, and that nearly all of these murders were committed by Negroes on their brother blacks." It seems evident, however, that this report was greatly exaggerated.

[4] McKay, "Texas under the Regime of E. J. Davis," pp. 57–58, MS.

[5] Louis M. Hacker and Benjamin B. Kendrick, *The United States since 1865,* p. 17.

[6] E. C. Barker, *Readings in Texas History,* p. 509.

[7] Hacker and Kendrick, *The United States since 1865,* p. 41.

settled once more crime among his race decreased, and the unsanitary jails ceased to be crowded.[8]

THE KU KLUX KLAN

Abolition of slavery had other consequences. Soon after the end of the Civil War certain Southern whites established secret organizations whose purpose was to prevent their area from being "Africanized" and to assure white supremacy. Of these the most widely known was the Ku Klux Klan,[9] which originated in Tennessee but soon spread to Texas. Klan members became famous for their night parades in which they appeared, mounted and armed, wearing long white or black robes, face masks, and high peaked hats. Their ghastly appearance terrified the superstitious Negroes and succeeded in restraining their activities, which was the hoped-for result. Sometimes, however, the consequences went far beyond this, for numerous outrages were committed by the Klan or at least in its name. Thus the peace-preserving purpose of the more responsible Klan founders was defeated, for the organization in these activities did anything but preserve law and order.[10] General J. J. Reynolds reported that between 1868 and 1869 East Texas units of the Ku Klux Klan were often guilty of intimidation, robbery, and murder:

Armed organizations, generally known as "Ku Klux Klans" exist independently or in concert with other armed bands, in many parts of Texas, but are more numerous, bold and aggressive east of the Trinity River.

The precise object of the organization cannot be readily explained, but

[8] *Daily State Journal,* May 4, 1870, I, 83. The prisoners placed in the various county jails, although fed well enough, were forced to live in dirty and uncomfortable cells, amid most unsanitary conditions. The account, quoted by the *Journal* from the Bryan *Appeal,* described the Bryan, Texas, jail as follows:

. . . First view, an old cat and three kittens; second view, a greasy cook; third view, a fine dinner, consisting of soup, roast beef, mutton, fish, coffee, etc. We almost wished ourselves a prisoner in order to share the luxuries supplied to prisoners by our generous sheriff. But all our anticipations of committing an offense against the law, in order to board at the jail, were dispelled when we visited the rain-beaten apartment of prisoners. There we found two stalwart Ethiopians, chained to a post surrounded by about two inches of water, and resembling two black islands in a sea of mud. Chains are necessary there, as the roof has an orifice sufficiently large to admit the egress and ingress of an elephant.

[9] Hacker and Kendrick, *The United States since 1865,* p. 39.

[10] Barker, *Readings in Texas History,* p. 510.

seem, in this State, to be to disarm, rob, and, in many cases, murder Union men and Negroes, and, as occasion may offer, murder United States officers and soldiers; also to intimidate every one who knows anything of the organization, but who will not join it. . . .

What political end, if any, is aimed at by these bands I cannot say, but they attend in large bodies the political meetings (barbecues) which have been and are still being held in various parts of this State, under the auspices of the democratic clubs of the different counties.

The speakers encourage their attendance, and in several counties men have been indicated by name from the Speaker's stand as those selected for murder. The men thus pointed out have no course left them but to leave their homes or be murdered on the first convenient opporunity.

The murder of Negroes is so common as to render it impossible to keep accurate account of them.[11]

The record of Klan activities during the Davis administration in Texas is far from complete. In March, 1869, the chief executive of the organization—the "Grand Wizard of the Invisible Empire"— ordered that the Klan be disbanded everywhere. This instruction, however, came from Klan headquarters in Tennessee, where a law prohibited newspaper publication of such items. Therefore, there was no way for the proclamation to be fully distributed.[12] Certainly, Klan chapters remained active in Texas and elsewhere, and some U.S. Army officers stated categorically that the Klan still operated in the Lone Star State in the spring of 1870. On May 5 General George P. Buell sent the following telegram from departmental headquarters in Austin to Army Captain Charles E. Morse, who was Secretary of Civil Affairs and acting Assistant Adjutant General on J. J. Reynolds' staff:

According to written report just received from Lieutenant Ekin at Nacogdoches, the murderers and Ku-Klux have commenced their work in that portion of my command. Some twenty-five attacked teamsters going to market in the night; one man killed, several missing, and one left supposed to be dead, who was able to tell the circumstances. Shall I send troops down?[13]

[11] *The Report of the Secretary of War, 1868–1869,* p. 704, reprinted in the Forty-second Congress, Second Session, *Report of the Committee on Affairs in the Late Insurrectionary States* (Serial No. 1529), p. 19.

[12] D. L. Wilson, "The Ku Klux Klan, Its Growth and Disbandment," *The Century Magazine,* XXVIII (May–October, 1884), 410.

[13] *Daily State Journal,* May 7, 1870, I, 85; *Flake's Daily Bulletin,* May 10, 1870, V, 273. Captain Charles Morse was stationed at Austin but was out of the city when the telegram was sent.

No record of dispatching any troops at this time was found, and possibly none were sent because there was no need for them.[14]

In mid-1870 the Radical Republican *Daily State Journal* was convinced that local organizations of the Klan were still active.[15] Early in June, of that year, the newspaper described a parade held in McKinney:

A short time since the quiet and slumbering citizens of McKinney were startled by the regular and heavy tramp of a squadron of horses, riding rapidly through the streets. On looking out they saw a company of horsemen, over fifty in number, drawn up in the square, silent and voiceless as the grave; each horse disguised with trappings, and every rider hidden in the deadly Ku-Klux mask.

After remaining about half an hour they rode off on the Denton road and vanished in the night.[16]

During the summer of 1871 Radical Republicans circulated a report alleging Klan activity in Bastrop County. The following open letter was sent to the Radical *Journal* from Bastrop on July 27, 1871, by a person who called himself "Observer":

. . . The existence of armed bands in disguise, prowling the country at night, burning school houses, whipping school teachers, and beating colored men who patronize schools, is no longer a myth, but an absolute fact, sustained by the most irrefragable testimony. The terrorism that these desperadoes and assassins exercise is not confined to the colored man; but the German inhabitants, especially those of Serbin, in this county, are con-

---

[14] *Daily State Journal,* May 7, 1870, I, 85. The *Journal* felt that troops should be sent to East Texas, and upon printing Buell's telegram stated:

From the above information it will be seen that the fell spirit of assassination is again on the *qui vive* in Texas, seeking its bloody occasions. But wherever it shows its ghastly front, it will be met and smitten with stern, uncompromising force. Whatever of power is required to enforce law and protect life in Texas, whether it be an armed and mounted police, a militia force, or regular troops, will be unhesitatingly used by the State Executive.

[15] The *Daily State Journal* of July 3, 1870, I, 134, stated that a Negro had been attacked by a group of masked men at Waxahachie and beaten with clubs to such an extent that his life had been despaired of, because it was alleged "that he had been guilty of the unpardonable sin of allowing his cotton to grow up in weeds." The freedman's wife was said to have gone to a white neighbor for assistance, but was told by him that he was "too sharp to interfere" and that the parties committing the crime were "white men and knew exactly what they were doing" and that she could have recourse to the law.

[16] *Ibid.,* June 8, 1870, I, 112.

tinually intimidated and outraged by these cowardly and infamous scoundrels.

The offense which the victims of this violence have committed is their devotion to good government, their love of law and order. Besides Mr. Hanna, a teacher of a colored school, who was taken out some time ago and almost whipped to death, on account of his vocation, several others have shared like treatment for sending children to such schools, and for voting with the Republican party. How long, I would like to know, shall such villains thus abuse the magnanimity of the Government? The seat and centre of these outrageous demonstrations can be readily ascertained and it is such a place that should be searched out. Martial law is terrible; but until certain bloated and pampered aristocrats here, who encourage and supply these gentlemen "Knights," are treated as the poor freedman and unoffending Germans have endured, there will be no peace in this county, to say nothing of a free Republican vote in the coming election.[17]

But the Bastrop County grand jury, after examining more than two hundred witnesses, reported to the district judge that they could find no proof of existence of Ku Klux Klan bands in that county.

The *Journal,* not satisfied with this finding, stated that it was well known that the testimony of six witnesses coincided in declaring that the disguised men had stated "they did not intend that a Negro school house should remain standing in the county, that they would drive out or hang every Negro school teacher and Radical in the county before they ceased operations." The newspaper further alleged that when the district attorney drew up his indictments he had deliberately stated that the masked men had called themselves "Ku Klux," and the newspaper expressed certainty that when these indictments were returned to the court they had been subjected to inspection of a counsel friendly to the Klan. As a consequence, the *Journal* declared, the grand jury reported that it had heard no testimony to justify the description given by the district attorney in the indictments—that the men had called themselves "Ku Klux." Concluding, the *Journal* offered the following evidence as proof that the jury had made a prejudiced decision:

It is well known that Marion Harrison, a Democrat, testified before the grand jury that fifteen disguised men, calling themselves "Ku Klux" came

[17] *Daily State Journal,* July 29, 1871, II, 156.

to his house at night, and stated they were hunting for "Negro school teachers, mean Negroes and Radicals."

C. C. Youngmichel testified that a like party came through Serbin once or twice, frightening the citizens, going the same way, and calling themselves the same name: i.e., "Ku-Klux."

Patrick Wormley, an aged and decrepit Negro, who was a victim to their outrages, says they called themselves "Ku-Klux."

A man by the name of Ryan states they called themselves "Ku-Klux."

Martin Bell, a Negro man who was almost beaten to death, and himself and family driven from home where he dare not return, testified that to frighten him, they put up the picture of a coffin on his door, writing on it "your coffin," and this because he complained to the justice of maltreatment at their hands after they had warned him not to do it. He also swears that they called themselves "Ku-Klux."[18]

On learning of this grand jury action Governor Davis wrote District Judge I. B. McFarland at Bastrop and expressed his doubt about the honesty of the decision. In his letter, dated July 31, 1871, Davis declared:

I am informed that the grand jury of the present term in Bastrop county have failed to find anybody to blame for the recent flagrant cases of violation of law in that county, and all the parties who have been arrested by the police, charged with Ku-Kluxing, school house burning, etc. have been discharged. Please let me hear from you in this matter. It is very strange that an *honest* grand jury of fifteen or eighteen men from different parts of the county can find nobody to blame for any of these acts. Is the grand jury honest, or is it a fixed up affair? . . . I enclose to you a statement of crimes committed within Bastrop county since the 16th of September last, and for persons evading arrest for crimes as reported from that county. It is true that some of those reported as evading arrest have since been arrested, but as near as I can ascertain not a single person has been tried and convicted for any of the offenses (including seven murders, three instances of whipping by disguised Ku-Klux, and one church and one school house burning) that have occurred within Bastrop during less than ten and a half months past.[19]

Governor Davis, however, never did use a favorite weapon—martial law—against Bastrop County; so he must have become con-

---

[18] *Daily State Journal*, August 6, 1871, II, 163.
[19] *Ibid.*

vinced that the Ku Klux Klan was at least not so active there as he had at first imagined. As for the *Journal* articles, it is quite possible that they were exaggerated. It would not have been the first time that newspapers had been guilty of such deception. Moreover, Davis' own appointee, State Police Captain L. H. McNelly, had declared only a few months earlier that other than the Loyal League no secret political society then existed in Texas. McNelly added that in 1867 a society had been organized to act against Negro uprisings, but that it had died out in a few months.[20]

The Conservative *Daily Telegraph,* published at Houston, also disputed the existence of a Texas Ku Klux Klan, declaring in March, 1872, that radical papers were wrong in saying that such an organization was active. The newspaper added that local chapters of the White Camelia and the Teutonic Band of Brothers were also dead, that none of them had held any meetings within the last two years. The *Telegraph* concluded:

If there be a Ku-Klux organization in Texas, in the name of justice to the State, why do the Radicals not show it? You have your police—why don't you arrest and punish them, and receive the thanks of every good citizen of the State?[21]

No record has been found showing that the State Police ever arrested any man wearing Ku Klux Klan regalia, and other than the possible exaggerated reports[22] of Klan activities in 1870 and 1871 no information of Klan operations during the Davis administration has been discovered. It is likely that the scattered Texas chapters, if not already dead, certainly ceased to exist following the passage of a Ku Klux act by Congress on April 20, 1871, giving the President author-

[20] *Ibid.,* March 17, 1871, II, 43. This particular statement was republished from the Galveston *News;* Walter Prescott Webb, *Handbook of Texas,* II, 125.

[21] *Daily Telegraph,* March 16, 1872, XXXIII, 107.

[22] J. C. De Gress, *J. C. De Gress to the editors of the New York Tribune,* November 18, 1871, Pamphlets in Pearson Newcomb Collection. A good example of such reports, this open letter was written by De Gress, then Treasurer of the Republican State Executive Committee, apparently for political purposes only and exaggerated actual conditions. Upon the subject of the Klan he declared, ". . . There is reason to believe that this organization numbers from fifteen to twenty thousand in Texas."

ity to suspend the writ of habeas corpus when dealing with secret societies. At the time of the passage of this act a congressional committee was named to investigate "affairs in the late insurrectionary states." Subcommittees visited the various reconstructed states, then published in twelve volumes the evidence they had obtained. This airing tended to break up the Klan all over the South[23] and probably destroyed the last vestige of the organization in Texas.

[23] J. S. Bassett, *A Short History of the United States*, p. 629.

IMMIGRATION

FOR A NUMBER OF REASONS, immigration into Texas increased during the early seventies. The problem of utilizing Negro labor immediately after the Civil War proved to be a baffling one. The former slaves, restless with their new freedom, left the plantations where they had lived and roamed at will. The excitement produced by their new status had largely subsided by 1866, and many of the Negroes returned to work. However, their employers found them irresponsible and unreliable. To the planters, faced with difficulties in utilizing Negro labor in the years that followed, immigration seemed to offer a solution to their problem.[1] An unsigned writer for the *Texas Almanac for 1870* stated: "Competition will dissipate many of the freedmen's conceited notions and lower their growing pretentiousness." This same writer suggested Chinese laborers as competitors to the freedmen. "To China the South is now looking with deep interest for a solution of the labor question, and there is reason to believe it will be solved favorably."[2] However, competition was not to be provided by this means. Indeed, a few Chinese immigrants were reported as moving into Texas, but not to the farms. The Galveston *Weekly Civilian* quoted an account from a St. Louis paper of December 28 as declaring: "Nearly five hundred Chinese will arrive here tonight. They will immediately proceed to Texas to work on the railroads."[3]

---

[1] Ellis Paxson Oberholtzer, *A History of the United States since the Civil War,* I, 297; H. H. Bancroft, *History of the North Mexican States and Texas,* II, 481.

[2] *Texas Almanac,* 1870, pp. 96–97.

[3] Galveston *Weekly Civilian,* December 30, 1869, XXXII, 206.

However, the planters were more successful in their encouragement of immigration from the other states. The farmers of Austin County for instance, held a meeting at Hempstead in September, 1871. There they appointed a committee of eight to report upon "such matters as the immigrant needed information upon" in the hope of inducing labor from the South to move to their county. In this report they included enthusiastic descriptions of the productivity of the soil in Austin County, telling in detail of the success of individual farmers. The achievements of a Southerner who had moved to their area was thus described:

Mr. Z. M. P. Motley, formerly from Alabama, farming on bottom land, has for the last four years averaged fifty bushels of corn and a half a bale of cotton per acre—the cotton cut off each year by worms. This year he will make from a bale to three-quarters of a bale per acre. Mr. M. states with good cultivation, bottom land here will give seventy five bushels of corn and three-fourths of a bale of cotton year after year, even with the worms every year.

The committee further declared that "owing to the changes produced in the labor system by the war," many of the finest plantations were "lying idle for want of laborers to cultivate them." The group also reported that besides those plantations "we have thousands of acres never as yet tilled which are as fertile as any in the world." So the committee, in concluding its report, resolved: "That we most cordially invite emigrants from our sister Southern States to come and settle here, promising them a cordial welcome and a helping hand in establishing homes in our midst." The meeting, after accepting the report, appointed Dr. D. L. Dardon, who was already en route to Alabama, to act as their representative there in procuring emigrants.[4]

Immigration was also encouraged by state legislation, since widespread settlement of the frontier was imperative to withstand the constant Indian attacks. Certain private immigration associations were chartered and a state bureau of immigration was established not only to bring new settlers to the West, but to attract white labor to the cotton plantations. The two homestead acts of 1870, described earlier, appealed to the prospective immigrant. By one of these measures, the head of a family might acquire a homestead of 160 acres of the public domain after occupying the land for three years, while a single

[4] *Texas Almanac*, 1872, p. 150.

man by fulfilling these conditions, could obtain eighty acres. The other law, growing out of a provision in the Constitution of 1869, exempted from foreclosure for debt a rural homestead not exceeding 200 acres or an urban homestead evaluated at not more than 5,000 dollars.[5]

Then, too, the immigrant himself was attracted by an abundance of fertile land available at very low prices and by the inducements of individual planters eager to secure his services. He was informed by the *Texas Almanac* that immigrants would find no difficulty in obtaining as much land as they wanted in Texas and "nearly on their own terms." The prospective newcomer was told that he actually needed "no money to secure him a good farm in almost any part of Texas." All the immigrant needed to bring with him was "a good character, industrious habits, and one or two boys old enough to help him" or one or two hired men if he had no boys.[6]

Finally, unfavorable social and economic conditions in other southern states were added incentives for coming to Texas. In these states people had been financially ruined, and many were ready to begin anew in another area. Emigration became heavy. "Every steamboat up Red River is crowded," was the statement of the *Daily State Journal* in June, 1870, regarding "the flow of immigration into Texas." To the same paper from Erath County came a letter stating that this portion of the frontier was rapidly filling up with emigrants from the older states—many of them from Kentucky. This correspondent added: "The disappearance of the red man and the advent of railroads are the coming events whose shadows are already cast athwart this section of Texas." Immigrants continued to arrive from the older states, and on October 12, it was announced in Austin that as many as fifty wagons loaded with new settlers from Arkansas, Missouri, Louisiana, and Tennessee had passed through the streets of the capital. The destination of these immigrants was said to be "the cheap lands near our frontier." The *Daily State Journal* was enthusiastic in its report:

The people are well dressed and seem to be in comfortable circumstances, and have handsomely painted wagons, and fine teams of horses or mules. Now that the ranger force has begun to operate on the border, there will

[5] H. P. N. Gammel, *Laws of Texas*, VI, 242–244, 301, 1029–1030, 1464; VII, 152–153; W. H. Nunn, *Texas Homestead and Other Exemptions*, p. 4.

[6] *Texas Almanac*, 1872, pp. 151–153.

be some practical protection, and the fine counties of Llano, Mason, San Saba and others will blossom with an energetic and civilized people.[7]

"Immigration seems to be pouring into Texas, early as it is, by every channel leading to that promised land." Thus declared the Vicksburg *Times,* as quoted by the *Daily State Journal* early in the fall of 1870.

Every steamship of the New Orleans and Galveston line is crowded with immigrants, while the railroad from New Orleans towards the Texas line is equally crowded with adventurers seeking locations and business in that prosperous State. Again we learn that train after train, with thousands of families, are crossing Red River at Natchitoches and Shreveport, wending their way to Central and Western Texas.

The account concluded in a burst of praise;

The fertile lands, delightful climate, and wonderful resources of Texas, all combine to attract within her borders the intelligent and enterprising of every State, and indeed of almost every land.

A tide of emigration from Tennessee and Georgia was directed towards Texas between September, 1870, and January, 1871. The total of wagons crossing at Memphis during that time was reported as being 1,664, while the number of people in these vehicles totaled 9,600.[8]

From still other states immigrants came. In December, 1870, they were arriving in large numbers from the Central states. "Thousands and thousands of immigrants are now pouring into our State from Illinois, Missouri, Iowa, Kansas," as well as those from the Southern state of Arkansas, wrote the Waco *Register,* as it further predicted that railroad lines and the Republican Administration would serve as motives for further immigration. Thus it declared:

The tide will rise higher and higher every year as our railroads and good government and the enforcement of law become assured. Let it be understood that Texas is to be a Republican State, and it will receive such an influx of immigration as has never been known before in the history of any State of the Union. We have a climate and soil unequalled by any State,

[7] *Daily State Journal,* June 15, 1870, I, 118; June 18, 1870, I, 121; October 12, 1870, I, 218.

[8] *Ibid.,* September 23, 1870, I, 202; October 12, 1870, I, 218; January 29, 1871, II, 3.

in variety and products. Convince the people that we are to be governed by true representative, American ideas, and they will come.[9]

That same autumn, a citizen of Clarksville, Texas who had but recently returned from Missouri by the overland route declared that at the crossing of the Canadian the ferryman told him he had transported sixty wagons over that stream the day before, and seventy were there to cross on that day. In reporting the story the *Daily State Journal* continued: "All these wagons were moving towards Sherman, thence, doubtless, to radiate through Northern Texas."[10]

In 1870 Gustav Loeffler, later appointed superintendent of immigration by Davis, arranged for the introduction of a group of Nebraskans and a colony of about forty families from Maryland.

European immigration was also steadily increasing, and Loeffler arranged in October, 1870, for settlement in Texas of about 500 Germans from the Duchy of Brunswick. Earlier in the year, in the month of April, 562 immigrants arrived at the port of Galveston. Of this number 115 were from Germany, 19 from France, 14 from Sweden, and most of the remainder from the Southern states. It was reported that "none were destitute or in need of relief, and nearly all proceeded to different points in the interior." Some of these German newcomers were moving into Washington County two months later, while in Houston a number of them were promised entertainment in June, and it was anticipated that "the German feast this month is to be the next sensation." "A number of German immigrants passed through San Antonio to Fredericksburg" wrote the *Daily State Journal* optimistically that same summer. "Six wagon loads of German newcomers direct from Saxony, well-to-do and hearty, entered our city yesterday. They will settle in Travis County." Thus exulted the same newspaper early that fall, adding, "Many others are on the way and will shortly arrive."[11]

By the early seventies several private immigration companies had been formed with the aim of acting as agents between those who had Texas lands to dispose of and newcomers who wanted to obtain homes. One such organization was the Texas and Southwestern Land and

[9] *Ibid.*, December 1, 1870, I, 260. The *Daily State Journal* reprinted this account from the Waco *Register*.

[10] *Daily State Journal,* November 4, 1870, I, 238.

[11] *Ibid.,* May 5, 1870, I, 83; June 2, 1870, I, 107; October 15, 1870, I, 221; November 27, 1870, I, 257.

Immigration Company, an association chartered under the laws of Missouri with an authorized capital of a million dollars. Governor Davis himself[12] was a director of this company.

The companies also proposed to import European labor. The European and Texas Immigration Association, for instance, was chartered in 1871 by the Twelfth Legislature. One of the officers in this association, Augustus B. Palm,[13] had already established a prosperous business contracting for and bringing Swedish immigrants into Texas. Planters and businessmen who desired employees might obtain them through Palm.[14] Still another association was the Texas Land and Immigration Company, chartered by the State Legislature in 1871.[15]

That same year, on May 23, the Twelfth Legislature passed an act organizing a bureau of immigration. The Governor was authorized to appoint, subject to State Senate consent, a superintendent of immigration to serve a four-year term. The superintendent was to be delegated responsibility for encouraging immigration and protecting immigrants. He was to appoint, with the Governor's approval, up to four immigrant agents, two to be stationed in the United States (one in the North and the other in the South) and two in Europe (one in the British Isles and the other on the continent). The Governor was also authorized to appoint one special agent or lecturer in each state of the United States and in each country of Europe. These special agents, who were to serve without pay, were to extoll the merits of Texas as a field for immigrants.[16] Even before addition of the bureau to the state organization Gustav Loeffler had been appointed superintendent of immigration. Now, under the new setup, he continued to serve in that capacity, appointing as immigrant agents Colonel J. H. Lippard of Hill County and General William H. Parsons of Harris County. Lippard, placed in charge of the southern and western states, originally made his headquarters at New Orleans but was soon moved to St. Louis. This transfer proved beneficial to the program, for by the end of 1872 he had formed colonies of residents in Missouri, Kansas, Iowa, Kentucky, and Indiana who were planning to relocate in Texas. One colony had, in fact, already moved to Texas and had settled in

---

[12] Austin *Daily Republican,* March 21, 1870, II, 244.
[13] Gammel, *Laws of Texas,* VI, 1464.
[14] Austin *Daily Republican,* June 7, 1870, III, 6.
[15] Gammel, *Laws of Texas,* VII, 152–153.
[16] *Ibid.,* VI, 1029–1030.

Robertson County. Many residents of northern and eastern states were also persuaded to move by the agent for that area, General Parsons, who made his headquarters at New York City.

European agents were John T. McAdam of Washington County, sent to the British Isles, and Theodore Hertzberg of Bexar County, stationed on the continent at Bremen. By the end of 1872 both men could claim successes. McAdam did not reach his headquarters at Manchester until June, 1872, but by the last of December he had sent to Texas more than 300 settlers. Most were farmers seeking more promising opportunities, but some were men of moderate wealth. Hertzberg had also accounted for several hundred new settlers by publishing in continental newspapers a number of articles about the state. Both men were hampered by lack of finances, a situation that prohibited the planned publication of a pamphlet describing Texas resources.

Altogether, 41,598 immigrants from other states and from Europe arrived at Galveston during 1872. This represented an increase of 4,802 over the previous year. Newcomers entering by land across the Red River numbered an estimated 50,000, making the grand total for 1872, 91,600, an increase of 31,600 over 1871.[17] During the following year, 1873, immigration again increased, for the panic that year evidently caused many residents of other states to seek new opportunity. Moreover, the cost of living was less in Texas than in other states. At least 125,000 new settlers arrived that year, 101,000 from other states[18] and the rest from Europe.

Whenever Europeans located in large colonies, they at first made little effort to assimilate American culture, and for many years continued to live as they had in their native lands. For instance, the Germans turned to fraternal organizations such as they had known in Europe for their social life, and a number of *turnvereins* were chartered by law in the early seventies. These clubs were formed, it was claimed, "for the practice of brotherly love and the promotion of physical and mental exercises and studies." Physical training was particularly emphasized. Texas Germans established singing societies as

[17] *Annual Report of the Superintendent of the Bureau of Immigration of the State of Texas, 1872,* p. 105.
[18] *Ibid., 1873,* pp. 2, 10.

well, and the largest gathering of these groups up to that time, was held at San Antonio in 1870.[19]

However, in time these immigrants were assimilated into the Texas life, and most of them proved to be assets to the state, bringing a new enrichment to the customs of the areas where they settled. Dance steps, choice additions to diet, improvements in musical tastes, and touches of beauty to religious edifices and ceremonies were among their contributions.

The newcomers from Germany and Sweden, arriving from lands where the culture of cotton was unknown, would in most instances become adept in producing that crop. Some of them were to become ranchers as well and would take pride in their fat livestock. Houses, neat and well kept, and large barns indicated their prosperity. The descendants of these European immigrants have long since adjusted to American ways of life. Worthy citizens, most of them have retained at least one Old World characteristic: thriftiness, which has contributed greatly to the wealth of their communities.

The newcomers from Europe, together with settlers from other states, joined forces with Texans to work for a better country much as other American colonists had done many years earlier. Their combined efforts, coming at a critical time in the history of the state, proved to be vital in leading Texas out of carpetbag confusion and shaping for the state a bright future. It took courage, self-reliance, determination, hard work, independence, ingenuity, and a certain zest for the new and strange and difficult to make a success of the life that these settlers had to face. This was a rough young land, and those who came to challenge it had to have the strength of youth to achieve. Yet succes was to come. Progress had been made in clearing and cultivating land, but the woodlands would yield still more to the plow, while the grasslands, dotted by windmills and crossed by barbed wire, must make a greater way for the herd. The locomotive was already whistling over the hill, while the public school bells had only begun to tinkle.

[19] Don H. Biggers, *German Pioneers in Texas*, pp. 55–56.

BIBLIOGRAPHY

PRIMARY SOURCES

MANUSCRIPTS

Brown, Frank. "Annals of Travis County and the City of Austin (From the Earliest Times to the Close of 1875)." Archives of the University of Texas, Austin, Texas.

Coke-Davis Imbroglio, Volumes of Miscellaneous Correspondence concerning. Archives of the State Library, Austin, Texas.

Davis, Governor E. J., Executive Letters of, 1870–1874. Archives of the State Library, Austin, Texas.

— Executive Record No. 204, in the Executive Records of Governor Davis. Archives of the State Library, Austin, Texas.

Frontier Forces, Letters of the, 1870–1871. Archives of the State Library, Austin, Texas.

Honey, George W. Letters of the State Treasurer, 1870–1872. Archives of the State Library, Austin, Texas.

Kiowa and Comanche Indians, Letters regarding, 1870–1874. Indian Library, Department of the Interior, Washington, D. C.

Martial Law in Freestone and Limestone counties, Letters relating to, 1871. Archives of the State Library, Austin, Texas.

Martial Law in Walker County, Letters relating to, 1871. Archives of the State Library, Austin, Texas.

Minute Men, Miscellaneous Letters of the, 1871. Archives of the State Library, Austin, Texas.

Miscellaneous Correspondence, Volume of. Archives of the State Library, Austin, Texas.

Newcomb, James P., Letters to, 1869–1874. Pearson Newcomb Collection of the Newcomb Papers, 106 West Market Street, San Antonio, Texas.

— Unpublished Manuscript of the Writings of. Pearson Newcomb Collection of the Newcomb Papers, 106 West Market Street, San Antonio, Texas.

Roberts, O. M., Papers of, Consisting of Letters, Pamphlets, and a Portion of an Autobiography. Archives of the University of Texas, Austin, Texas.

Sherman, W. T., Semi-official Letters of, 1872–1878. Manuscript Division, Library of Congress, Washington, D. C.

State Comptroller, Letters of, 1869–1874. Archives of the State Library, Austin, Texas.

State Police, Muster Roll of the, 1870, 1873. Archives of the State Library, Austin, Texas.

263

Bibliography

State Police, Reserve Militia and State Guard, Letters of, July 1870–April 1873. Archives of the State Library, Austin, Texas.
U. S. Circuit Court Minutes, Book E. File Room of the United States District Court, Federal Building, Austin, Texas.

NEWSPAPERS

Miscellaneous Newspapers, Daily, Volume I, 1869–1904; Weekly, Volume II, 1851–1904. A collection of newspapers located at the University of Texas Library, Austin, Texas.
Civilian. Galveston, Texas, May 1869–May 1873. This paper appeared at various times as the *Weekly Civilian,* the *Daily Civilian,* the *Civilian and Gazette,* and the *Civilian and Galveston Gazette.*
Daily Express. San Antonio, Texas, 1871.
Daily Herald. San Antonio, Texas, July 1870–January 1874.
Daily News. Galveston, Texas, January 1873–December 1873.
Daily Republican. Austin, Texas, January 1870–July 1871.
Daily State Gazette. Austin, Texas, October 1870–September 1871. Appeared also as the *Tri-Weekly State Gazette* (January 1870–January 1874).
Daily State Journal. Austin, Texas, February 1870–January 1874.
Daily Telegraph. Houston, Texas, February 1870–March 1872.
Democratic Statesman. Austin, Texas, August 1871–October 1877. This paper appeared at various times as the *Daily Democratic Statesman,* the *Tri-Weekly Democratic Statesman,* the *Weekly Democratic Statesman,* and the *Daily Statesman.*
Flake's Bulletin. Galveston, Texas, January 1870–April 1872. This paper appeared as both *Flake's Daily Bulletin and Flake's Semi-Weekly Bulletin.*
Herald. Dallas, Texas, January 1873–December 1873. This paper appeared as both the *Daily Herald* and the *Weekly Herald.*
Norton's Union Intelligencer. Dallas, Texas, January 1872–April 1873.
Union. Houston, Texas, November 1869–March 1872. This paper appeared as both the *Daily Union* (1869–1870) and the *Tri-Weekly Union* (1870–1872).
Weekly News. Denison, Texas, December 1870–December 1873.

PUBLIC DOCUMENTS

Adjutant General's Reports, 1870–1881. See *Report of the Adjutant General of Texas for 1870, 1871, 1872, 1873.*
Annual Report of the Comptroller of Public Accounts of the State of Texas, from September 1, 1870 to August 31, 1871. Austin: J. G. Tracy, State Printer, 1872.
Annual Report of the Comptroller of Public Accounts of the State of Texas

Bibliography

from September 1, 1871 to August 31, 1872. Austin: James P. Newcomb and Company, 1873.

Annual Report of the Comptroller of Public Accounts of the State of Texas for the Fiscal Year Ending August 31, 1874. Houston: A. C. Gray, State Printer, 1874.

Annual Reports of the Commissioner of Indian Affairs to the Secretary of the Interior for 1870, 1871, 1872, and 1873. Washington: Government Printing Office, 1871, 1872, 1873, 1874.

Annual Reports of the Superintendent of the Bureau of Immigration of the State of Texas, 1871, 1872, 1873. Austin: James P. Newcomb and Company, 1872, 1873; Cardwell and Walker Printers, 1874.

Congress, 42d, Second Session. *Report of the Joint Select Committee to Inquire into the Condition of Affairs in the Late Insurrectionary States Made to the Two Houses of Congress, February 19, 1872.* Washington: Government Printing Office, 1872 (Serial No. 1529).

Congress, 43d, First Session. *Executive Document No. 257:* "Depredations on the Frontiers of Texas," in *Executive Documents, Nos. 256–290.* Washington: Government Printing Office, 1873–1874 (Serial No. 1615).

Congress, 47th, Second Session. *Executive Documents, XVIII.* Washington: Government Printing Office, 1882–1883 (Serial No. 2107).

Gammel, H. P. N. *Laws of Texas.* Vols. IV, V, VI, and VII of 23 vols. Austin: The Gammel Book Company, 1898.

The House and Senate Journals of the 12th Legislature. Austin: Tracy, Siemering, and Company, 1870 (first session); J. C. Tracy, 1871 (second and third sessions).

The House and Senate Journals of the 13th Legislature. Austin: John Cardwell, printer, 1873.

The House Journal of the 16th Legislature of the State of Texas. Galveston, Texas: A. H. Belo and Company, state printers, 1879.

Paschal, George W. *A Digest of the Laws of Texas,* Fourth Edition. Vol. II of 2 vols. Washington: W. H. and O. H. Morrison, 1874.

Report of the Adjutant General of Texas for 1870, 1871, 1872, 1873, and the *Adjutant General's Report to Honorable E. B. Pickett, President of the Constitutional Convention.* Austin: September, 1875. These reports are in a bound volume, entitled *Adjutant General's Reports 1870–1881,* and are in the Archives of the State Library, Austin, Texas.

Report of the Attorney General of the State of Texas for the Year 1872, William Alexander, Attorney General. Austin: James P. Newcomb and Company, 1873.

Report of the Secretary of State of the State of Texas for the Year 1872, James P. Newcomb, Secretary of State. Austin: James P. Newcomb and Company, 1873.

Bibliography

Report of the State Treasurer from July 1 to December 31, 1872, B. Graham, Treasurer of State of Texas. Austin: James P. Newcomb and Company, 1873.

Richardson, James D. *Messages and Papers of the Presidents, 1789–1897.* Vol. VII of 20 vols. Washington: Government Printing Office, 1896–1899.

Second Annual Report of the Superintendent of Public Instruction of the State of Texas for the Year 1872, J. C. De Gress, Superintendent of Public Instruction. Austin: James P. Newcomb and Company, 1873.

Texas Department of Insurance, Statistics and History. *The Resources, Soil and Climate of Texas.* (Report of the commissioner of insurance, statistics and history, A. W. Spaight.) Galveston, Texas: A. H. Belo and Company, 1882.

Texas Supreme Court Reports, XXXI, XXXIX, and XL. St. Louis, Missouri: Gilbert Book Company, 1882.

U. S. Bureau of the Census. *Ninth Census of the United States, 1870.* 3 vols. Washington: Government Printing Office, 1872.

U. S. Department of Agriculture. *Report of the Secretary of Agriculture.* Washington: Government Printing Office, 1869, 1870, 1871.

U. S. Office of Education. *Report of the Commission of Education.* Washington: U. S. Department of the Interior, 1869–1870, 1870–1871, 1873–1874.

PAMPHLETS

De Gress, J. C. *J. C. De Gress to the Editors of the New York Tribune.* Austin: November 18, 1871. A copy is to be found in the Pearson Newcomb Collection of the Newcomb Papers, 106 West Market Street, San Antonio, Texas.

Miscellaneous Pamphlets, in the Pearson Newcomb Collection of the Newcomb Papers, 106 West Market Street, San Antonio, Texas.

Proceedings of the Taxpayer's Convention of the State of Texas. Galveston, Texas: News Steam Book and Job Office, 1871. A copy is to be found in the Texas Collection of the University of Texas, Austin, Texas.

Ritual, Constitution and By Laws of the National Council, Union League of America. Together with All the Necessary Information for the Complete Working of Subordinate Councils. New York: M. B. Brown and Co., 1870.

SCHOLARLY JOURNALS

Wheeler, T. B. "Reminiscences of Reconstruction in Texas," *The Quarterly of the Texas State Historical Association,* XI (1908).

Bibliography

BOOKS

Haltom, Richard W. *History and Description of Nacogdoches County.* Nacogdoches, Texas: Richard W. Haltom, 1880.

Hardin, John W. *Life of John Wesley Hardin.* Seguin, Texas: Smith and Moore, 1896. Republished, Bandera, Texas: Frontier Times, 1925.

Matthews, Sallie Reynolds. *Interwoven.* Houston, Texas: Anson Jones Press, 1936.

McCoy, Joseph G. *Historical Sketches of the Cattle Trade of the West and Southwest.* Kansas City, Missouri: Ramsey, Millett, and Hudson, 1874.

Memorial and Biographical History of Johnson and Hill Counties, Texas. Chicago: Lewis Publishing Company, 1892.

Memorial and Biographical History of Navarro, Henderson, Anderson, Limestone, Freestone, and Leon Counties, Texas. Chicago: Lewis Publishing Company, 1893.

Texas Almanac and Emigrants Guide for 1867, 1869, 1870, 1871, 1872, 1873, and 1874. Galveston, Texas: W. and D. Richardson and Company, 1867; Richardson, Belo, and Company, 1869–1874.

Wood, William D. *Reminiscences of Reconstruction in Texas and Reminiscences of Texas and Texans Fifty Years Ago.* n.p.: 1902.

Wooten, Dudley G. *A Comprehensive History of Texas.* Vol. II of 2 vols. Dallas: W. G. Scarff, 1898.

SECONDARY SOURCES

MANUSCRIPTS

Haley, J. E. "A Survey of the Texas Cattle Drives to the North, 1866–1895." Unpublished Master's Thesis, University of Texas, Austin, Texas, 1926.

McKay, Seth S. "Texas under the Regime of E. J. Davis." Unpublished Master's Thesis, University of Texas, Austin, Texas, 1919.

NEWSPAPERS

Standard Times. San Angelo, Texas, May 3, 1934, Vol. 51, No. 1.

SCHOLARLY JOURNALS

Denman, C. P. "The Office of the Adjutant General in Texas, 1835–1881." *Southwestern Historical Quarterly,* XXVIII (July 1924–April 1925).

Potts, Charles Shirley. "Railroad Transportation in Texas," *Texas Magazine,* II (May–October, 1910).

Wilson, D. L. "The Ku Klux Klan, Its Growth and Disbandment," *The Century Magazine,* XXVIII (May–October, 1884).

Wood, W. D. "The Ku Klux Klan," *The Quarterly of the Texas State Historical Association,* IX (1905–1906).

Bibliography

BOOKS

Appleton, C. (ed.). *American Annual Cyclopaedia*, X, XI, XII, and XIII. New York: D. Appleton & Company, Inc., 1871, 1872, 1873, and 1874.

Bailey, Thomas A. *The American Pageant*. Boston: D. C. Heath and Company, 1956.

Bancroft, H. H. *History of the North Mexican States and Texas* (being Volumes XV and XVI of the Works of *Hubert Homer Bancroft*). 2 vols. San Francisco: A. L. Bancroft and Company, 1884–1889.

Barker, E. C. *Readings in Texas History*. Dallas: Southwest Press, 1929.

Bassett, J. S. *A Short History of the United States*. New York: The Macmillan Company, 1916.

Biggers, Don H. *German Pioneers in Texas*. Fredericksburg: Fredericksburg Publishing Company, 1925.

Brown, John Henry. *History of Texas from 1685 to 1892*. 2 vols. St. Louis, Missouri: L. E. Daniell, 1892.

Cox, James. *Historical and Biographical Records of the Cattle Industry and the Cattlemen of Texas and Adjacent Territory*. St. Louis, Missouri: Woodward and Tiernan Printing Company, 1895.

Davenport, J. H. *The History of the Supreme Court of the State of Texas*. Austin: Southern Law Book Publishers, 1917.

Eby, Frederick. *The Development of Education in Texas*. New York: The Macmillan Company, 1925.

Hacker, Louis M. and Kendrick, Benjamin B. *The United States since 1865*. New York: F. S. Crofts & Company, 1932.

Hammond, Matthew Brown. "Cotton Production in the South," *The South in the Building of the Nation*, VI. Richmond, Virginia: The Southern Historical Publication Society, 1909–1913.

Hebison, W. O. *Early Days in Texas and Rains County*. Emory, Texas: Leader Printers, 1917.

Hunter, J. Marvin. *The Trail Drivers of Texas*. Nashville, Tennessee: Cokesbury Press, 1925.

Kittrell, Norman G. *Governors Who Have Been and Other Public Men of Texas*. Houston: Dealy-Adey-Elgin Company, 1921.

Lane, J. J. *History of Education in Texas*. Washington: Government Printing Office, 1903.

Miller, E. T. *A Financial History of Texas* (Bulletin of the University of Texas No. 37). Austin: 1916.

Nunn, W. H. *Texas Homestead and Other Exemptions*. Austin: A. C. Baldwin and Sons, 1931.

Oberholtzer, Ellis Paxson. *A History of the United States since the Civil War*. 5 vols. New York: The Macmillan Company, 1917.

Bibliography

Potts, Charles Shirley. *Railroad Transportation in Texas* (University of Texas Bulletin No. 119). Austin: 1909.

Ramsdell, Charles W. *Reconstruction in Texas.* New York: Columbia University, Longmans-Green & Co., Inc., agents, 1910.

— "Texas in the New Nation," *The South in the Building of the Nation,* III. Richmond, Virginia: The Southern Historical Publication Society, 1909.

Reed, S. G. *A History of the Texas Railroads.* Houston, Texas: The St. Clair Publishing Co., 1941.

Rister, Carl Coke. *The Southwestern Frontier.* Cleveland, Ohio: Arthur H. Clark, 1928.

Siringo, Charles A. *Riata and Spurs.* Boston and New York: Houghton Mifflin Company, 1927.

Texas Almanac 1958–1959. Dallas: Dallas Morning News, 1959.

Thrall, Homer S. *A History of Texas from Earliest Settlements to the Year 1876.* New York: University Publishing Company, 1876.

— *A Pictorial History of Texas.* St. Louis, Missouri: N. D. Thompson and Company, 1879.

Webb, Walter Prescott. *Handbook of Texas.* 2 vols. Austin: Texas State Historical Association, 1952.

— *The Great Plains.* Boston: Ginn & Company, 1931.

Wharton, Clarence R. *Texas under Many Flags.* 5 vols. Chicago and New York: American Historical Society, Inc., 1930.

Wilbarger, J. W. *Indian Depredations in Texas.* Austin: Hutchings Printing House, 1889. A fascimile reproduction of the original, Austin: Steck and Company, 1935.

Winkler, E. W. *Platforms of Political Parties in Texas* (Bulletin of the University of Texas No. 53). Austin: 1916.

Wortham, Louis J. *A History of Texas from Wilderness to Commonwealth,* Vol. V of 5 vols. Fort Worth, Texas: Wortham-Molyneaux, 1924.

INDEX

Abercrombie, Colonel ———: and Walker County incident, 82
Abilene, Kansas: cattle drives to, 136–137, 138, 139, 140; description of, 233
Adams, David: death of, 193
Adams, G. H.: and Minute Men, 199
Adams, John Quincy II: 112
Adams, Scott J.: death of, 59–62
Add-Ran College: founding of, 244; and Texas Christian University, 244
adjutant general: salary of, 30 n; James Davidson as, 44; Frank L. Britton as, 68
ad valorem tax: SEE tax, ad valorem
agricultural and mechanical college: attempts to found, 171–172
Agricultural, Mechanical and Blood Stock Association of Texas: 237
agriculture: decline in, 135–137; during Davis administration, 135–147
Alabama: cotton production in, 145; immigration from, 255
Alexander, Jno.: and Minute Men, 199
Alexander, William: and E. J. Davis, 102–105; indictment of, 102; and George Honey and J. H. Burns, 106–107; on International Railroad bonds, 117
Alford, Senator E. L.: expulsion of, from Senate, 29–30; arrest of, 29 n
Alford, H. E.: as commissioner of Indian affairs, 187
allegiance, oath of: 3
Allen, Richard: in Legislature, 23 n
Amole, Mexico: border thieves at, 222
amusements on the frontier: 234
Anahuac, Texas: packeries at, 144
Anderson County: mineral deposits in, 149 n, 150
Angelina River: transportation on, 158–159
antimony: deposits of, 147, 150
Apaches: and stagecoach routes, 157; national policy toward, 177; depredations by, 178, 207, 210, 218; treaties with, 179 n; and Jacksboro trouble, 183; peace talks with, 187; at council meeting, 188; kidnapping of Smith boys by, 215
———, Mescalero: SEE Mescalero Apaches
Applewhite, D. C.: murder of, 87

appointive powers of governor: 30–31
apprenticeship law: provisions of, 8
Aransas Bay: rendering plants on, 144
Arapahoes: thefts by, 182; peace talks with, 187
Archer County: mineral deposits in, 148, 149 n, 150
Arizona: railroads through, 161, 162
Arkansas: election fraud in, 104; movement of Negroes from, 135; attacks on cattle drives in, 136; immigration from, 256, 257
Armour and Company: sale of cattle to, 139
Army, Mexican: and Indians, 221
———, United States: A. J. Hamilton in, 3; General Griffin in, 9; and Indians, 177, 177–178, 180, 181; and ranging companies, 197–198
arsenal, state: in Coke-Davis Imbroglio, 128–129; 129
asphaltum: deposits of, 147, 150
asylum lands: restrictions on sale of, 169
asylums: costs of, 166
Atascosa County: lignite deposits in, 148
Atchison, Topeka, and Santa Fe Railroad: and cattle drives, 139, 140–141
Atkins, Joseph: at Democratic meeting, 70
Atkinson, H. M.: and removal of Kickapoos, 208
Atkinson, N: and Minute Men, 199
attorney general: salary of, 30 n
attorneys, district: salaries of, 30 n
attorneys, prosecuting: fees paid to, 166
Augur, General C. C.: and Coke–Davis Imbroglio, 126; in command of frontier defense, 183; and removal of Kickapoos, 208
Austin, Texas: 34, 63, 67; conventions in, 6, 93, 98, 118, 168; railroad to, 34, 160, 161, 163, 235, 240; Greeley meeting in, 68–69; as state capital, 113, 240; Fourteenth Legislature in, 122; inauguration of Richard Coke and R. B. Hubbard in, 126; stagecoach to, 156, 157; railroad excursion to, 235–236; appearance of, 240; population of, 240; schools in, 240; Colonel De Gress as mayor of, 242; immigration through, 256

271

Index

Index

Bryant, A. M.: as candidate for Congress, 99, 101
Buckmeyer family: Indian attack on, 211
Buell, General George P.: on Ku Klux Klan, 248
buffalo: and Indians, 230–231
Buffalo Bayou: and Houston, 239
Buffalo Bayou, Brazos, and Colorado Railway: 163
buffalo drives: holding of, 229–230; and the "Flat," 230; profits from, 230
builders: number of, 152
Bulletin, Indianola: on rendering plants, 143–144
Burleson, A. B.: on treasury commission, 107
Burleson County: State Police in, 50–51
Burley, D. W.: in Legislature, 23 n
Burnet, David G.: sent to U. S. Senate, 7
Burnet, Texas: Indians near, 214–215
Burnet County: mineral deposits in, 147, 149 n; Minute Men in, 198, 199, 200; Indians in, 213, 213–215
Burnett, Crawford: sale of cattle by, 139
Burnett, Judge J. R.: and Walker County incident, 81, 82
Burney, Mat: in Madison County affair, 54
Burns, J. H.: and treasury muddle, 105–106, 106, 106–107; at opening of safes, 107
Burton, Texas: disturbance at, 53
Bush, ————: and Walker County incident, 82

Cache Creek: 179
Caddoes: at council meeting, 188
Caddo Lake: commerce on, 154, 155
Cairo and Fulton Railroad: 34, 160
Caldwell, Texas: State Police in, 50–51
California: horses in, 144; stagecoach to, 157; railroads through, 161, 162
Callahan County: coal deposits in, 148; Minute Men in, 200
Calvert, Texas: railroads to, 159–160; baseball team in, 235
Camargo, Texas: railroads to, 162
Camden, Arkansas: railroads to, 161
Cameron County: 1869 election in, 19
Campbell, Don: as lieutenant governor, 23

Camp Colorado, Texas: ranging company at, 196
Camp Radziminski: 179
Camp County: iron deposits in, 149 n
Canadian River: immigrants' crossing of, 258
Canadians in Texas: 238
cannon: use of, in Coke-Davis Imbroglio, 127, 128
capital (city): location of, 112, 113
capital (money): loss of, after Civil War, 135
capitol: struggle for, in Coke-Davis Imbroglio, 123, 125–129; in Austin, 240
Cardwell, John: as editor of *Democratic Statesman*, 69; at Greeley meeting, 69
carpenters: number of, 152
Caruthers, William: in Indian fight, 196
Casey, B. F.: and Minute Men, 199
Cass County: iron deposits in, 149 n
Castro, Old: as chief of Lipans, 193
Catholic College in Galveston: 238
cattle: prices of, 138, 139, 141–142, 143
——, feeder: demand for, 140
cattle business: 136; importance of, 138; and rendering plants, 143–144
cattle country: area of, 136
cattle drives: before Civil War, 136; attacks on, 136; after Civil War, 136–137; and railroads, 138, 140, 140–141, 143; size of, 138, 139, 140, 141, 143; losses from, 139, 140, 142; and panic of 1873, 142–143; decrease in, 143; to Kansas, 154; description of, 232
cattle products: export of, 154
cattle ranching: development of, 231–232
cattle thieves, Mexican: and Kickapoos, 204–205; depredations of, 205–206, 207, 209, 210, 218, 221–222; Congress on, 206; commissioners' report on, 207; Levi English on, 221
Cedar Bayou, Texas: James Davidson at, 53
Cedar Creek, Texas: lignite deposits near, 148
Cedar Mills, Texas: Indians near, 213–215
Cedar Mountain: 196–197
Central Texas: value of land in, 147; immigration into, 257
Chaparozo Creek: 193

274

Index

—, public: 172
—, total: 174
defense, frontier: SEE frontier protection
deficiency appropriation act: 201
Degener, Edward: as congressman, 17; as candidate for Congress, 99, 101
De Gress, Colonel Jacob C.: on election fraud, 102 n; and Coke-Davis Imbroglio, 126, 127, 127–128; background of, 241; and Freedman's Bureau, 241; as state school superintendent, 241; legislative investigation of, 241; as a Republican, 242; as mayor of Austin, 242; extravagance of, 243; on Ku Klux Klan, 252 n
Delano, C.: as secretary of interior, 179; and Indian depredations, 179, 180; to General Townsend, 180; and E. J. Davis, 187, 188; from General Sherman, 187–188; on release of Indians, 188
delegates: to 1866 constitutional convention, 5–6, 6
Democratic convention: SEE convention, Democratic
Democratic meeting: at Galveston, 70
Democratic party: SEE Democrats
Democratic Statesman, Austin: on Brown County incident, 61–62; on State Police, 66–67; on Greeley meeting, 68–70; John Cardwell as editor of, 69; founding of, 99–100; influence of, 99–100; on Radicals, 100; on indictment of E. J. Davis, 104–105; on Thirteenth Legislature, 117; SEE ALSO *Tri-Weekly Democratic Statesman*, Austin; *Weekly Democratic Statesman*, Austin
Democrats: and 1869 constitution, 13; and A. J. Hamilton, 16, 99; in Legislature, 23, 114, 123; and militia bill, 29; and public printing law, 32; on railroad legislation, 35, 37, 111; victories of, 58, 100–102, 102, 112–113, 119; and State Police, 73; and taxpayers' convention, 93; and Conservative Republicans, 98, 99; strength of, 98; meetings of, 100; and San Antion *Herald*, 100; and President Grant, 110, 122; convention of, 110–111, 118; candidates of, 111, 112; on Davis administration, 111; on education, 111;

on frontier protection, 111; on governor's term of office, 111; platform of, 111; on school fund, 111; on state problems, 111; and B. Gratz Brown, 112; and Horace Greeley, 69, 112; on election law, 121. SEE ALSO Conservatives
Denison, Texas: railroads to, 160, 162
Denmenber, James: arrest of, 78
Deno, Lottie: gambling of, 230
Denton, Joe: and Coke-Davis Imbroglio, 127
Denton, Texas: 74; C. J. Wilkerson in, 235 n
Denton County: C. J. Wilkerson of, 147; Indians in, 195
Department of Texas: SEE Texas, Department of
Department of the Gulf: E. J. Davis in, 21
Devil's River Mountains: 193
DeWitt County: 65; State Police in, 45
Diaz, Martina: kidnapping of, by Indians, 216–217
Dickerson, Henry: at Greeley meeting, 96
Dillard, Senator ——: unseating of, 29 n–30 n
Disciples of Christ: founding of Add-Ran College by, 244
discrimination: Republican convention on, 118
disfranchisement of qualified voters: 16–17
district attorneys: salaries of, 30 n
district court, clerk of: bond paid by, 26
District Court, Travis County: railroad bond case in, 35
District Court, United States: indictment of E. J. Davis by, 102
district school supervisors: SEE school supervisors, district
Dobs, ——: murder of, 181
doctors: description of, 229
Dodge, Judge ——: 57
Dodge, Henry W.: on treasury commission, 106
Dodge, Sam: at Radical convention, 57
Dofflemeyer, J. A.: murder of, 197
Dohoney, Senator ——: arrest of, 29 n
Dorn, A. H.: 118
Douglas, Senator ——: arrest of, 29 n

279

Index

Lanham, S. W. T.: prosecution of Satanta and Big Tree by, 186

Laredo, Texas: 21, 136; E. J. Davis in, 19; railroads to, 34, 160; coal deposits near, 149 n; commissioners at, 207; Indians near, 216; Indian sympathizers in, 220

Latimer, Senator ———: arrest of, 29 n

law: enforcement of, 245–253

lawlessness: in Texas, 8

Lawrence, Justice ———: and Hill County troubles, 7

laws: about Negroes, 7–8; about state officers, 27–28

lead: deposits of, 147, 149

leaders, Southern flight of, to Mexico, 3

leather workers: number of, 152

Leavenworth, Lawrence, and Galveston Railroad: and cattle drives, 140–141

Ledbetter, W. H.: and Minute Men, 199

Lee, ———: murder of, 90

Lee, Sheriff George: in Brown County incident, 60–62; death of, 61

Lee, Milly F.: as captive of Indians, 218

Lee, John: as captive of Indians, 218

Lee, Robert E.: and E. J. Davis, 20 n; J. P. Newcomb on, 20 n

Lee, Susanna: as captive of Indians, 218

Lee family: murder of, 181

legislation: about freedmen, 7–8

Legislature: Secessionists in, 7; spending by, 165–166; and education, 169, 241

Legislature, Twelfth: sessions of, 22–25, 25–27; composition of, 23; Negroes in, 23; measures passed by, 27–32, 38–39; and martial law, 28, 92; militia bill in, 29; and public printing law, 33; and railroad legislation, 34–38, 160, 161, 162–166; and homestead acts, 38, 227; and frontier protection, 38; and education, 39; and M. C. Hamilton, 40; and State Police, 43; and Limestone County, 87–88, 90–91, 92; and Freestone County, 92; and taxpayers' convention, 94; and Democratic convention, 118; and manufacturing, 153; and ranging companies, 190–191; on Indians, 202, 203, 222; and immigration, 255–256, 259

Legislature, Thirteenth: railroad legislation in, 36; and State Police, 73–74; on treasury muddle, 108–109; first session

of, 114; Democrats in, 114; and E. J. Davis, 114–115; work of, 114–117; and martial law, 116; and State Police act, 116; and enabling act, 116; printing act of, 116; school acts of, 116; and State Guards, 116; and militia act, 116; and railroad bonds, 117; *Democratic Statesman* on, 117; reapportionment act of, 117; and 1873 election, 117, 119; and party conventions, 117–118, 118; and election law, 120; and Fourteenth Legislature, 123, 125; on liberation of Satanta and Big Tree, 187; and Minute Men, 200; and Colonel De Gress, 241; and education, 243

Legislature, Fourteenth: San Antonio *Daily Herald* on, 120; and Coke-Davis Imbroglio, 122, 124, 125, 131; and Democrats, 123; organization of, 123; and Thirteenth Legislature, 123, 125; possession of legislative chambers by, 124; assembly of, 125; and election returns, 125; House of Representatives of, 125; and secretary of state, 125; and Minute Men, 201; and ranging companies, 201

Lewisville, Texas: railroads to, 164

Liberal Republican party: and Horace Greeley, 68, 112; and B. Gratz Brown, 112

Liberty, Texas: river transportation to, 158

lieutenant governor: SEE governor, lieutenant

lignite: deposits of, 148, 149 n

Limestone County: martial law in, 69 n, 76, 87–92; and Legislature, 87–88, 90–91, 92; conditions in, 91–92; rejection of votes in, 101

Lindsay, L.: as candidate for lieutenant governor, 6

Lipans: H. J. Richarz on, 193; depredations by, 202; in Mexico, 202; Jefferson Smith as prisoner of, 215; fight of, with Kickapoos, 219

Lippard, Colonel J. H.: as immigrant agent, 259

liquor: use of, by Negroes, 246

Live Oak County: Indians in, 220

Liverpool, England: steamers from, 154

livestock: export of, 154

Index

McCormick, ———: at Radical meeting, 57–58

McCormick, A. P.: as candidate for lieutenant governor, 14

McCoy, Joseph G.: *Historical Sketches of the Cattle Trade of the West and Southwest*, 141

McCulloch, Henry E.: and Coke-Davis Imbroglio, 123; as adjutant general, 126, 129

McCulloch County: mineral deposits in, 147–148, 149 n; ranging company in, 201

McDade, Texas: railroad excursion through, 235

McFarland, Judge I. B.: from E. J. Davis, 251

McIver, Tider: in Madison County affair, 59

Mackenzie, General R. S.: pursuit of Indians by, 183–184, 185; and Kickapoos, 206

McKenzie College: and Southwestern University, 243

McKinney, James P.: on treasury commission, 107

McKinney, Texas: Ku Klux Klan in, 249

McLemore, ———: and Coke-Davis Imbroglio, 129

McLennan County: 79; Major Erath from, 93

McMillion, J. H.: in Brown County incident, 60

McMullen County: rejection of votes from, 113

McNelly, Captain L. H.: shooting of, 81; and Walker County incident, 81–82, 85–86; pursuit of Indians by, 221; on Loyal League, 252; on Ku Klux Klan, 252

McParrish, John: arrest and trial of, 81, 82

Meader, John: and murder of the Kelly brothers, 45–48

meat packers: number of, 152

mechanical college: SEE agricultural and mechanical college

Medina County: Minute Men in, 199, 200

Medlock, David: in Legislature, 23 n

Melville, Andrew: death of, 71

Memorial to the Legislature: from Limestone County, 90–91

Memphis, Tennessee: immigration through, 257

Memphis and El Paso Railway: 160

Memphis, El Paso, and Pacific Railroad: chartering of, 161; and constitutional convention, 161; credit of, 161; and other railroads, 161

Menard County: rejection of votes from, 113; frontier protection in, 182; Minute Men in, 200

Merrick, ———: and Limestone County troubles, 88

"Merrick's Quarters": 88

Mescalero Apaches: in Mexico, 209; depredations by, 210, 216, 218, 222–223; fight of, with Kickapoos, 219

metalware businesses: number of, 152

Methodists: and Southwestern University, 243; and Wiley University, 244

Mexican Army: SEE Army, Mexican

Mexican cattle thieves: SEE cattle thieves, Mexican

Mexicans: and Indians, 219, 221; in Texas, 238

Mexico: flight of Southern leaders to, 3; French in, 5; E. J. Davis in, 20–21; Indians in, 182, 202–203, 204–205, 208–209

Mexico City: railroads to, 160, 162

Milam County: 1869 election in, 18; lignite deposits in, 149 n

military authorities: and civil courts, 3–4; in Texas, 5

Military Division of the Southwest: General Sheridan as commander of, 5

military forces: and J. W. Throckmorton, 8; in Texas, 8; and control of crime, 245

military government: SEE government, military

military governor: SEE governor, military

military rule: in Texas, 8–9, 25, 28

militia: E. J. Davis on, 27, 115; and governor, 28; contributions of, 53; and John Hunter, 59; and elections, 99, 112

Militia, Reserve: creation of, 28; and governor, 28–29

militia bill: provisions of, 28–29; in Legislature, 29, 116; and Democrats, 29, 118; petition to Congress on, 33 n;

Index

Paris, Texas: State Police in, 72
Parish, J. D.: on murder of D. C. Applewhite, 87
Parker, Colonel E. S.: commissioner of Indian affairs, 178, 180
Parker, F. J.: on river transportation, 158
Parker County: copper deposits in, 149; Indian depredations in, 184; Minute Men in, 198, 199; ranging company in, 201
Parks, Fred: arrest and trial of, 81
Parsons, General William H.: as immigrant agent, 259–260
Patrick, State Police Captain ———: in Madison County affair, 54
Patrick, Mrs. ———: 54
Patton, C. A.: and Minute Men, 199
peaceful Indians: SEE Indians, peaceful
peace officers: and 1872 election, 112
"peace policy": purposes of, 177; flaws in, 177–178, 181; reaction of settlers to, 180–181; General Sherman on, 181–182
peace talks: with Indians, 187
Pease, E. M.: as candidate for governor, 6; as military governor, 9, 15; at 1868 constitutional convention, 9; and Conservatives, 9, 13–14; and A. J. Hamilton, 15; to President Grant, 17–18; and 1869 election, 18; and M. C. Hamilton, 25 n; and petition to Congress, 33; and taxpayers' convention, 93; on state finances, 93, and Texas Historical Society, 237 n
Pecos County: rejection of votes from, 113; copper deposits in, 148; frontier protection in, 182
Pendencia, Texas: ranging company at, 193
Pendleton, George C.: at Democratic convention, 118
penitentiary: upkeep of, 166
Pennsylvania: hogs in, 144–145
Peoples, ———: murder of, 181
per diem measure: cost of, 165
permanent school fund: SEE school fund, permanent
Perry, William: and State Police, 61
Perryman Station: Indians near, 195
petition to Congress: 33–34
Philips, Mrs. ———: 20 n
Pickett, Senator, E. B.: arrest of, 29 n; on

unseating of Senator Dillard, 29 n–30 n
picnics, Sunday school: 236
Piedras Negras, Mexico: Indians near, 193, 219; Jefferson Smith rescued at, 215; border thieves near, 222
pillaging: in San Antonio, 4; in La-Grange, 4
Pine and Palm, Boston: and G. T. Ruby, 23 n
Piotes, Mexico: Trompo Garcia in, 222
Pitts, William A.: defense of capitol by, 124, 125
plantations: after Civil War, 135
plantation system: breakup of, 227
Platt, Ratcliff: at Greeley meeting, 69
Plumley, Major B. Rush: as speaker of the House, 22
Poe, Wylie: as buffalo hunter, 230
police, city: and State Police, 43
police, special: salaries of, 31 n; and elections, 55–56, 68, 112; and State Police, 55–56; at political meetings, 56
Police, State: 43–75; and E. J. Davis, 27, 28–29, 30, 43, 53–54, 73, 115; salaries of, 31 n, 44–45; recruiting for, 41; and Legislature, 43, 73–74; reputation of, 43, 66; purpose of, 43, 345; composition of, 43; creation of, 43; and other law officers, 43, 55; James Davidson as chief of, 44, 53, 54, 66; accomplishments of, 44, 45, 52, 53, 55, 58–59, 70–71; financing of, 44–45, 54–55, 55; criminal files of, 45; abuses by 45, 74; murders by, 45–48; in Madison County, 54; and elections, 55–56, 56–58, 58, 68; political activities of, 67, 70–71; and Conservatives, 68–70; F. Britton as chief of, 71; and Democrats, 73, 118; advantages of, 74; disadvantages of, 74; cost of, 165–166; and Ku Klux Klan, 252
Police law, State: in legislature, 30; and governor, 31 n; petition to Congress on, 33 n; and M. C. Hamilton, 39; emendation to, 55; repeal of, 73–74, 116; and taxpayers' convention, 94; and Democratic convention, 98–99
police court: justice of the peace as, 26
Polish settlers in Texas: 238
political machine of Radicals, 4
political meetings: special policemen at,

294

Index

Willie, A. H.: as candidate for Congress, 111

Willingham, J. J.: and Minute Men, 199

Wilson, Captain Dave: and Coke-Davis Imbroglio, 129

Wilson County: rejection of votes from, 113; value of land in, 147

Wise County: value of land in, 147; coal mining in, 149 n; plow made in, 151; ranging company in, 191, 201; Indians in, 195; Minute Men in, 198, 199, 200

women: situation of, 233

women's suffrage movements: development of, 234

Woodbridge, Dr. ———: and ranging company, 193–194

Wood County: 51; lignite deposits in, 149 n

wool: export of, 154

wool carding businesses: number of, 152

woolen mills: locations of, 151

Woolfork, J. A.: defense of Satanta and Big Tree by, 186

Wormley, Patrick: and Ku Klux Klan, 251

Wright, J. A.: and Minute Men, 199

Wright, Jo: arrest and trial of, 81, 82

Wyoming: cattle sent to, 143

Young, Sheriff ———: and Limestone County troubles, 88–89

Young, James: as temperance leader, 234

Youngcost (Indian): Martina Diaz as prisoner of, 216

Young County: coal deposits in, 148; ranging company in, 201

Youngmichel, C. C.: and Ku Klux Klan, 251

Zadek, A., Jr.: and murder of D. C. Applewhite, 87; and Limestone County troubles, 88

Zapata County: ranging company in, 191

Zimpleman, Sheriff George B.: and treasury muddle, 107; and Coke-Davis Imbroglio, 123, 126, 129

304